GENERAL MOTORS
Buick · Chevrolet · Oldsmobile · Pontiac
1972-1985
TUNE-UP · MAINTENANCE

By
KALTON C. LAHUE

SYDNIE A. WAUSON
Editor

JEFF ROBINSON
Publisher

CLYMER PUBLICATIONS

*World's largest publisher of books
devoted exclusively to automobiles and motorcycles*

12860 MUSCATINE STREET · P.O. BOX 4520 · ARLETA, CALIFORNIA 91333-4520

FIRST EDITION
First Printing June, 1983

SECOND EDITION
Revised by Kalton C. Lahue to include 1983-1984 models
First Printing March, 1984

THIRD EDITION
Revised by Kalton C. Lahue to include 1985 models
First Printing April, 1985

Printed in U.S.A.

ISBN: 0-89287-375-2

Production coordinator, Doug Achterman

Technical illustrations courtesy of General Motors Corporation.

Cover: Photographed by Michael Brown Photographic Productions, Los Angeles, CA. Assisted by Bill Masho and Tim Lunde. Cars courtesy of Chevrolet and Pontiac Divisions of General Motors Corporation.

CONTENTS

GENERAL MOTORS
Buick · Chevrolet · Oldsmobile · Pontiac
1972-1985
TUNE-UP · MAINTENANCE

CHAPTER ONE

GENERAL INFORMATION

This book provides lubrication, general maintenance and tune-up information for the following domestic rear-wheel drive General Motors passenger cars manufactured between 1972-1985:

1. Buick.
   a. Centurion.
   b. Le Sabre.
   c. Le Sabre Estate Wagon.
   d. Riviera (1972-1978).
   e. Skyhawk.
2. Chevrolet.
   a. Biscayne.
   b. Bel Air.
   c. Caprice.
   d. Impala
   e. Monza.
3. Oldsmobile.
   a. Delta 88.
   b. Custom Cruiser.
   c. Starfire.
4. Pontiac.
   a. Bonneville (1972-1981).
   b. Catalina (1972-1981).
   c. Grand Ville.
   d. Safari/Grand Safari.
   e. Parisienne.
   f. Sunbird.

Due to the large number of vehicle/engine combinations used over this span of time, many of the maintenance procedures provided here are general in nature and may require some interpretation. Every effort has been made, however, to be as specific as possible.

Major mechanical procedures, such as rebuilding of the engine, transmission, differential, etc., are not provided. Many special tools and extensive experience are required for such work. Such service and repair should be entrusted to a dealer or automotive specialist.

Procedures requiring the use of special tools have been kept to a minimum. Where special tools are required, their designation is provided. Such tools may often be borrowed or rented or can be purchased directly from Kent-Moore Tool Division, 28635 Mound Road, Warren, Michigan 48092. The resourceful mechanic can, in many cases, think of acceptable substitutes for special tools–there is always another way. However, using a substitute for a special tool is not recommended, as it can be dangerous to you and may damage the part.

The terms NOTE, CAUTION and WARNING have specific meanings in this manual. A NOTE provides additional information to make a step or procedure easier or clearer. Disregarding a NOTE could cause inconvenience, but would not cause damage or personal injury.

A CAUTION emphasizes areas where equipment damage could result. Disregarding a CAUTION could cause permanent mechanical damage; however, personal injury is unlikely.

A WARNING emphasizes areas where personal injury or even death could result from negligence. Mechanical damage may also occur. WARNINGS *are to be taken seriously.* In some cases serious injury or death has resulted from disregarding similar warnings.

MANUAL ORGANIZATION

This chapter describes the scope of this manual and provides some service hints and precautions to be observed. Recommended tools and test instruments necessary for proper tune-up and diagnostic work are also described.

Chapter Two provides procedures for isolating common automotive problems.

Chapter Three provides a plan for scheduled lubrication and preventive maintenance.

Chapter Four provides engine tune-up information and procedures.

Carburetor adjustment and fuel pump testing is covered in Chapter Five.

Chapter Six provides procedures for servicing major electrical components such as the battery, alternator, starter motor and lighting systems.

Cooling system maintenance is discussed in Chapter Seven. Procedures are given for checking, cleaning and maintaining the system.

Instructions for bleeding, adjusting and relining brakes are provided in Chapter Eight.

Chapter Nine covers clutch adjustment procedures for all models equipped with a manual transmission.

Chapter Ten provides replacement procedures for shock absorbers.

Each chapter provides disassembly, repair and assembly procedures in easy-to-follow, step-by-step form. All procedures are given in the most practical sequence. Complex and lengthy operations are described in detail and are thoroughly illustrated. The exploded views show the correct sequence of parts as well as a listing of the parts needed for replacement. These can be of considerable help as a reference during disassembly and reassembly.

U.S. standards are used throughout and are accompanied by metric equivalents in parentheses where such reference might have practical value. Metric to inch conversion is given in **Table 1**.

SERVICE HINTS

Time, effort and frustration can be saved by following the practices suggested here.

1. "Front," as used in this manual, refers to the front of the vehicle; the front of any component is the end closest to the front of the vehicle. The left side of the vehicle is the driver's side; the right side of the vehicle is the passenger side.

2. Never trust any jack, mechanical or hydraulic. Use jackstands to hold the car when working under it and always set the parking brake and block the wheels remaining on the ground.

3. Disconnect the negative battery cable when working on or near the electrical system and before disconnecting any wires. On most batteries, the negative terminal will be marked with a minus (-) sign and the postive terminal with a plus (+) sign. Never run the engine with the battery disconnected, as this can cause serious damage to the alternator.

4. When disassembling a part or component, a good practice is to tag the parts for location and mark all parts which mate together for location. Small parts, such as bolts, can be identified by placing them in plastic sandwich bags. Seal the bags and label them with masking tape and a marking pen. When reassembly will take place immediately, an accepted practice is to place small parts in a cupcake tin or egg carton in the order of disassembly.

5. Finished surfaces should be protected from physical damage or corrosion. Keep gasoline and brake fluid off painted surfaces.

6. Use penetrating oil on frozen or tight bolts, then strike the bolt head a few times with a hammer and punch (use a screwdriver on screws). Avoid the use of heat where possible, as it can warp, melt or affect the temper of parts and also ruins finishes, especially paint.

7. Keep flames and sparks away from a charging battery or inflammable fluids and do not smoke in the area. It is a good idea to have a fire extinguisher handy in the work area.

8. No parts removed or installed in the procedures given in this book should require unusual force during disassembly or assembly. If a part is hard to remove or install, find out why before proceeding.

9. Cover all openings after removing parts or components to prevent dirt, small tools, etc. from falling in.

10. Read each procedure *completely* while looking at the actual parts before starting a job. Make sure you *thoroughly* understand what is to be done and then carefully follow the procedure, step-by-step.

11. Recommendations are occasionally made to refer service or maintenance to a dealer or a specialist in a particular field. In these cases, work will probably be done more quickly and economically than if you performed the job yourself.

12. In procedural steps, the term "replace" means to discard a defective part and replace it with a new or exchange unit. "Overhaul" means to remove, disassemble, inspect, measure, repair or replace defective parts, reassemble and install major systems and parts.

RECOMMENDED TOOLS

Some of the procedures in this manual specify special tools, which are generally expensive. Such tools can often be rented or bought, but it is usually more practical to have a dealer or repair shop perform the step which requires the special tool. Most of the procedures in this manual can be carried out with simple hand tools and test equipment familiar to the average home mechanic.

For proper servicing, you will need an assortment of ordinary hand tools. Recommended are:

   a. Combination wrenches.
   b. Sockets, socket extension(s) and a socket wrench.
   c. Plastic mallet.
   d. Small hammer.
   e. Snap ring pliers.
   f. Assorted pliers.
   g. Phillips and flat-blade screwdrivers.
   h. Feeler gauges (flat and round).
   i. Tire pressure gauge.

Any home mechanic intent on saving money and aggravation by doing repair and maintenance work should invest in the following test instruments.

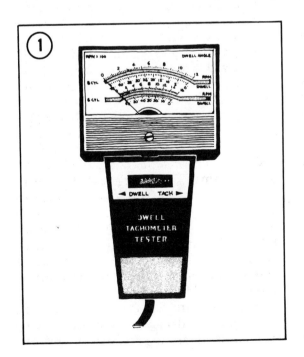

Dwell Meter

A dwell meter (**Figure 1**) is useful for 1972-1974 cars equipped with a breaker point ignition. It measures the distance of distributor cam rotation (in degrees) from the time the breaker points close until they open again while the engine is running. Since this angle is determined by the breaker point gap setting, dwell angle is an accurate indication of breaker point gap.

A dwell meter is not necessary for 1975 and later cars equipped with a breakerless ignition. Dwell is determined by an electronic control unit and cannot be changed.

Many tachometers intended for tuning and testing incorporate a dwell meter. Follow the manufacturer's instructions when using a combination instrument to measure dwell.

Tachometer

A tachometer is necessary for tune-up work, as ignition timing and carburetor adjustments must be made at specified speeds. The best instrument for this work is one with 2 ranges: a low range of 0-1,000 to 0-2,000 rpm for setting low or "curb" idle and a high range of 0-4,000 or more rpm for setting fast idle and checking ignition timing at faster engine speeds. Tachometers with only one extended range (0-6,000 to 0-8,000 rpm) lack accuracy at lower speeds. The instrument should be capable of detecting changes of 25 rpm on the low range.

Timing Light

This instrument is required for accurate timing adjustment. The light is connected to flash each time the No. 1 spark plug fires, making the position of the timing mark visible at that instant. When the engine is properly timed, the timing marks will be aligned.

Suitable timing lights range from inexpensive neon bulb types to powerful xenon strobe lights. See **Figure 2**. Neon timing lights are difficult to see and must be used in dimly lit areas. Xenon strobe timing lights can be used outside in bright sunlight.

Xenon timing lights can be obtained for either AC or DC operation; DC types can be operated from the car's battery. Timing lights with an inductive pickup are recommended for use with breakerless ignitions.

Compression Tester

The compression tester measures the pressure built up in each cylinder as the engine is turned over. The results, when properly interpreted, can indicate general cylinder and valve condition. Many compression testers have long flexible extensions as accessories (**Figure 3**).

Vacuum Gauge

The vacuum gauge (**Figure 4**) is one of the easiest instruments to use, but one of the hardest for the inexperienced mechanic to interpret. When interpreted with other findings, test results can give valuable clues to possible troubles and help isolate the cause of a problem.

Figure 5 shows a number of typical vacuum gauge readings with interpretations. Results

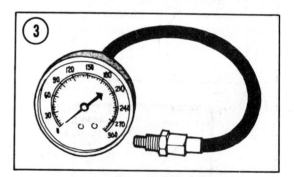

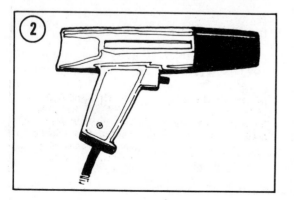

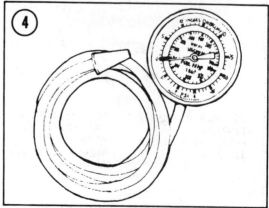

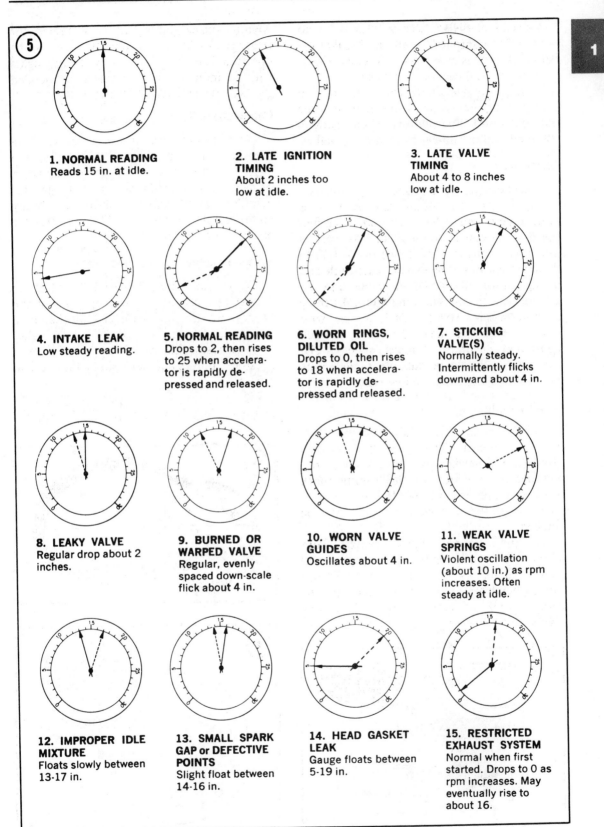

1. NORMAL READING
Reads 15 in. at idle.

2. LATE IGNITION TIMING
About 2 inches too low at idle.

3. LATE VALVE TIMING
About 4 to 8 inches low at idle.

4. INTAKE LEAK
Low steady reading.

5. NORMAL READING
Drops to 2, then rises to 25 when accelerator is rapidly depressed and released.

6. WORN RINGS, DILUTED OIL
Drops to 0, then rises to 18 when accelerator is rapidly depressed and released.

7. STICKING VALVE(S)
Normally steady. Intermittently flicks downward about 4 in.

8. LEAKY VALVE
Regular drop about 2 inches.

9. BURNED OR WARPED VALVE
Regular, evenly spaced down-scale flick about 4 in.

10. WORN VALVE GUIDES
Oscillates about 4 in.

11. WEAK VALVE SPRINGS
Violent oscillation (about 10 in.) as rpm increases. Often steady at idle.

12. IMPROPER IDLE MIXTURE
Floats slowly between 13-17 in.

13. SMALL SPARK GAP or DEFECTIVE POINTS
Slight float between 14-16 in.

14. HEAD GASKET LEAK
Gauge floats between 5-19 in.

15. RESTRICTED EXHAUST SYSTEM
Normal when first started. Drops to 0 as rpm increases. May eventually rise to about 16.

1

should be compared with other test results, such as compression, before reaching a conclusion.

Fuel Pressure Gauge

This instrument is needed for evaluating fuel pump performance. Usually a vacuum gauge and a fuel pressure gauge are combined.

Voltmeter, Ammeter and Ohmmeter

A good voltmeter is required for testing ignition and other electrical systems. An instrument covering 0-20 volts is satisfactory. It should also have a 0-2 volt scale for testing relays, points or individual contacts where voltage drops are much smaller. Accuracy should be ± 1/2 volt.

An ohmmeter measures electrical resistance. This instrument is useful in checking continuity (for open and short circuits) and testing fuses and lights.

The ammeter measures electrical current. Ammeters for automotive use should have scales covering 0-50 amperes and 0-250 amperes. These are useful for checking battery starting and charging currents.

Several inexpensive multimeters combine all 3 instruments (**Figure 6**) into one unit which fits into any toolbox. The ammeter ranges of such units are usually too low for automotive work. However, combination instruments designed especially for automotive diagnostic work are available at a reasonable price.

Hydrometer

Hydrometer testing is the best way to check the condition of unsealed batteries. The most efficient type is a temperature-compensated hydrometer with numbered gradations (**Figure 7**) from 1.100 to 1.300 rather than one with color-coded bands.

To use the hydrometer, squeeze the rubber ball, insert the tip into a battery cell and release the ball (**Figure 8**). Draw enough electrolyte into the instrument so that the weighted float is riding freely in the liquid. Note the number on the float in line with the liquid surface level; this is the specific gravity of the cell. Return the electrolyte to the cell from which it was taken and continue to test all cells.

Specific gravity gives an indication of cell condition. A fully-charged cell will read 1.275-1.380, while a cell in good condition may read 1.250-1.280. A cell in fair condition reads from 1.225-1.250 and anything below 1.225 is practically dead. Any variation between cells in excess of 0.050 indicates a battery problem.

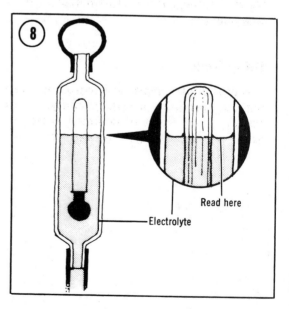

Read here

Electrolyte

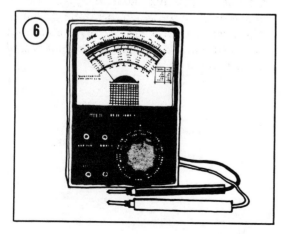

If the cells test in the poor range, the battery requires recharging. The hydrometer may also be used for checking the progress of the charging operation. A reading from 1.200 to about 1.225 indicates a half charge, while 1.275-1.380 indicates full charge.

CAUTION
Always disconnect both battery cables before hooking up charging equipment.

Remote Starter Button

An optional but convenient item of equipment is a remote starter button. This is connected to the starter solenoid and permits cranking the engine from outside the car. It eliminates the need for an assistant during certain procedures, such as setting the breaker points.

Expendable Supplies

Certain expendable supplies are also required to correctly service your vehicle. These include greases, oil, gasket cement, shop rags, cleaning solvent and distilled water. Special fastener locking compounds and silicone lubricants are available from a dealer or auto parts specialist to make maintenance simpler and easier. Solvent is available at auto parts stores and distilled water for the battery is available at most supermarkets.

Safety Hints

A professional mechanic can work for years without sustaining a serious injury. If you observe a few rules of common sense and safety, you can safely service your own vehicle. You can also hurt yourself or damage your vehicle if you ignore these rules.

1. Never use gasoline as a cleaning solvent.
2. Never smoke or use a torch around flammable liquids such as cleaning solvents.
3. Never smoke or use a torch in areas where batteries are being charged. Highly explosive hydrogen gas is formed during the charging process.
4. Never arc the terminals of a battery to see if it is charged. The sparks can ignite the explosive hydrogen as easily as an open flame.
5. If welding or brazing is required on the vehicle, make sure that it is not in the area of the fuel tank or lines. In such case, the work should be entrusted to a specialist.
6. Always use the correct size wrench for loosening and tightening fasteners.
7. When replacing a fastener, make sure to use one with the same measurements and strength as the old one. Incorrect or mismatched fasteners can result in damage to the vehicle and possible personal injury.
8. Keep your work area clean and uncluttered.
9. Wear safety goggles in all operations involving drilling, grinding, or the use of a chisel or an air hose.
10. Do not use worn tools or tools that are not appropriate to the job.
11. Keep a fire extinguisher handy. Be sure it is rated for gasoline and electrical fires.
12. When drying bearings or other rotating parts with compressed air, never allow the air jet to rotate the bearing or part; the jet is capable of rotating them at speeds far in excess of those for which they were designed. The likelihood of a bearing or rotating part disintegrating and causing serious injury and damage is very great.

Table 1 CONVERSION CHART—MILLIMETERS TO INCHES

mm	in.	mm	in.	mm	in.
0.01	0.0004	0.51	0.0201	1	0.0394
0.02	0.0008	0.52	0.0205	2	0.0787
0.03	0.0012	0.53	0.0209	3	0.1181
0.04	0.0016	0.54	0.0213	4	0.1575
0.05	0.0020	0.55	0.0217	5	0.1969
0.06	0.0024	0.56	0.0221	6	0.2362
0.07	0.0028	0.57	0.0224	7	0.2756
0.08	0.0032	0.58	0.0228	8	0.3150
0.09	0.0035	0.59	0.0232	9	0.3543
0.10	0.0039	0.60	0.0236	10	0.3937
0.11	0.0043	0.61	0.0240	11	0.4331
0.12	0.0047	0.62	0.0244	12	0.4724
0.13	0.0051	0.63	0.0246	13	0.5118
0.14	0.0055	0.64	0.0252	14	0.5512
0.15	0.0059	0.65	0.0256	15	0.5906
0.16	0.0063	0.66	0.0260	16	0.6299
0.17	0.0067	0.67	0.0264	17	0.6693
0.18	0.0071	0.68	0.0268	18	0.7087
0.19	0.0075	0.69	0.0272	19	0.7480
0.20	0.0079	0.70	0.0276	20	0.7874
0.21	0.0083	0.71	0.0280	21	0.8268
0.22	0.0087	0.72	0.0284	22	0.8661
0.23	0.0091	0.73	0.0287	23	0.9055
0.24	0.0095	0.74	0.0291	24	0.9449
0.25	0.0098	0.75	0.0295	25	0.9843
0.26	0.0102	0.76	0.0299	26	1.0236
0.27	0.0106	0.77	0.0303	27	1.0630
0.28	0.0110	0.78	0.0307	28	1.1024
0.29	0.0114	0.79	0.0311	29	1.1417
0.30	0.0118	0.80	0.0315	30	1.1811
0.31	0.0122	0.81	0.0320	31	1.2205
0.32	0.0126	0.82	0.0323	32	1.2598
0.33	0.0130	0.83	0.0327	33	1.2992
0.34	0.0134	0.84	0.0331	34	1.3386
0.35	0.0138	0.85	0.0335	35	1.3779
0.36	0.0142	0.86	0.0339	36	1.4173
0.37	0.0146	0.87	0.0343	37	1.4567
0.38	0.0150	0.88	0.0347	38	1.4961
0.39	0.0154	0.89	0.0350	39	1.5354
0.40	0.0158	0.90	0.0354	40	1.5748
0.41	0.0161	0.91	0.0358	41	1.6142
0.42	0.0165	0.92	0.0362	42	1.6535
0.43	0.0169	0.93	0.0366	43	1.6929
0.44	0.0173	0.94	0.0370	44	1.7323
0.45	0.0177	0.95	0.0374	45	1.7716
0.46	0.0181	0.96	0.0378	46	1.8110
0.47	0.0185	0.97	0.0382	47	1.8504
0.48	0.0186	0.98	0.0386	48	1.8898
0.49	0.0193	0.99	0.0390	49	1.9291
0.50	0.0197			50	1.9685

TROUBLESHOOTING

Troubleshooting mechanical problems can be relatively simple if you use orderly procedures and keep a few basic principles in mind.

The troubleshooting procedures in this chapter analyze typical symptoms, and show logical methods of isolating causes. These are not the only methods. There may be several ways to solve a problem, but only a systematic, methodical approach can guarantee success.

Gather as many symptoms together as possible to aid in diagnosis. Note whether the engine lost power gradually or all at once, what color smoke (if any) came from the exhaust, and so on. After the symptoms are defined, areas which could cause the problem are tested and analyzed. Guessing at the cause of a problem may eventually provide the solution, but it can lead to frustration, wasted time and a series of expensive, unnecessary parts replacements.

You don't need exotic, complicated test equipment to determine whether repairs can be made at home. A few simple checks could save a large repair bill and time lost while the car sits in a dealer's service department. On the other hand, be realistic and don't attempt repairs beyond your abilities. Service departments tend to charge heavily to correct other people's mistakes.

During the years covered by this manual, Buick, Chevrolet, Oldsmobile and Pontiac Divisions used a large number of different displacement engines in their passenger car lines. These engines were used in an almost infinite number of combinations with various manual and automatic transmissions, carburetors and distributors. Because of these factors, it would be impossible to provide specific check-out procedures for all of the numerous combinations. Instead, the troubleshooting procedures given below have been purposely kept general in nature in order to cover the largest possible number of engine, transmission, carburetor and distributor combinations.

The following are commonly encountered problems.

STARTER

Starter system troubles are relatively easy to isolate. The following are common symptoms.

Engine Cranks Very Slowly or Not At All

Turn on the headlights. If the lights are very dim, the battery or connecting wires are most likely at fault. Check the battery with a hydrometer. Check wiring for breaks, shorts and dirty connections. If the battery and wires are all right, turn the headlights on and crank the engine. If the lights dim drastically, the starter is probably shorted to ground.

If the lights remain bright or dim slightly when cranking, the trouble may be in the starter, starter solenoid or wiring. If the starter spins, check the starter solenoid and wiring to the ignition switch.

Note whether solenoid plunger is pulled into solenoid when starter circuit is closed (ordinarily, the plunger makes a loud click when pulled in). If plunger is pulled in, the solenoid circuit is not the problem. The trouble is in the solenoid switch, starter motor or the starter motor circuit. Remove the starter motor for repairs to either motor or switch.

If plunger does not pull into solenoid, solenoid circuit is open or solenoid is at fault. Connect a jumper wire between the solenoid battery terminal and the terminal on the solenoid switch to which the purple lead wire is attached. If the starter works, the solenoid is good and the trouble is in the neutral start switch, ignition switch or in the wires and connections between the switches.

Some 1974-1975 models are equipped with seat belt/starter interlock systems. If the battery, cables and connections are satisfactory, and no solenoid click is heard when the starter circuit is closed, the problem may be a malfunction in the interlock system.

If the starter still will not crank properly, refer the problem to a dealer or automotive electrical specialist.

Starter Turns, But Does Not Engage With Engine

This is usually caused by a defective pinion. The teeth on the pinion, flywheel ring gear, or both may be worn too far to engage properly.

Starter Engages, But Does Not Crank Engine

This is usually caused by an open circuit in the solenoid armature or field coils, or by a short or ground in the starter motor field coil or armature. Check out both systems to isolate the problem and then repair or replace the faulty component.

Starter Engages, But Will Not Disengage When Ignition Switch Is Released

Usually caused by a sticking starter solenoid, but occasionally the pinion may jam on the flywheel. A sticking solenoid can sometimes be temporarily remedied by lightly tapping the solenoid with a piece of wood or a rubber mallet. The pinion can be temporarily freed on manual transmission cars by rocking the car in high gear.

Loud Grinding Noises When Starter Runs

The teeth on the pinion and/or flywheel are not meshing properly or the overrunning clutch mechanism is broken. Remove the starter and examine gear teeth and pinion drive assembly.

CHARGING SYSTEM

Charging system troubles may be in the alternator, voltage regulator, or drive belt. When troubleshooting the charging system, observe the following precautions.
 a. Do not polarize the alternator.
 b. Do not short across or ground any of the charging system terminals unless specifically directed to do so in a procedure.
 c. Never operate the alternator with the output terminal open circuited.
 d. Make sure the alternator and battery are of the same ground polarity.
 e. When connecting booster cables or a charger to the battery, connect negative terminal to negative terminal and positive terminal to positive terminal.
The following symptoms are typical:

Instrument Panel Light Shows Continuous Discharge

This usually means that battery charging is not taking place. Check drive belt tension. Check battery condition with hydrometer and electrical connections in the charging system. Finally, check the alternator and/or voltage regulator using procedures in Chapter Five.

Instrument Panel Light Shows Intermittent Discharge

Check drive belt tension and electrical connections. The trouble may be traced to worn alternator brushes or bad slip rings.

Battery Requires Frequent Addition of Water or Lamps Require Frequent Replacement

The alternator may be overcharging the battery or the voltage regulator is defective.

Noisy Alternator

Check for loose mountings and/or worn bearings.

ENGINE

These procedures assume the starter cranks the engine over normally. If not, refer to the *Starter* section.

Engine Won't Start

Could be caused by the ignition system or fuel system. First, determine if high voltage to spark plugs occurs. To do this, disconnect one of the spark plug wires and connect A.C. Delco Tester ST-125. If the tester is not available, hold the exposed wire terminal about 1/4 to 1/2 in. from ground (any metal in the engine compartment) with insulated pliers. Crank the engine. If sparking does not occur or if the sparks are very weak, the trouble may be in the ignition system. If sparks occur properly, the trouble may be in the fuel system.

Engine Misses Steadily

Remove and ground each spark plug wire, one at a time. If engine miss increases, that cylinder is working properly. When a wire is disconnected and engine miss remains the same, that cylinder is not firing. Check spark as described above. If no spark occurs for one cylinder only, check distributor cap, wire and spark plug. If spark occurs properly, check compression and intake manifold vacuum.

Engine Misses Erratically at All Speeds

Intermittent trouble can be difficult to find. It could be in the ignition system, intake system or fuel system. Follow troubleshooting procedures for these systems to isolate the trouble.

Engine Misses at Idle Only

Trouble could be in the ignition system or carburetor idle adjustment. Check idle mixture adjustment. Inspect for restrictions in the idle circuit. Check for inlet manifold and vacuum leaks.

Engine Misses at High Speed Only

Trouble is in the fuel system or ignition system. Check accelerator pump operation, fuel pump delivery, fuel line, etc. Check spark plugs and wires.

Low Performance at All Speeds, Poor Acceleration

Trouble is usually in the ignition, fuel or exhaust system.

Excessive Fuel Consumption

Could be caused by a number of seemingly unrelated factors. Check for clutch slippage, brake drag, defective wheel bearings, poor front end alignment, faulty ignition, leaky gas tank or lines and carburetor condition.

Low Oil Pressure Shown by Oil Pressure Gauge or Light

If the oil pressure gauge shows a low pressure reading or if the indicator lamp lights with the engine running, stop the engine immediately. Coast to a stop with the clutch disengaged or the automatic transmission in neutral. The trouble may be caused by low oil level, blockage in the oil line, defective oil pump, overheated engine or a defective oil pressure gauge/light. Check the oil level and drive belt tension. Check for shorted oil pressure sender with an ohmmeter or other continuity tester. Do not restart the engine until you know why the low indication was given and you are sure the problem has been corrected.

Engine Overheats

Usually caused by trouble in the cooling system. Check the level of coolant in the radiator, condition of the drive belt and connecting hoses for leaks and loose connections. Check the operation of the fan fluid clutch, if so equipped. This problem can also be caused by late ignition or valve timing.

Engine Stalls As It Warms Up

The choke valve may be stuck closed, the manifold heat control valve may be stuck, the engine idling speed may be set too low or the emission control (PCV) valve may be faulty.

Engine Stalls After Idling or Slow-Speed Driving

Can be caused by defective fuel pump, overheated engine, high carburetor float level, incorrect idle adjustment or a defective PCV valve.

Engine Stalls After High-speed Driving

Vapor lock within the fuel lines caused by an overheated engine is usually the cause of this trouble. Inspect and service the cooling system. If the trouble persists, changing to a different fuel or shielding the fuel line from engine heat may prove helpful.

Engine Backfires

Several causes can be suspected; ignition timing, overheating, excessive carbon, wrong heat range spark plugs, hot or sticking valve, cracked distributor cap, a hole in the exhaust system, excessively rich fuel/air mixture or a defective air pump diverter valve.

Smoky Exhaust

Blue smoke indicates excessive oil consumption usually caused by worn rings or valve guides. Black smoke indicates an excessively rich fuel mixture.

Excessive Oil Consumption

Can be caused by external leaks through broken seals or gaskets or by burning oil in the combustion chamber. Check the oil pan and the front and rear of the engine for oil leaks. If the oil is not leaking externally, valve stem-to-guide clearances may be excessive, piston rings may be worn, cylinder walls may be scored or the PCV valve may be plugged.

Noisy Engine

1. *Regular clicking sound*–Valve and/or tappets out of adjustment.

2. *Ping or chatter on load or acceleration*–Spark knock due to low octane fuel, carbon buildup, overly advanced ignition timing and causes mentioned under engine backfire.

3. *Light knock or pound with engine not under load*—Indicates worn connecting rod bearings, worn camshaft bearings, misaligned crankpin and/or lack of engine oil.

4. *Light metallic double knock, usually heard during idle*–Worn or loose piston pin or bushing and/or lack of oil.

5. *Chattering or rattling during acceleration*–Worn rings, cylinder walls, low ring tension and/or broken rings.

6. *Hollow, bell-like muffled sound when engine is cold*–Piston slap due to worn pistons, cylinder walls, collapsed piston skirts, excessive clearances, misaligned connecting rods and/or lack of oil.

7. *Dull, heavy metallic knock under load or acceleration, especially when cold*–Regular noise: worn main bearings; irregular noise: worn thrust bearings.

IGNITION SYSTEM (BREAKER-POINT)

The following procedures assume the battery is in good enough condition to crank the engine at a normal rate.

2

No Sparks to One Plug

The only causes are defective distributor cap or spark plug wire. Examine the distributor cap for moisture, dirt, carbon tracking caused by flashover and cracks. Check spark plug wire for breaks or loose connectors.

No Spark to Any Plug

This could indicate trouble in the primary or secondary ignition circuits. First, remove the coil wire from the center tower of the distributor cap. Hold the wire end about 1/4 in. from ground with insulated pliers. Crank the engine. If sparks are produced, the trouble is in the rotor or distributor cap. Remove the cap and check for burns, moisture, dirt, carbon tracking, cracks, etc. Check rotor for excessive burning, pitting and cracks. Check rotor continuity with a test light.

If the coil does not produce any spark, check the secondary wire for a break. If the wire is good, turn the engine over so the breaker points are open. Examine them for excessive gap, burning, pitting or loose connections. With the points open, check voltage from the coil to ground with a voltmeter or test lamp. If voltage is present, the coil is probably defective. Have it checked or substitute a coil known to be good.

If voltage is not present, check wire connections to coil and distributor. Disconnect the wire leading from the coil to the distributor and measure it from the coil terminal to ground. If voltage is present, the distributor is shorted. Examine breaker points and connecting wires carefully. If voltage is still not present, measure the other coil terminal. Voltage on the other terminal indicates a defective coil. No voltage indicates a broken wire between the coil and battery.

If voltage is not present, check wire connections to coil and distributor. Disconnect the wire leading from the coil to the distributor and measure from the coil terminal to ground. If voltage is present, the distributor is shorted. Examine breaker points and connecting wires carefully. If voltage is still not present, measure the positive coil terminal. Voltage on the positive terminal, but not on the negative terminal, indicates a defective coil. No voltage indicates a broken wire between the coil and battery.

If there is no spark or a weak one from the coil wire on a breakerless ignition system, the problem is in the primary circuit. To isolate the exact cause, a series of electrical tests must be performed on the primary circuitry with a sensitive volt-ohmmeter. Refer this testing to your dealer or a qualified electrical shop.

Weak Spark

If the spark is so small it cannot jump from the wire to ground, check the battery. Other causes are bad breaker points, condenser, incorrect point gap, dirty or loose connections in the primary circuit, or a dirty or burned rotor/distributor cap. Check for worn cam lobes in breaker point distributors.

Missing

This is usually caused by fouled or damaged plugs, plugs of the wrong heat range, incorrect plug gap or defective plug wires.

IGNITION SYSTEM (BREAKERLESS)

The following procedures are for the diagnosis of basic problems in High Energy Ignition (HEI) ignition systems.

Engine Cranks But Will Not Start

Turn the ignition on and place the transmission selector in PARK (automatic transmission) or NEUTRAL (manual transmission). Connect a test lamp to the BAT lead terminal on the side of the distributor. See **Figure 1**. Connect the other test lamp lead to a good ground. If the light goes on, remove a spark plug wire and connect it to A.C. Delco Tester ST-125. If this tester is not available, hold the spark plug wire 1/4 in. from the engine block with a pair of insulated pliers while cranking the engine. If a good spark is present, the problem is not in the ignition system. Check the spark plugs, fuel system, or for a flooded condition.

If the test lamp did not light, check the ignition switch and repair or replace as required. If the engine still does not start, perform the spark test described above. If no spark resulted from the spark test, connect the test lamp to the distributor B plus terminal on the side of the distributor (**Figure 1**) by inserting the test lead into the red B plus wire. If the test lamp does not light, repair or replace B pius wire or connector. If the test lamp lights, or if the engine fails to start after repairs, have a dealer check the electronic control module (ECM) and replace if necessary.

If the ECM is good, remove the distributor cap assembly and disconnect the 3-wire connector. Inspect cap and distributor for signs of moisture, dust, cracks, burns, etc., and repair or replace as required. If no defects are noted, remove the green and white leads from the distributor module and connect an ohmmeter from either lead to ground. If any reading less than infinity is obtained on the X 1,000 scale, replace the pickup coil.

If the engine still does not start, connect an ohmmeter between the 2 outside terminals in the distributor cap connector. If a reading above one ohm is obtained on the X 1 scale, replace the ignition coil.

If the reading from the green or white module lead to ground was infinite, connect the ohmmeter between the 2 leads (green and white). If the reading is between 500 and 1,500 ohms repeat the reading while moving the vacuum advance with a screwdriver. If the reading is still within the 500-1,500 ohm limits, check the ignition coil as described in the paragraph above.

If a reading of less than 500 or more than 1,500 ohms is obtained, replace the pickup

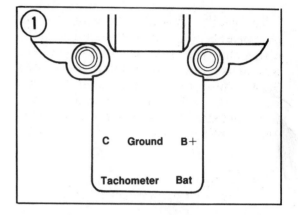

coil. If the engine still does not start, check the ignition coil as outlined above.

If the ohmmeter reads less than one ohm on the X 1 scale when the ignition coil is checked, connect the ohmmeter between the center terminal in the distributor cap side connector and the ignition coil case. If the reading is above 30,000 ohms or less than 6,000 ohms, replace the coil. If the reading is between 6,000-30,000 ohms, repeat the procedure above until the problem is isolated.

Engine Runs Rough or Cuts Out

Check the spark plugs and plug wires and repair or replace as needed. If engine still runs rough, have a dealer check the ECM and replace if indicated. If this is not the problem, remove the distributor cap and inspect cap and distributor for signs of moisture, dust, cracks, burns, etc., and repair or replace as necessary.

If the ECM is good, remove the green and white distributor module leads. Connect an ohmmeter between either lead and a good ground. If the reading is less than infinity on the X 1,000 scale, replace the pickup coil. If the reading is infinity, connect the ohmmeter between the green and white leads. If the reading is between 500 and 1,500 ohms, retake the reading while moving the vacuum advance with a screwdriver. If the reading is still within the 500-1,500 ohm limits, check the ignition coil as outlined below. If the reading is not within the 500-1,500 ohm limits, replace the pickup coil. If engine still does not function properly, check the ignition coil as outlined below.

To check ignition coil, connect an ohmmeter between the center terminal of the distributor cap side connector and the ignition coil case. If the reading is more than 30,000 ohms, or less than 6,000 ohms, replace the ignition coil. If the reading is between 6,000 and 30,000 ohms, repeat the procedure above until the problem is isolated.

BODY AND CHASSIS ELECTRICAL SYSTEMS

Circuit failures are usually caused by open or short circuits. Open circuits are generally caused by breaks in wiring, faulty connections or by failure of a switch, fuse or circuit breaker. Short circuits are usually caused by components of one circuit coming into contact with each other, or by a wire or component ground to the car body because of screws driven through wires, cut or abraded insulation, etc.

Finding electrical problems is usually a matter of painstakingly checking out the circuit involved to isolate the cause. Complete troubleshooting procedures covering all possible situations and corrective action for the complete electrical system are beyond the scope of this book. The following pointers, however, may be of help in locating and correcting body electrical wiring failures.

1. If all or the major portion of the electrical circuit fails at the same time, check for poor connections at connectors between the front and rear wiring harnesses, or between the front harness and the chassis wiring connector on top of the fuse block.

2. If only one of the circuits (all headlights, etc.) fails, the cause is probably due to an open or short in the affected circuit. Short circuits usually result in blown fuses or tripped circuit breakers. If the appropriate fuse or circuit breaker is not blown and the circuit affected is a lamp circuit, check the bulb or sealed beam unit before proceeding. If bulbs are good, check the circuit for continuity.

3. Dome and courtesy lamp circuits are designed so that switches are in the "ground" side of the circuit. If lamps remain on when switches are not activated, the problem is probably due to a defective switch or the wire leading to the switch being grounded.

FUEL SYSTEM

Fuel system troubles must be isolated to the carburetor, fuel pump, fuel filter or lines. The following procedures assume the ignition system has been checked and is properly adjusted and that there is sufficient fuel in the fuel tank.

Engine Will Not Start

First, determine that fuel is being delivered to the carburetor. Remove the air cleaner and look into the carburetor throat while depressing the accelerator pump several times. There should be a stream of fuel from the accelerator pump discharge nozzle each time the accelerator is depressed. If not, check fuel pump delivery, float valve and float adjustment, fuel filter, and fuel pump and lines. If fuel is present and the engine still will not start, check the automatic choke for sticking or damage. If necessary, rebuild or replace the carburetor.

Engine Runs at Fast Idle

Misadjustment of fast idle screw or defective carburetor, vacuum leak, intake manifold leak, carburetor gasket leak.

Rough Idle or Engine Miss With Frequent Stalling

Check carburetor idle mixture and idle screw and/or solenoid adjustments (Chapter Five).

Engine Diesels When Ignition is Shut Off

Check carburetor adjustments, particularly the idle stop or "anti-dieseling" solenoid, if so equipped.

Engine Misses or Stumbles at High Speed or Lacks Power

This indicates possible fuel starvation. Check fuel filter and fuel pump pressure/capacity (Chapter Five). If this does not solve the problem, clean the main jet and float needle valve.

Black Exhaust Smoke

This means that the air/fuel mixture is excessively rich with fuel. Make sure that the automatic choke is working properly. Check idle mixture and idle speed settings (Chapter Five). Check for excessive fuel pump pressure, a leaky float or a worn float needle valve.

EXHAUST EMISSION CONTROLS

Failure of the emission control systems to maintain exhaust output within acceptable limits is usually due to a defective carburetor, improper carburetor adjustment, incorrect engine timing, general engine condition or defective emission control devices.

CLUTCH

Several clutch troubles may be experienced. Usually, the trouble is quite obvious and will fall into one of the following categories:
1. Slipping, chattering or grabbing when engaging.
2. Spinning or dragging when disengaged.
3. Clutch noises, clutch pedal pulsations and rapid clutch disc facing wear.

Clutch Slips While Engaged

Improper adjustment of clutch cable or linkage, weak or broken pressure spring, worn friction disc facings and grease or oil on clutch disc.

Clutch Chatters or Grabs While Engaging

Usually caused by misadjustment of clutch cable or linkage, dirt or grease on the friction disc facing, or broken, worn clutch parts or warped or burned flywheel.

Clutch Spins or Drags When Disengaged

The clutch friction disc normally spins briefly after disengagement and takes a moment to come to rest. This should not be confused with drag. Drag is caused by the friction disc not being fully released from the flywheel or pressure plate as the clutch pedal is depressed. The trouble can be caused by clutch cable or linkage misadjustment, defective or worn clutch parts or a warped flywheel.

Clutch Noises

Clutch noises are usually most noticeable when the engine is idling. First, note whether the noise is heard when the clutch is engaged or disengaged. Clutch noises when engaged cold be due to a loose friction disc hub, loose friction disc springs or a possible misalignment or looseness of engine or transmission mountings. When disengaged, noises can be due to a worn release bearing, defective pilot bearing or a misaligned release lever.

Clutch Pedal Pulsates

Usually noticed when slight pressure is applied to the clutch pedal with the engine running. As pedal pressure is increased, the pulsation ceases. Possible causes include misalignment of engine and transmission, bent crankshaft flange, distortion or shifting of the clutch housing, release lever misalignment, warped friction disc, damaged pressure plate or warped flywheel.

Rapid Friction Disc Facing Wear

This trouble is caused by any condition that permits slippage between facings and the flywheel or pressure plate. Probable causes are "riding" the clutch, slow releasing of the clutch after disengagement, weak or broken pressure springs, pedal linkage or cable misadjustment, warped clutch disc or pressure plate.

MANUAL TRANSMISSION

Hard Shifting Into Gear

Common causes are the clutch not releasing, misadjustment of linkage, linkage needing lubrication, detent ball stuck or gears tight on shaft splines.

Transmission Slips Out of First or Reverse Gear

Causes are gearshift linkage out of adjustment, gear loose on main shaft, gear teeth worn, excessive play, insufficient shift lever spring tension or worn bearings.

Transmission Slips Out of Gear

Gearshift linkage is out of adjustment, misalignment between engine and transmission, excessive main shaft end play, worn gear teeth, gear loose on main shaft, insufficient shift lever spring tension, worn bearings or a defective synchronizer.

No Power Through Transmission

May be caused by clutch slipping, stripped gear teeth, damaged shifter fork linkage, broken gear or shaft and stripped drive key.

Transmission Noisy in NEUTRAL

Transmission misaligned, bearings worn or dry, worn gears, worn or bent countershaft or excessive countershaft end play.

Transmission Noisy in Gear

Defective clutch disc, worn bearings, loose gears, worn gear teeth and faults listed above.

Gears Clash During Shifting

Caused by the clutch not releasing, defective synchronizer or gears sticking on main shaft.

Oil Leaks

Most common causes are foaming due to use of wrong lubricant, lubricant level too high, broken gaskets, damaged oil seals, loose drain plug and cracked transmission case.

AUTOMATIC TRANSMISSION

Many automatic transmission problems are caused by improper linkage adjustment or a low fluid level. If linkage adjustment and fluid level is satisfactory, refer further troubleshooting to a dealer or qualified tranmission specialist.

DIFFERENTIAL

Noise usually draws attention to trouble in the differential. It is not always easy to diagnose the trouble determining the source of noise and the operating conditions that produce the noise. Defective conditions in the universal joints, wheel bearings, muffler or tires may be wrongly diagnosed as trouble in the differential or axles.

Some clue as to the cause of trouble may be gained by noting whether the noise is a hum, growl or knock; whether it is produced when the car is accelerating under load or coasting; and whether it is heard when the car is going straight or making a turn.

1. *Noise during acceleration*—May be caused by shortage of lubricant, incorrect tooth contact between drive gear and drive pinion, damaged or misadjusted bearings in axles or side bearings or damaged gears.

2. *Noise during coasting*–May be caused by incorrect backlash between drive gear and drive pinion gear or incorrect adjustment of drive pinion bearing.

3. *Noise during turn*—This noise is usually caused by loose or worn axle shaft bearing, pinion gear too tight on shafts, side gear jammed in differential case or worn side gear thrust washer and pinion thrust washer.

4. *Broken differential parts*—Breaking of differential parts can be caused by insufficient lubricant, improper use of clutch, excessive loading, misadjusted bearings and gears, excessive backlash, damage to case or loose bolts. A humming noise in the differential is often caused by improper drive pinion or ring gear adjustment which prevents normal tooth contact between gears. If ignored, rapid tooth wear will take place and the noise will become more like a growl. Repair as soon as the humming is heard so that new gears will not be required.

Tire noise will vary considerably, depending upon the type of road surface. Radial tire noise at some road speeds is considered normal and may not even be cured by tire replacement. Differential noises will be the same regardless of road surface. If noises are heard, listen carefully to the noise over different road surfaces to help isolate the problem.

BRAKE SYSTEM

Brake Pedal Goes to Floor

Worn linings or pads, air in the hydraulic system, leaky brake lines, leaky wheel cylinders or leaky/worn master cylinder may be the cause. Check for leaks and worn brake linings or pads. Bleed and adjust the brakes. Rebuild wheel cylinders and/or master cylinder.

Spongy Pedal

Usually caused by air in the brake system. Bleed and adjust the brakes.

Brakes Pull

Check brake adjustment and wear on linings and disc pads. Check for contaminated linings, leaking wheel cylinders, loose calipers, lines, or hoses. Check front end alignment and suspension damage such as broken front or rear springs and shock absorbers. Tires also affect braking; check tire pressures and tire condition.

Brakes Squeal or Chatter

Check brake and pad lining thickness and brake drum/rotor condition. Ensure that shoes are not loose. Clean away all dirt on shoes, drums, rotors and pads.

Brakes Drag

Check brake adjustment, including handbrake. Check for broken or weak shoe return springs, swollen rubber parts due to improper or contaminated brake fluid. Check for defective master cylinder. Also check the brake pedal-to-master cylinder clearance.

Hard Pedal

Check brake linings for contamination. Check for brake line restrictions and frozen wheel cylinders and calipers.

High Speed Fade

Check for distorted or out-of-round drums and rotors. Check linings or pads for contamination.

Pulsating Pedal

Check for distorted or out-of-round brake drums or rotors. Check for excessive disc runout.

COOLING SYSTEM

Engine Overheats

May be caused by insufficient coolant, loose or defective drive belt, defective thermostat, defective water pump, clogged coolant lines or passages, incorrect ignition timing, and/or defective or loose hoses, or a defective fan clutch. Inspect radiator and all parts for leaks.

Engine Does Not Warm Up

Usually caused by defective thermostat or extremely cold weather.

Coolant Loss

Radiator leaks, loose or defective hoses, defective water pump, leaks in cylinder head gasket, cracked cylinder head or engine block, or defective radiator cap may be the cause.

Noisy Cooling System

Usually caused by defective water pump bearings, loose or bent fan blades, or a defective drive belt.

STEERING AND SUSPENSION

Trouble in the suspension or steering is evident when any of the following occur:
  a. Hard steering.
  b. Car pulls to one side.
  c. Car wanders or front wheels wobble.
  d. Excessive play in steering.
  e. Abnormal tire wear.

Unusual steering, pulling or wandering is usually caused by bent or misaligned suspension parts. If the trouble seems to be excessive play, check wheel bearing adjustment first. Next, check steering free play and kingpins or ball-joints. Finally, check tie rod ends by shaking each wheel.

Tire Wear Analysis

Abnormal tire wear should always be analyzed to determine the cause. The most common are incorrect tire pressure, improper driving, overloading and incorrect wheel alignment. **Figure 2** identifies wear patterns and their most probable causes.

Underinflation—Worn more on sides than in center.

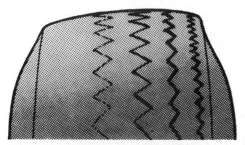

Wheel Alignment—Worn more on one side than the other. Edges of tread feathered.

Road Abrasion—Rough wear on entire tire or in patches.

Overinflation—Worn more in center than on sides.

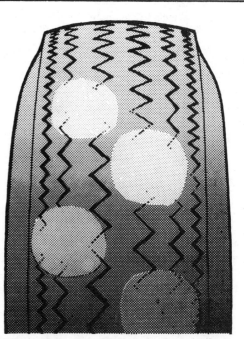

Wheel Balance — Scalloped edges indicate wheel wobble or tramp due to wheel unbalance.

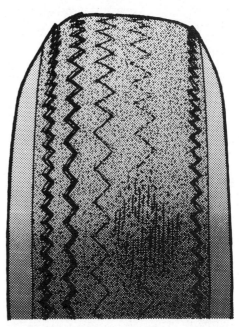

Combination—Most tires exhibit a combination of the above. This tire was overinflated (center worn) and the toe-in was incorrect (feathering). The driver cornered hard at high speed (feathering, rounded shoulders) and braked rapidly (worn spots). The scaly roughness indicates a rough road surface.

Wheel Balancing

All 4 wheels and tires must be in balance along 2 axes. To be in static balance (**Figure 3**), weight must be evenly distributed around the axis of rotation. (A) shows a statically unbalanced wheel. (B) shows the result–wheel tramp or hopping. (C) shows proper static balance.

To be in dynamic balance (**Figure 4**), the centerline of the weight must coincide with the centerline of the wheel. (A) shows a dynamically unbalanced wheel. (B) shows the result–wheel wobble or shimmy. (C) shows proper dynamic balance.

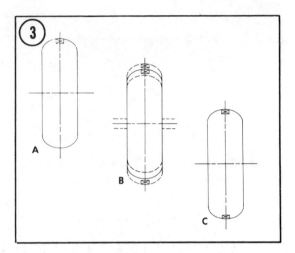

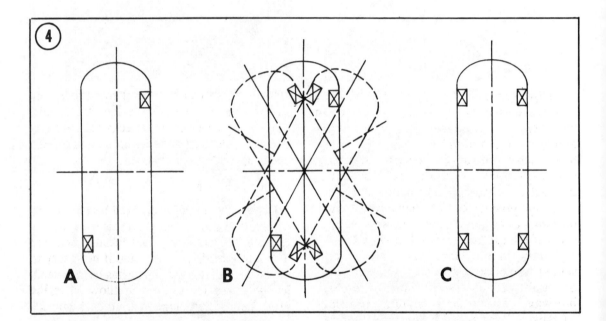

NOTE: If you own a 1985 model, first check the Supplement at the back of the book for any new service information.

CHAPTER THREE

LUBRICATION AND PREVENTIVE MAINTENANCE

Following a careful program of lubrication and preventive maintenance will result in longer engine and vehicle life. It will also pay dividends in fewer and less expensive repair bills. Such a program is especially important if the car is used in remote areas or on heavily traveled freeways where breakdowns are not only inconvenient but dangerous. Such breakdowns or failures are much less likely to occur if the car has been well maintained.

Certain maintenance tasks and checks should be performed weekly. Others should be performed at certain time or mileage intervals. Still others should be done whenever certain symptoms appear. Maintenance schedules are given in **Tables 1-5.**

Oil viscosity recommendations are provided in **Table 6** and **Table 7**. **Table 8** gives GM recommended lubricants. **Tables 1-8** are at the end of the chapter.

WEEKLY CHECKS

Many of the following checks were once routinely made by service station attendants when you stopped for fuel. With the advent of the self-service station and the extra cost for "full-service," you may want to perform the checks yourself. Even though they are simple, they are important. Such checks help prolong the car's life and give an indication of the need for other maintenance.

Engine Oil Level

Engine oil should be checked before the car is started in the morning. At this time, all the oil is in the crankcase and the dipstick will give a true reading. If you find it necessary to check the oil after the engine has been started, let the car sit for an hour to allow oil in the upper part of the engine to drain back into the crankcase.

To check engine oil level, remove the dipstick and wipe clean with a cloth or paper towel. Reinsert the dipstick in the tube until it seats firmly. Wait a moment, then remove it again and read the oil level on the lower end. Reinsert the dipstick after taking the reading. **Figure 1** shows a typical dipstick location for all engines.

The oil level should be maintained in the "SAFE" zone on the dipstick. Oil should be added whenever the level drops below the "ADD" mark. Do not overfill the engine. Too much oil can be as harmful to the engine as too little.

Coolant Level

> *WARNING*
> *Do not remove the radiator cap when*
> *the engine is warm or hot, especially if*
> *an air conditioner has been in use. You*
> *may be seriously scalded or burned.*

On vehicles equipped with coolant recovery systems, check coolant level by observing the liquid level in the reservoir (**Figure 2**, typical). The radiator cap should not be removed. Coolant should be at the "COLD FULL" mark on the reservoir with the engine coolant at ambient temperature or at the "HOT FULL" mark with the engine at operating temperature.

Coolant level on cars without a recovery system should be maintained 3 inches below the bottom of the filler neck when the cooling system is cold.

> *NOTE*
> *The coolant level in crossflow radiators*
> *cannot be checked with the engine*
> *running. Check the level when the*
> *engine is cold.*

Any significant loss of coolant could mean a leak in the cooling system. If the system consistently loses coolant, see Chapter Seven for system testing.

Battery Electrolyte Level

Unsealed batteries will have individual cell vent caps, or a bar with vented plugs which fits across 3 cells. To check electrolyte level with this type of battery, remove the vent caps or vent bars and observe the liquid level. It should touch the bottom of the vent well (**Figure 3**). If it does not, add distilled water until the level is satisfactory. Do not overfill, as this will result in loss of electrolyte and shorten the battery life. Carefully wipe any spilled water from the battery top before installing the vent caps or bars.

Periodic electrolyte level checks are not required on Delco Freedom II or other sealed maintenance-free batteries.

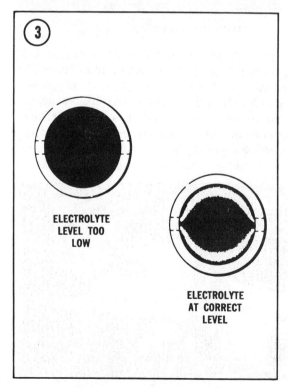

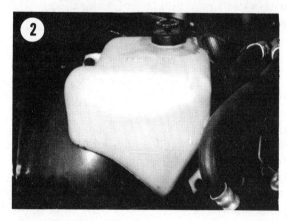

ELECTROLYTE LEVEL TOO LOW

ELECTROLYTE AT CORRECT LEVEL

Windshield Wipers and Washers

Check the wiper blades for breaks or cracks in the rubber. Blade replacement intervals will vary with age, the weather, amount of use and the degree of chemical reaction from road salts or tar.

Operate the windshield washer and wiper blades. At the same time, check the amount and direction of the sprayed fluid. If the blades do not clean the windshield satisfactorily, wash the windshield and the blades with a mild undiluted detergent. Rinse with water while rubbing with a clean cloth or paper towels.

If the wiper pattern is uneven and streaks over clean glass, replace the blades.

Fill the fluid reservoir (**Figure 4**, typical) with a mixture of water and windshield washer fluid. A mixture of ammonia and water works equally well. In cold weather areas, do not fill the reservoir more than 3/4 full to allow for expansion in freezing weather. Never use radiator antifreeze in the windshield washer reservoir, as it can damage painted surfaces.

OWNER SAFETY CHECKS

The following simple checks should be performed on a daily basis during normal operation of the car. Some are driveway checks. The others can be performed while driving. If any result in unsatisfactory operation, see your dealer to have the condition corrected.

Steering Column Lock

The ignition key should turn to the LOCK position only when the transmission selector is in PARK (automatic transmission) or REVERSE (manual transmission).

Parking Brake and Transmission PARK Mechanism

Check holding ability by setting the parking brake with the car on a fairly steep hill. Check automatic transmission PARK mechanism by placing the transmission selector in PARK and releasing all brakes.

WARNING

*You should not expect the PARK mechanism to hold the car by itself even on a level surface. **Always** set the parking brake after placing the transmission selector in PARK. When parking on an incline, you should also turn the wheels to the curb before shutting off the engine.*

Transmission Shift Indicator

Make sure the automatic transmission shift indicator accurately indicates the gear selected.

Starter Safety Switch

The starter should operate only in PARK or NEUTRAL positions (automatic transmission) or in NEUTRAL with the clutch fully depressed (manual transmission, if equipped with starter safety switch).

Steering

Check the steering mechanism to make sure it operates freely and does not have excessive play or make harsh sounds when turning or parking.

Wheel Alignment and Balance

Visually check tires for abnormal wear. If the car pulls either to the right or left on a straight, level road (with correct tire pressure), have the wheel alignment checked. Excessive vibration of the steering wheel or front of the car while driving at normal highway speeds usually indicates the need for wheel balancing.

Brakes

Observe brake warning light (if so equipped) during braking action. Also check for changes in braking action, such as pulling to one side, unusual sounds or increased brake pedal travel. If the brake pedal feels spongy, there is probably air in the hydraulic system. Bleed the brakes (Chapter Eight).

Exhaust System

Be alert to any smell of fumes in the car or to any change in the sound of the exhaust system that might indicate leakage.

Defroster

Turn on the heater, then move the control to defrost (DEF) and check the amount of air directed to the windshield.

Rear View Mirrors and Sun Visors

Make sure that the friction mounts are adjusted so that mirrors and visors stay in selected positions.

Horn

Check the horn to make sure that it works properly.

Lap and Shoulder Belts

Check all components for proper operation. Make sure that the anchor bolts are tight. Check the belts for fraying.

Head Restraints

If the seats are equipped with head restraints, check to see that they will adjust up and down properly and that no components are missing, loose or damaged.

Seat Back Latches

If the car is equipped with automatic seat back latches, pull forward on the seat backs with the doors closed to make sure the latches hold properly.

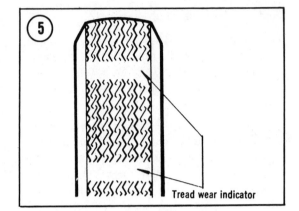

Tread wear indicator

Lights and Buzzers

Verify that all interior lights and buzzers are working. These include seat belt reminder light and buzzer, ignition key buzzer, interior lights and instrument panel illumination and warning lights.

Check all exterior lights for proper operation. These include the headlights, license plate lights, side marker lights, parking lights, turn or directional signals, backup lights and hazard warning lights.

Glass

Check for any condition that could obscure vision or be a safety hazard. Correct as required.

Door Latches

Verify positive closing, latching and locking action.

Hood Latches

Verify that the hood closes firmly by lifting up on the hood after closing it. Check for missing, broken or damaged parts.

Fluid Leaks

Check under the vehicle after it has been parked for awhile for evidence of fuel, water or oil leaks. Water dripping from the air conditioner drain tube after use is normal. Immediately determine and correct the cause of any leaking gasoline fumes or liquids to avoid possible fire or explosion.

Tires and Wheels

Visually check tire condition. Look for nails, cuts, excessive wear or other damage. Remove all stones or other objects wedged in the tread. Check tire side walls for cuts or other damage. Check tire valve for air leaks; replace valve if necessary. Replace any valve caps that are missing. Check tire pressure with a reliable pressure gauge and adjust air pressure to agree with that specified for the tires. If the tread wear indicators are visible, replace the tire. See **Figure 5**.

SCHEDULED MAINTENANCE

Maintenance intervals differ with model years. See **Tables 1-5**. These services are required to assure that emissions are maintained at the levels required by law. If your car is subjected to conditions such as heavy dust, continuous short trips or pulling trailers, more frequent servicing is necessary.

Following is a brief explanation of each of the services required by your car. Use only those which apply to your vehicle.

Engine Oil and Filter

Engine oil should be selected to meet the demands of the temperatures and driving conditions anticipated. Refer to **Table 6** (gasoline engine) or **Table 7** (diesel engine) to select a viscosity that is appropriate for the temperatures you expect to encounter during the next maintenance interval. The rating and viscosity range are usually printed on top of the can.

All General Motor divisions recommend the use of a high grade motor oil with an API classification of SE or SF for all gasoline engine vehicles in this manual. SF is preferred. Diesel engines require the use of an oil with an API classification of SF/CC, SF/CD or SE/CC. Oils not marked with these letter codes will not provide the protection necessary for diesel engines and their use could lead to engine damage.

Change the oil and filter at specified intervals.

CAUTION

Non-detergent, low quality oil should never be used. The regular use of oil additives is not recommended.

To drain the oil and change the filter, proceed as follows:

1. Drive the car until the engine warms up thoroughly. Place a suitable container under the oil pan.
2. Set the parking brake and block the rear wheels.
3. Raise the front of the car with a jack and place it on jackstands.
4. Remove the drain plug. **Figure 6** shows a typical drain plug location.
5. Clean the drain plug and check its gasket. Replace the gasket if damaged.
6. Allow the oil to drain completely (10-15 minutes), then reinstall the plug snugly.
7. Move the drain pan beneath the oil filter. **Figure 7** shows a typical oil filter location on

gasoline engines; **Figure 8** shows a typical diesel oil filter location.

8. Loosen the filter with a filter wrench (**Figure 9**). Remove and discard the filter. Wipe the filter mounting pad on the engine clean with a lint-free cloth or paper towel.

9. Coat the neoprene gasket on the new filter with a thin film of clean engine oil. Screw the filter in place *by hand* until it contacts the mounting pad surface. Tighten 1/2-2/3 turn further by hand. Do not overtighten as this can cause an oil leak.

10. Remove the filler cap on the valve cover. **Figure 10** shows a typical gasoline engine; **Figure 11** shows a diesel engine. Fill the crankcase with the required amount of oil:

  a. 4-cylinder–4 qt. with filter change, 3 qt. without.

  b. 231 cid V6–4 qt. with or without filter change.

  c. Diesel V8–7 qt. with filter change, 6 qt. without.

  d. All others–5 qt. with filter change, 4 qt. without.

Wipe up any spills on the valve cover with a clean cloth and reinstall the filler cap.

11. Start the engine. The engine warning or oil pressure light will stay on for several seconds. Allow the engine to idle for several minutes.

> *CAUTION*
> *Do not operate the engine at more than idle speed until the oil has a chance to circulate thoroughly through the engine or damage could result.*

12. Check the area under and around the drain plug and filter for leaks while the engine is idling. Correct as required. Shut the engine off.

Air Cleaner

A disposable paper element filter is used in all air cleaners. Service to a paper element filter consists only of replacement. Elements must not be cleaned with an air hose, tapped, washed or oiled.

Air cleaner filters should be replaced at specified intervals. The entire air cleaner is

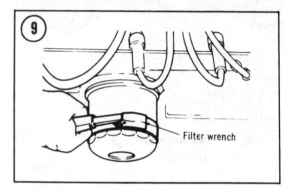

Filter wrench

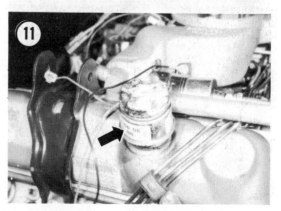

replaced at 50,000 mile intervals on 4-cylinder engines covered by this manual.

To change the filter on 6-cylinder and V8 engines:

1. Remove the wing nut at the center of the air cleaner cover (**Figure 12**). Remove the cover.
2. Remove and discard the filter (**Figure 13**).
3. Wipe the inside of the air cleaner housing with a damp rag to remove any dust, dirt or debris.

4. Install a new filter element. Install the cover and tighten the wing nut snugly.

To change the air cleaner on 4-cylinder engines:

1. Remove the 2 wing nuts on the air cleaner cover.
2. Disconnect air cleaner housing from carburetor air horn and snorkel ducting. Remove and discard the air cleaner.
3. Installation of a new air cleaner is the reverse of removal.

Check hoses and ducts on the air cleaner every 12,000 miles. Replace any hose or ducting that is damaged. Check to make sure the air control valve in the air cleaner tube operates freely. Locate and correct any cause of valve binding or sticking.

Crankcase Ventilation Filter

The crankcase ventilation filter pack in the air cleaner housing (**Figure 14**) should be replaced each time the air cleaner filter is changed. Disconnect the hose leading to the filter pack, slide the retaining clip off and remove the filter pack from inside the air cleaner. Install a new filter pack through the air cleaner hole, slide the retaining clip in place on the outside of the housing and reconnect the hose.

Fuel Filter/Fuel Lines (Gasoline Engines)

All gasoline engines use a pleated paper filter and check valve assembly located in the carburetor fuel inlet. See **Figure 15** (typical).

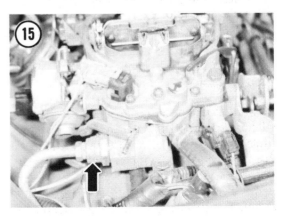

3

A clogged fuel filter can cause stumbling or cutting out at high speed and will eventually lead to complete fuel starvation. Change the filter every 15,000 miles as follows:

1. Remove the air cleaner as necessary to provide access to the fuel inlet fitting.

2. Hold the inlet nut with an open-end wrench and loosen the fuel line attaching nut with a second open-end wrench.

3. Disconnect the fuel line from the inlet nut. Cap the line and move it out of the way.

4. Remove the fuel inlet nut. Remove the filter and spring.

5. Install the spring and new filter in the inlet (**Figure 16**). The gasket end or hole in the filter must face outward.

6. Install a new gasket on the inlet nut. Install the nut in the carburetor and tighten to 25 ft.-lb. (34 N•m).

7. Install fuel line to inlet nut. Hold inlet nut with an open-end wrench and tighten fuel line fitting to 18 ft.-lb. (24 N•m).

8. Install the air cleaner, if removed. Start the engine and check for fuel leaks.

Check all fuel lines for abrasion, cracks, pinched spots, etc. when the fuel filter is changed.

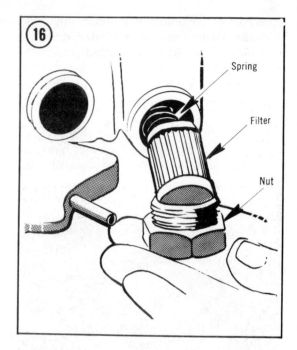

Spring

Filter

Nut

Fuel Filter/Fuel Lines (Diesel Engines)

The fuel filter on all diesel engines is located in a line between the mechanical fuel pump and the injection pump. Diesel fuel filters should be replaced when engine temperature is below 125° F to reduce initial cranking time.

To replace, disconnect the filter from the line and install a new one. Disconnect the wire connector at the engine temperature switch (near the oil filter) and use a jumper wire to bridge the connection. Once the engine is running, remove the jumper wire and reconnect the temperature switch wire connector.

Battery (Unsealed)

Water is lost from the battery as the result of charging and discharging. It must be replaced before the electrolyte level falls to the tops of the battery plates. If the plates become exposed, they may become sulphated, which would reduce performance and eventually destroy the battery. Also, the plates cannot provide full battery power in the battery action unless they are completely covered by the electrolyte. Add distilled water as often as necessary to keep the fluid level approximately 1/2 in. above the top of the battery plates or at the bottom of the filler vent wells. Do not overfill.

The charging action of a battery creates heat. A battery that requires frequent addition of water may be subject to overcharging. This is a signal to have the charging system checked to see if the alternator and voltage regulator are doing their job properly.

When working with batteries, use extreme care to avoid spilling or splashing the electrolyte. Battery electrolyte is sulphuric acid, which can destroy clothing and cause serious chemical burns. If any electrolyte is spilled or splashed on clothing or body, immediately neutralize it with a solution of baking soda and water, then flush the affected area with plenty of clean water.

WARNING
Electrolyte splashed into the eyes is extremely dangerous. Always wear

safety glasses when working with batteries. If electrolyte is splashed into the eyes, call a physician immediately, force the eyes open and flood with cool, clean water for about 5 minutes.

If electrolyte is spilled or splashed onto painted or unpainted surfaces, neutralize it immediately with a baking soda and water solution and then rinse with clean water.

Keep the battery clean. Electrolyte which escapes through the vents will create a surface charge on the top of the battery which lowers battery performance. It also attacks metal surfaces such as the battery cable clamps. Periodically remove the battery from the engine compartment and clean it as described in Chapter Six.

Exhaust Gas Recirculation (EGR) System

Remove and inspect the EGR valve (**Figure 17**) at specified intervals. Replace the valve every 30,000 miles. Check the orifice hole in the valve body for deposits. At the same time, inspect the EGR passages in the intake manifold and clean if required. To service the EGR valve:

1. Remove the EGR valve from the engine. **Figure 18** shows a typical V8 engine installation; others are similar.
2. Inspect the valve and spacer passages for carbon buildup. Remove exhaust deposits around valve and on mounting surface with a wire wheel.
3. Depress valve diaphragm. Check valve seating and outlet areas. If not completely clean, repeat Step 2.
4. Remove exhaust deposits in the valve outlet with a screwdriver.
5. Clean intake manifold and valve mounting surfaces. Sandwich the spacer between new gaskets and install on the manifold. Install the valve and tighten the mounting bolts to 15-22 ft.-lb. (20-30 N•m).
6. Check vacuum lines for damage or deterioration and replace as necessary.
7. If the EGR system is suspected of a malfunction other than a dirty valve, have it tested by a dealer or other competent mechanic.

Positive Crankcase Ventilation (PCV) System

The PCV valve and fittings should be checked for proper operation and replaced at specified intervals. More frequent checks and/or replacement should be made if the car is operated under severe conditions.

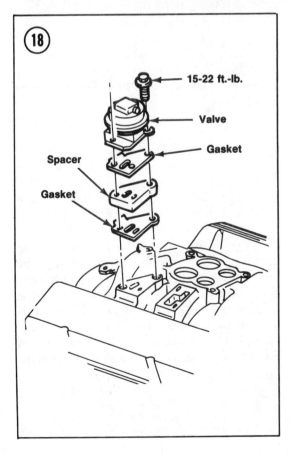

To check the valve, pull it from its rubber grommet (**Figure 19**) in the intake manifold or rocker arm cover. Run the engine at idle. Put a finger over the end of the valve. If no vacuum is felt, check for plugged hoses or valve. Replace as required. Shut the engine off and shake the valve. If the valve rattles, it is working; if not, replace it.

Evaporative Emission Canister

Canister design, location and hose connections differ according to model year and engine application. **Figure 20** shows a typical installation. Inspect the canister lines and connections and change the filter in the canister lower section (if so equipped) at specified intervals.

Replace the canister if it has been damaged or flooded with oil or gasoline. To remove the canister, disconnect the vapor hoses. Remove the bolt(s) holding the canister and lift it from the engine compartment. Install a new canister in the reverse order.

Drive Belts

Check all engine drive belts for cracks, fraying and tension at specified intervals. Adjust tension or replace belts as required. See Chapter Seven.

Brake Master Cylinder

Fluid level should be checked every 6,000 miles on 1972-1974 models and every 7,500 miles on 1975-on models. Clean all dirt and grime from the edge of the cover so it will not fall into the reservoir.

1A. To check fluid level on 1972-1980 master cylinders (**Figure 21**), insert a wide-blade screwdriver under the wire bail and pry it off the cover. Remove the cover.

1B. With 1981-on master cylinders (**Figure 22**), lift up on the cover to unsnap the plastic cover tabs at one side, then remove the cover.

2. If the fluid level is more than 1/4 in. below the reservoirs, top up with a brake fluid marked DOT 3.

3A. On 1972-1980 master cylinders, install the cover and pry the wire bail back in place

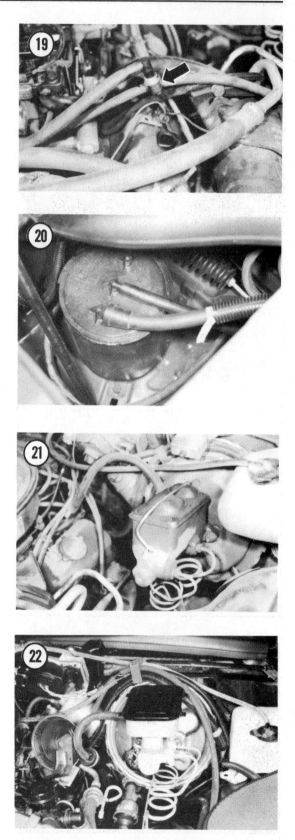

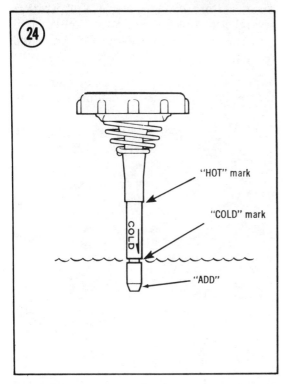

"HOT" mark

"COLD" mark

"ADD"

until it snaps back into the cover depressions. 3B. On 1981-on master cylinders, snap the cover in place on the reservoir.

Inspect brake lines and fittings for abrasion, kinks, leakage and other damage.

Manual Steering Gear Housing

Inspect the area around the pitman arm and housing for seal leakage at specified intervals. Leakage (solid grease, not just an oily film) should be corrected immediately. Seasonal change is not necessary and no lubrication is required for the life of the steering gear.

Power Steering

Check the power steering fluid in the power steering pump reservoir (**Figure 23**, typical) at each oil change period. Add GM power steering fluid (or DEXRON or DEXRON II automatic transmission fluid) as required to bring the level to the proper range on the filler cap dipstick. See **Figure 24**. If at operating temperature, fluid level should be between the "HOT" and "COLD" marks. If at outdoor temperature, fluid level should be between "ADD" and "COLD" marks.

Check all power steering hoses and lines for proper connections, leaks and deterioration. If abrasion or undue wear is evident, locate and correct the cause immediately.

Cooling System

The cooling system should be serviced at special intervals. Test the system for leaks and check or replace the pressure cap. Tighten hose clamps (**Figure 25**) and inspect all cooling and heater hoses for cracks, checks, swelling or other signs of deterioration. Replace hoses at every coolant change.

Clean exterior of radiator and air conditioning compressor with compressed air every 12 months. Drain and flush cooling system and replace coolant at specified intervals.

3

Rear Axle and Manual Transmission Lubrication

Remove the rear axle filler plug and check the lubricant level at specified intervals. Rear axle and manual transmission lubricants normally do not require changing during the life of the vehicle. However, if the vehicle is used consistently for trailer pulling, rear axle lubricant should be changed at specified "severe service" intervals.

Positraction rear axles require a special lubricant (GM part No. 1051052 or equivalent). Drain and refill to level of filler plug hole at first specified interval, then maintain as a standard differential.

With Limited Slip rear axles used from 1979-on, drain and refill to level of filler plug hole at first 7,500 miles. Change lubricant at 15,000 mile intervals when using vehicle to pull a trailer. Add 4 ounces of GM lubricant additive (part No. 1052358) or equivalent, then fill with GM gear lubricant part No. 1052271, 1052272 or equivalent.

Check manual transmission fluid level every 12 months or 7,500 miles. With the transmission at operating temperature, the fluid level should be level with the bottom of the filler plug hole. When the transmission is cold, the level should be 1/2 in. below the filler plug hole. If not, top up with the recommended lubricant (**Table 8**) and install the filler plug.

Automatic Transmission

Check the fluid level at each engine oil change. Change the fluid at specified intervals. Checking the fluid level is basically the same for all models:

1. Check fluid level with the transmission at operating temperature, engine running, the car parked on level ground with the parking brake set and the transmission selector in PARK.

2. Clean all dirt from the transmission dipstick cap (**Figure 26**, typical). Pull the dipstick from the tube, wipe clean (with a second clean lint-free cloth) and reinsert until cap fully seats. Remove dipstick and note reading. See **Figure 27**.

3. If the fluid level is low, add sufficient automatic transmission fluid of the

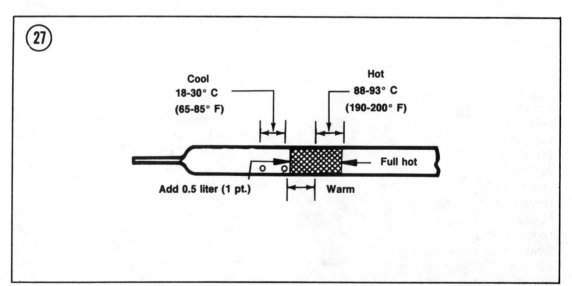

recommended type (**Table 8**) through the dipstick tube to bring it to the proper level on the dipstick. Reinsert dipstick and make sure it is fully seated in the tube.

CAUTION
Do not overfill the transmission. Too much fluid can cause damage to the transmission.

If the car has been driven under severe service conditions such as those described under *Engine Oil and Filter* in this chapter, drain and refill the fluid as follows:
1. Raise the front of the car with a jack and place it on jackstands.
2. Place a drain pan under the transmission.
3. Loosen all pan attaching bolts a few turns. Tap one corner of the pan with a rubber hammer to break it loose and let the fluid drain.
4. When the fluid has drained to the level of the pan flange, remove the pan bolts at the rear and along both sides of the pan. This will let the pan drop at one end and drain slowly.
5. When all fluid has drained, remove the pan and let the strainer or filter drain.
6. Discard the pan gasket and clean pan thoroughly with solvent and lint-free cloths or paper towels.
7. Remove the strainer or filter-to-valve body bolts. Remove the strainer or filter.
8. Clean strainer assembly thoroughly in solvent and dry with compressed air. Replace paper or felt-type filters.
9. Install a new gasket or O-ring to the strainer or filter assembly, as required. Install the strainer or filter to the valve body and tighten attaching bolts securely.
10. Install the pan with a new gasket and tighten the bolts in an alternating pattern to 12 ft.-lb. (16 N•m).
11. Lower the vehicle and fill the transmission through the dipstick tube with approximately 2.5 quarts of the recommended automatic transmission fluid (**Table 8**). Use a clean funnel inserted in the tube and a clean pouring spout installed in the fluid container to help prevent spillage.
12. Start the engine and let it idle for 2 minutes.

13. Set the parking brake, block the wheels and move the transmission selector lever through each gear range, pausing long enough for the transmission to engage. Return to the PARK position.
14. Remove the dipstick (**Figure 26**) and wipe it clean. Reinsert the dipstick in the tube until it seats completely.
15. Remove the dipstick and check the fluid level. Add sufficient automatic transmission fluid to bring to proper level on the dipstick.

Transmission Shift Linkage

Lubricate all pivot points in the shift linkage and manual transmission floor control lever with engine oil every 4 months or 6,000 miles, whichever comes first.

NOTE
If chassis lubricant has been used previously on linkage, continue using this lubricant.

Clutch Cross Shaft

Periodic lubrication of the clutch cross shaft is not required. However, at 36,000 miles, remove the plug, install a grease fitting and apply chassis lubricant with a grease gun.

Clutch Adjustment

Adjust the clutch as required. See Chapter Nine for this procedure.

**Rear Universal Joint Fitting
(1974-1975 Chevrolet Only)**

Lubricate the rear universal joint every 4 months or 6,000 miles (7,500 miles, 1975 models). Use water resistant EP chassis lubricant, GM part No. 1050679 or equivalent.

Steering Linkage and Front Suspension

Lubricate all grease fittings in the front suspension, steering linkage and universal joint at specified intervals with recommended lubricant (**Table 8**). During winter weather, the car should be placed in a heated garage for at least 30 minutes prior to lubrication so the joints will accept lubricant.

Wipe around the plugs with a clean rag to remove accumulated dirt before removing the plugs for greasing. On ball-joints, force lubricant into the joint until the joint boot can be felt or seen to swell slightly, indicating that the boot is full of lubricant.

CAUTION
Do not overfill until lubricant escapes from boot. This will destroy the weathertight seal.

Install the plugs after greasing.

Front Wheel Bearings

Lubricate at specified intervals. See Chapter Eight for procedure. Use a high melting point, water resistant, front wheel bearing lubricant meeting the requirements of GM Specification GM6031M or equivalent. If equipped with disc brakes, use GM wheel bearing lubricant part No. 1051344 or equivalent.

CAUTION
General Motors warns against the use of "long fiber" or "viscous" type lubricants on front wheel bearings, and also against the mixing of lubricant types. To avoid bearing damage, use the recommended lubricants and thoroughly clean bearings and hubs of old lubricants before repacking.

Disc Brakes

Check brake pad and rotor condition when wheels are removed for tire rotation.

Drum Brakes and Parking Brake

Inspect the brakes at specified intervals. Remove the drums and check for cracked drums, shoe or lining wear, wheel cylinder leakage and other possible defects. See Chapter Eight for procedure.

Lubricate the parking brake cable and lever mechanism with chassis lubricant.

Exhaust System

Check the entire exhaust system from exhaust manifold to tailpipe(s). Look for broken, damaged, missing, corroded or misaligned components, open seams, holes, loose connections or any other defect that could allow exhaust gases to enter. Replace as necessary.

Inspect the catalytic converter heat shields (if so equipped) for looseness or damage. Tighten or replace as required. Make sure there is adequate clearance between the exhaust system components and nearby body areas.

Tire Rotation

Rotate steel belted tires at the first 7,000 miles, then every 15,000 miles thereafter. Rotate bias belted tires every 7,500 miles. Refer to **Figure 28** for recommended rotation patterns. Tires should be inflated to the pressures shown on the tire placard on the rear face of the driver's door (late models) or to the values given in the owner's manual.

Hood Hinges and Latches

At each oil change interval, lubricate the hood hinge and latch assemblies as follows:
1. Wipe hinge and latch areas of accumulated dirt or contamination.
2. Apply Lubriplate or equivalent to latch pilot bolts and locking plate.
3. Apply engine oil to all pivot points in hood release mechanism and to primary and secondary latch mechanism.
4. Lubricate hinges with engine oil.
5. Make a functional check to verify that all parts of the hinge and latch assemblies are functioning properly.

Engine Tune-up

The purpose of a tune-up is to restore power and performance lost over a gradual period of time due to normal wear.

Because of Federal laws limiting exhaust emissions, it is important that an engine tune-up is done accurately, using the latest. information available.

Trouble-free and economical operation can be assured if a complete engine tune-up is performed at specified intervals. A tune-up generally consists of 3 distinct categories: compression, ignition and carburetion. Carburetion adjustments should not be attempted until the compression and ignition work has been completed.

Refer to Chapter Four and Chapter Five for tune-up procedures.

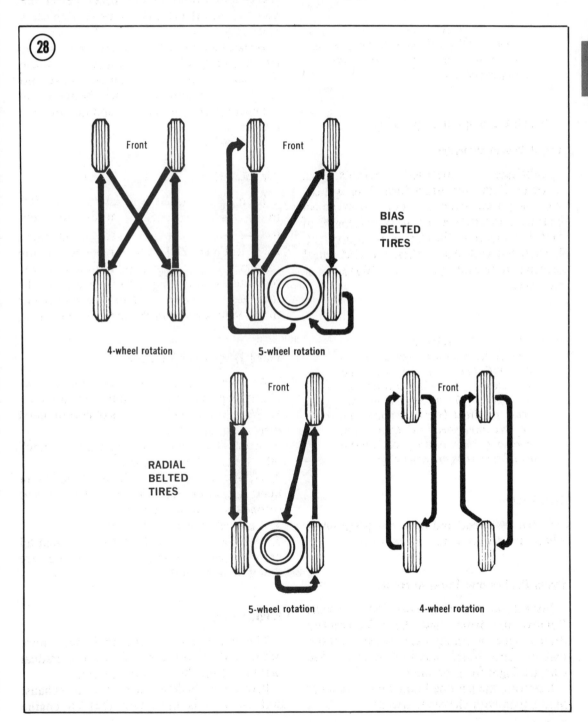

(28)

Front

Front

BIAS
BELTED
TIRES

4-wheel rotation

5-wheel rotation

RADIAL
BELTED
TIRES

Front

Front

5-wheel rotation

4-wheel rotation

Table 1 MAINTENANCE SCHEDULE (1972-1974)

Every 6,000 miles **(4 months)**	• Change engine oil[1] • Check fluid levels • Replace spark plugs (leaded fuels) • Lubricate chassis • Lubricate rear universal joint[2] • Rotate tires • Check exhaust system • Check and adjust drive belts • Check disc brakes • Check power steering operation • Check suspension and steering
At first 6,000 miles, **then every 12,000 miles**	• Change oil filter • Check air cleaner operation • Check carburetor choke • Check ignition timing • Check and adjust idle speed • Check distributor cap, coil, and ignition wiring
Every 12,000 miles **(12 months)**	• Check drum brakes and parking brake • Replace spark plugs (unleaded fuels) • Check cooling system operation • Check coolant condition and protection • Check rear axle lubricant level[1] • Replace breaker points • Replace air cleaner filter (6-cylinder only) • Check throttle linkage operation • Check EGR system operation (leaded fuels) • Replace fuel filter • Check PCV system operation • Check vacuum hose condition
Every 24,000 miles **(24 months)**	• Clean, repack and adjust wheel bearings • Check EGR system operation (unleaded fuels) • Change automatic transmission fluid and filter[1] • Check engine compression • Check fuel cap, tank and lines • Replace distributor cam lubricator • Check AIR system operation • Replace air cleaner filter (V8 only) • Replace PCV filter[1] • Drain, flush and refill cooling system • Change evaporative canister filter (if so equipped) • Replace cooling system hoses • Check spark plug and ignition coil wires
Every 36,000 miles **(36 months)**	• Check manual steering gear housing seals • Lubricate clutch cross shaft

1. SEVERE SERVICE OPERATION: If the vehicle is operated under any of the following conditions, change engine oil @ 3,000 miles or 2 months and oil filter @ alternate oil changes. Change rear axle lubricant every 12,000 miles. Replace PCV filter every 12,000 miles. Change automatic transmission fluid and service filter every 12,000 miles.

  a. Extended idle or low-speed operation (short trips, stop-and-go driving).

  b. Trailer towing.

  c. Operation at temperatures below 10° F for 60 days or more, with most trips under 10 miles.

  d. Sustained high-speed driving in hot weather.

  e. Very dusty conditions.

2. 1974 Chevrolet models only.

Table 2 MAINTENANCE SCHEDULE (1975-1976)

Every 7,500 miles **(12 months)**	• Change engine oil [1] • Check fluid levels • Lubricate chassis • Lubricate rear universal joint [2] • Check exhaust system • Check and adjust drive belts [3] • Check disc brakes • Check power steering operation • Check suspension and steering
At first 7,500 miles, **then every 15,000 miles**	• Change oil filter
At first 7,500 miles, **then every 22,500 miles**	• Check air cleaner operation • Check carburetor choke • Check ignition timing • Check and adjust idle speed • Check distributor cap, coil, and ignition wiring
Every 12,000 miles	• Check manual transmission fluid
Every 15,000 miles **(12 months)**	• Check drum brakes and parking brake • Check cooling system operation • Check coolant condition and protection • Check rear axle lubricant level [1] • Check throttle linkage operation • Replace fuel filter • Check PCV system operation • Check vacuum hose condition
Every 22,500 miles	• Replace spark plugs
Every 30,000 miles **(24 months)**	• Clean, repack and adjust wheel bearings • Check EGR system operation • Change automatic transmission fluid and filter[1] • Check engine compression • Check fuel cap, tank and lines • Check AIR system operation • Replace air cleaner filter (except 4-cylinder) • Replace PCV filter [1] • Drain, flush and refill cooling system • Change evaporative canister filter (if so equipped) • Replace cooling system hoses • Check spark plug and ignition coil wires • Check manual steering gear housing seals
Every 50,000 miles	• Replace air cleaner filter (4-cylinder only)

3

1. **SEVERE SERVICE OPERATION:** If the vehicle is operated under any of the following conditions, change engine oil @ 3,000 miles or 3 months and oil filter @ alternate oil changes. Change rear axle lubricant every 15,000 miles. Replace PCV filter every 15,000 miles. Change automatic transmission fluid and service filter every 15,000 miles (1975) or 30,000 miles (1976).
   a. Extended idle or low-speed operation (short trips, stop-and-go driving).
   b. Trailer towing.
   c. Operation @ temperatures below 10° F for 60 days or more, with most trips under 10 miles.
   d. Sustained high-speed driving in hot weather.
   e. Very dusty conditions.
2. 1975 Chevrolet models only.
3. 1976, every 15,000 miles.

Table 3 MAINTENANCE SCHEDULE (1977-ON GASOLINE ENGINE)

Every 7,500 miles (12 months)	• Change engine oil[1] • Check fluid levels • Lubricate chassis • Check exhaust system • Check power steering operation • Check suspension and steering
At first 7,500 miles, then every 15,000 miles	• Change oil filter • Check disc brakes
At first 7,500 miles, then every 22,500 miles (Schedule 1) or 30,000 miles (Schedule 2 and all 1983-on)	• Check air cleaner operation • Check carburetor choke • Check ignition timing • Check/adjust idle speed • Check distributor cap, coil and ignition wiring
Every 12,000 miles	• Check manual transmission fluid
Every 15,000 miles (12 months)	• Check drum brakes and parking brake • Check cooling system operation • Check coolant condition and protection • Check rear axle lubricant level[1] • Check throttle linkage operation • Replace fuel filter • Check PCV system operation • Check vacuum hose condition
Every 22,500 miles (Schedule 1) or 30,000 miles (Schedule 2 and all 1983-on)	• Replace spark plugs • Check spark plug and ignition coil wires • Check EFE valve operation
Every 30,000 miles (24 months)	• Clean, repack and adjust wheel bearings • Check EGR system operation • Check engine compression • Check fuel cap, tank and lines • Check AIR system operation • Replace air cleaner filter (except 4-cylinder) • Replace air cleaner crankcase ventilation filter • Replace PCV valve[1] • Drain, flush and refill cooling system • Change evaporative canister filter (if so equipped) • Replace cooling system hoses • Check manual steering gear housing seals
Every 50,000 miles	• Replace air cleaner filter (4-cylinder only)
Every 60,000 miles	• Change automatic transmission fluid and filter (1976-1978)
Every 100,000 miles	• Change automatic transmission fluid and filter (1979-on)

1. SEVERE SERVICE OPERATION: If the vehicle is operated under any of the following conditions, change engine oil and filter @ 3,000 miles or 3 months. Change rear axle lubricant every 15,000 miles. Replace PCV valve every 15,000 miles. Change automatic transmission fluid and service filter/screen every 15,000 miles.
   a. Extended idle or low-speed operation (short trips, stop-and-go driving).
   b. Trailer towing.
   c. Operation @ temperatures below 10° F for 60 days or more, with most trips under 10 miles.
   d. Sustained high-speed driving in hot weather.
   e. Very dusty conditions.

Table 4 MAINTENANCE SCHEDULE (1980 DIESEL)

Every 3,000 miles	• Change engine oil and filter
First 3,000 miles, then every 30,000 miles	• Adjust idle speed
Every 6,000 miles	• Check rear axle lubricant level • Rotate bias-belted tires
At first 6,000 miles, then every 12,000 miles	• Rotate radial tires
Every 9,000 miles (12 months)	• Check fluid levels • Lubricate chassis • Check exhaust system • Check power steering operation • Check suspension and steering • Check disc brakes
Every 15,000 miles (12 months)	• Check drum brakes and parking brake • Check and adjust drive belts • Service crankcase ventilation system • Check cooling system operation • Check coolant condition and protection
Every 30,000 miles (24 months)	• Clean, repack and adjust wheel bearings • Check fuel cap, tank and lines • Replace air cleaner filter element • Replace fuel filter • Drain, flush and refill cooling system • Replace cooling system hoses • Clean ventilation regulator valve • Replace breather cap assembly
Every 100,000 miles	• Change automatic transmission fluid and filter [1]

1. SEVERE SERVICE OPERATION: If the vehicle is operated under any of the following conditions, change rear axle lubricant every 6,000 miles. Change automatic transmission fluid and service filter every 15,000 miles.
   a. Extended idle or low-speed operation (short trips, stop-and-go driving).
   b. Trailer towing.
   c. Operation @ temperatures below 10° F for 60 days or more, with most trips under 10 miles.
   d. Sustained high-speed driving in hot weather.
   e. Very dusty conditions.

Table 5 MAINTENANCE SCHEDULE (1981-ON DIESEL)

Every 5,000 miles	• Change engine oil and filter [1] • Check fluid levels • Lubricate chassis • Check rear axle lubricant level [1] • Rotate bias-belted tires
First 5,000 miles, then every 15,000 miles	• Check exhaust pressure regulator valve • Check exhaust system • Rotate radial tires
First 5,000 miles, then every 30,000 miles	• Check/adjust idle speed
Every 10,000 miles (12 months)	• Check suspension and steering • Check power steering operation • Check disc brakes
Every 15,000 miles (12 months)	• Check drum brakes and parking brake • Check/adjust drive belts • Check throttle linkage operation • Service crankcase ventilation system • Check cooling system operation • Check coolant condition and protection
Every 30,000 miles (24 months)	• Clean, repack and adjust wheel bearings • Check fuel cap, tank and lines • Replace air cleaner filter element • Replace fuel filter • Drain, flush and refill cooling system • Replace cooling system hoses • Replace breather cap/ventilator valve assembly [2] • Have fuel injection pump timing checked/adjusted
Every 100,000 miles	• Change automatic transmission fluid and filter [1]

1. SEVERE SERVICE OPERATION: If the vehicle is operated under any of the following conditions, change engine oil and filter every 2,500 miles or 3 months. Change rear axle lubricant every 5,000 miles. Change automatic transmission fluid and service filter/screen every 15,000 miles.
   a. Extended idle or low-speed operation (short trips, stop-and-go driving).
   b. Trailer towing.
   c. Operation @ temperatures below 10° F for 60 days or more, with most trips under 10 miles.
   d. Sustained high-speed driving in hot weather.
   e. Very dusty conditions.
2. 1982 California only.

Table 6 ENGINE OIL VISCOSITY CHART (GASOLINE)

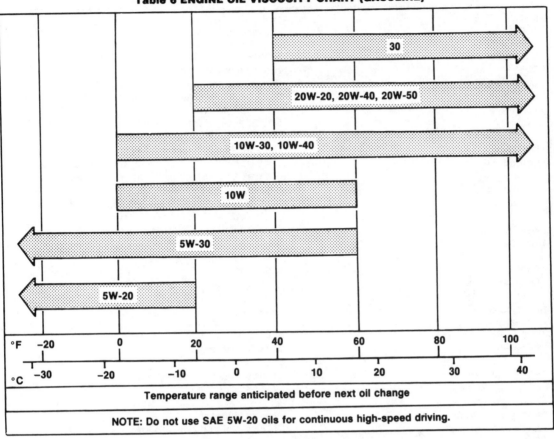

NOTE: Do not use SAE 5W-20 oils for continuous high-speed driving.

Table 7 ENGINE OIL VISCOSITY CHART (DIESEL)

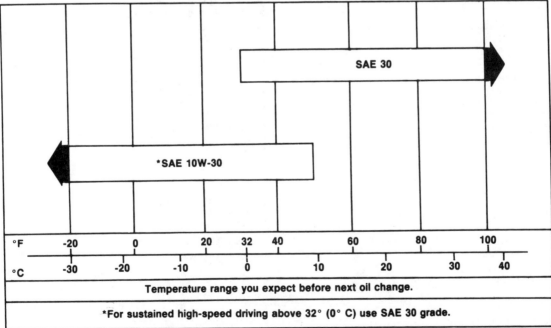

*For sustained high-speed driving above 32° (0° C) use SAE 30 grade.

Table 8 RECOMMENDED LUBRICANTS AND FLUIDS

Use	Recommendation
Engine oil	
Gasoline	API designation SE or SF
Diesel	API designation SF/CC, SF/CD or SE/CC
Power steering	GM power steering fluid (if not available, DEXRON II automatic transmission fluid)
Rear axle	
Standard	SAE 80W GL-5 or SAE 80W-90 GL-5 gear lubricant (only SAE 80W GL-5 in Canada)
Positraction	GM part No. 1051022 lubricant or equivalent
Limited slip	GM part No. 1052271 and 4 oz. GM part No. 1052358
Steering gear (manual)	GM part No. 1052182 lubricant or equivalent
Transmission	
Manual	SAW 80W GL-5 or SAE 80W-90 GL-5 gear lubricant (only SAE 80W GL-5 in Canada)
Automatic	DEXRON II automatic transmission fluid
Brake master cylinder	Delco Supreme 11 or other DOT 3 brake fluid
Clutch linkage (manual transmission)	
Pivot points	Engine oil
Cross shaft grease fitting and pushrod-to-clutch fork joint	EP chassis lubricant meeting GM specification GM 6031-M
Shift linkage (all)	Engine oil
Hood latch and hinge assemblies	
Pivots and spring anchor	Engine oil
Release pawl	Chassis lubricant
Hinges	Engine oil
Chassis lubrication (front suspension, steering linkage, etc.)	Chassis lubricant meeting GM specification GM 6031-M
Parking brake cable	Chassis lubricant
Front wheel bearings	GM lubricant part No. 1051344 or equivalent
Door, tailgate, seat and trunk hinges	Engine oil
Windshield washer	GM Optikleen washer solvent or equivalent
Cooling system	Mixture of water and ethylene glycol base antifreeze meeting GM specification 1899-M

NOTE: If you own a 1985 model, first check the Supplement at the back of the book for any new service information.

CHAPTER FOUR

ENGINE TUNE-UP

GASOLINE ENGINE TUNE-UP

A tune-up consists of a series of inspections, adjustments and parts replacements to compensate for normal wear and deterioration of engine components. Regular tune-ups are important for proper emission control and fuel economy.

Since proper engine operation depends upon a number of interrelated system functions, a tune-up consisting of only one or two corrections will seldom give lasting results. For improved power, performance and operating economy, a thorough and systematic procedure of analysis and correction is necessary.

Always refer to the Vehicle Emission Control Information (VECI) decal in the engine compartment for the correct tune-up specifications for your car. If the decal has been lost or damaged, refer to **Tables 1-4** for tune-up specifications for all 1972-1980 cars. These specifications are provided by General Motors, but due to changes in emission calibrations during a model year, they should be used only as a general guide. Specifications are not provided for 1981-on models because most carburetion and ignition functions are controlled by an on-board computer system which requires special equipment and training to service. Refer to the VECI decal for the proper specifications and to your dealer for service.

TUNE-UP SEQUENCE

The procedures presented in this chapter require a series of visual and mechanical checks and adjustments, followed by an instrument checkout. The instruments are described in detail in Chapter One. Tune-up specifications are given in **Tables 1-5** at the end of this chapter.

Because different systems in an engine interact, the tune-up should be carried out in the following order:

1. Tighten cylinder head bolts. See **Table 5**.
2. Adjust valve lash (1975 Monza 4-cylinder only).
3. Check engine compression.
4. Ignition system work consisting of:
   a. Spark plug replacement.
   b. Breaker point replacement and/or adjustment (if so equipped).
   c. Condenser replacement (if so equipped).
   d. Distributor cap and rotor inspection (replacement if necessary).
   e. Spark plug wire inspection (replacement if necessary).
   f. Ignition timing check and adjustment.
5. Adjust carburetor.

CYLINDER HEAD BOLTS

Because of the many variations in placement of engine compartment components, the following procedure is generalized but can be adapted to cover your particular engine.

1. Remove the air cleaner.
2. Disconnect all electrical connectors, vacuum lines or hoses which will prevent valve cover removal.

3. Disconnect spark plug wires which pass over the valve cover(s) and place out of the way.
4. Disconnect the PCV valve hose. Remove the oil filler cap.
5. Remove the capscrews holding the valve cover(s) to the cylinder head(s) and remove the valve cover(s).
6. Tighten the cylinder head bolts in the appropriate pattern shown in **Figure 1** to the torque specified in **Table 5**.

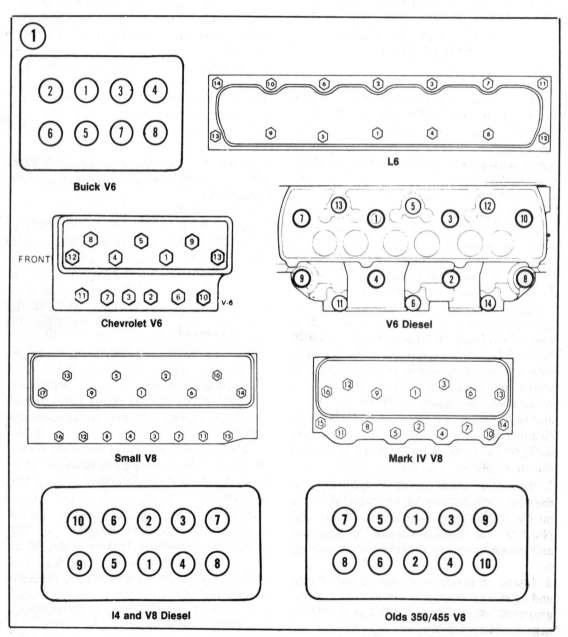

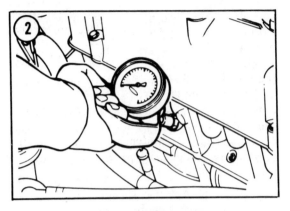

VALVE CLEARANCE ADJUSTMENT

(1975 Monza 4-cylinder Only)

Valves should be adjusted every 30,000 miles. Valves are adjusted with the engine off and cold. The adjustment is made with the tappet on the base circle of the cam lobe. Valve arrangement is I-E-I-E-I-E-I-E, from front to rear.

1. Disconnect the negative battery cable.
2. Remove the air cleaner.
3. Remove the PCV valve from the camshaft cover grommet.
4. Remove camshaft cover-to-cylinder head screws. Remove cover from cylinder head.
5. Turn the camshaft timing sprocket to align the timing mark on the sprocket with the inverted V-notch on the timing belt upper cover. This is the firing position for cylinder No. 1. The following valves can be adjusted without changing position: No. 1 exhaust and intake, No. 2 intake and No. 3 exhaust.
6. Measure the clearance between the tappet and cam lobe with a feeler gauge. Adjust the clearance to 0.014-0.017 in. for intake and 0.029-0.032 in. for exhaust valves by turning the tappet screw.
7. Rotate camshaft timing sprocket 180° to the 10 o'clock position (in line with the notch on the timing belt upper cover). Adjust the No. 2 exhaust, No. 3 intake and No. 4 exhaust and intake valves to the specifications in Step 6.
8. Install camshaft cover and gasket. Install and tighten cover screws. Install PCV valve in grommet, install air cleaner and reconnect negative battery cable.

COMPRESSION TEST

An engine with low or uneven compression cannot be properly tuned. A compression test measures the compression pressure built up in each cylinder. Its results can be used to assess general cylinder and valve condition. In addition, it can warn of developing problems inside the engine.

1. Warm the engine to normal operating temperature (upper radiator hose hot).
2. Shut the engine off. Remove the air cleaner from the carburetor and block the throttle and choke valves in a wide-open position.
3. On breaker point ignitions, remove the distributor primary lead from the negative post on the ignition coil. On High Energy Ignition (HEI) systems, disconnect the pink wire (ignition switch connector) at the distributor.
4. Connect a remote starter to the starter solenoid according to manufacturer's instructions.
5. Remove all spark plugs.
6. Firmly insert a compression gauge in the No. 1 cylinder spark plug hole. See **Figure 2**.

NOTE
The No. 1 cylinder is the front cylinder on 4-cylinder and inline 6-cylinder engines and the front cylinder in the left bank on V6 and V8 engines.

7. Crank the engine at least 5 compression strokes with the remote starter switch or until there is no further increase in compression shown on the cylinder gauge.
8. Remove the compression tester and record the reading. Relieve the tester pressure valve.
9. Test the remaining cylinders in the same manner.

When interpreting the results, actual readings are not as important as the differences in readings. If there is more than 20 pounds difference between the high and low reading cylinders, corrective maintenance is beyond the scope of this book. The engine cannot be properly tuned until the necessary repairs have been made.

If the compression test indicates a problem (excessive variation in readings), isolate the cause with a wet compression test. This is done in the same way as the dry compression test above, except that about 1 tablespoon of oil is poured down the spark plug hole before checking each cylinder. If the wet compression readings are much greater than the dry readings, the trouble is probably caused by worn or broken piston rings. If there is little difference between the wet and dry readings, the problem is probably due to leaky or sticking valves. When 2 adjacent cylinders read low in the dry test and do not increase in the wet test, the problem may be a defective head gasket.

SPARK PLUG REPLACEMENT

CAUTION
Whenever the spark plugs are removed, dirt from around them can fall into the spark plug holes. This can cause expensive engine damage.

1. Blow out any foreign matter from around the spark plugs with compressed air. Use a compressor if you have one. Cans of compressed inert gas are available from photo stores.

NOTE
It is a good idea to identify each spark plug wire with a piece of masking tape and a felt-tip pen before removing the wires in Step 2. Another way of identifying the wires is to write the wire location on a wooden clothes pin which is then clipped to the wire. See Figure 3.

2. Disconnect the spark plug wires by twisting the wire boot back and forth on the plug insulator while pulling upward. Pulling on the wire instead of the boot may cause internal damage to the wire. The use of spark plug terminal pliers as shown in **Figure 4** is recommended.
3. Remove the spark plugs with a 5/8 in. or 13/16 in. spark plug socket, as appropriate.

Keep the plugs in order so you know which cylinder they came from.
4. Examine each spark plug. Compare its condition with **Figure 5**. Spark plug condition indicates engine condition and can warn of developing trouble.
5. Discard the plugs. Although they could be cleaned, regapped and reused if in good condition, they seldom last very long. New plugs are inexpensive and far more reliable.
6. Remove the plugs from the box. Tapered seat plugs do not use gaskets. Some plug brands may have small end pieces that must

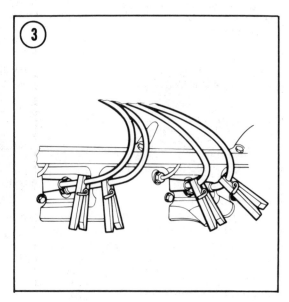

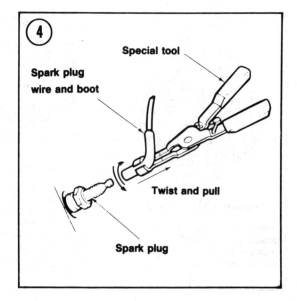

(5) **SPARK PLUG CONDITION**

NORMAL
• Identified by light tan or gray deposits on the firing tip.
• Can be cleaned.

GAP BRIDGED
• Identified by deposit buildup closing gap between electrodes.
• Caused by oil or carbon fouling. If deposits are not excessive, the plug can be cleaned.

OIL FOULED
• Identified by wet black deposits on the insulator shell bore electrodes.
• Caused by excessive oil entering combustion chamber through worn rings and pistons, excessive clearance between valve guides and stems, or worn or loose bearings. Can be cleaned. If engine is not repaired, use a hotter plug.

CARBON FOULED
• Identified by black, dry fluffy carbon deposits on insulator tips, exposed shell surfaces and electrodes.
• Caused by too cold a plug, weak ignition, dirty air cleaner, too rich a fuel mixture, or excessive idling. Can be cleaned.

LEAD FOULED
• Identified by dark gray, black, yellow, or tan deposits or a fused glazed coating on the insulator tip.
• Caused by highly leaded gasoline. Can be cleaned.

WORN
• Identified by severely eroded or worn electrodes.
• Caused by normal wear. Should be replaced.

FUSED SPOT DEPOSIT
• Identified by melted or spotty deposits resembling bubbles or blisters.
• Caused by sudden acceleration. Can be cleaned.

OVERHEATING
• Identified by a white or light gray insulator with small black or gray brown spots and with bluish-burnt appearance of electrodes.
• Caused by engine overheating, wrong type of fuel, loose spark plugs, too hot a plug, or incorrect ignition timing. Replace the plug.

PREIGNITION
• Identified by melted electrodes and possibly blistered insulator. Metallic deposits on insulator indicate engine damage.
• Caused by wrong type of fuel, incorrect ignition timing or advance, too hot a plug, burned valves, or engine overheating. Replace the plug.

4

be screwed on (**Figure 6**) before the plugs can be used.

7. Determine the correct gap setting from the VECI label. Use a spark plug gapping tool to check the gap. **Figure 7** shows one common type. Insert the appropriate size wire gauge between the electrodes. If the gap is correct, there will be a slight drag as the wire is pulled through. If there is no drag or if the wire will not pull through, bend the side electrode with the gapping tool (**Figure 8**) to change the gap and then remeasure with the wire gauge.

NOTE
Never try to close the electrode gap by tapping the spark plug on a solid surface. This can damage the plug internally. Always use the special tool to open or close the gap.

8. Check spark plug hole threads and clean, if necessary, before installing plugs. Apply a thin film of oil to the spark plug threads.

9. Screw each plug in by hand until it seats. Very little effort is required. If force is necessary, the plug is cross-threaded. Unscrew it and try it again.

10. Tighten the spark plugs by hand. If you have a torque wrench, tighten 5/8 in. spark plugs to 15 ft.-lb. (20 N•m) and 13/16 in. plugs to 25 ft.-lb. (34 N•m).

11. Inspect the spark plug wires before reinstalling them. If the insulation is oil soaked, brittle, torn or otherwise damaged, replace the wire.

BREAKER POINT
IGNITION SYSTEM

Inspection

1. Disconnect secondary wire between coil and distributor at the coil.

2. Remove 6-cylinder distributor cap by releasing hold-down screws. Remove 8-cylinder distributor cap by placing a screwdriver blade in the slotted head of each latch screw, pressing down and rotating 1/4 turn in either direction. See **Figure 9**.

3. Lift the cap off the distributor housing and remove.

4. Remove V8 rotor screws with a screwdriver. Remove 6-cylinder rotor by pulling straight up and off distributor cam. See **Figure 10**.

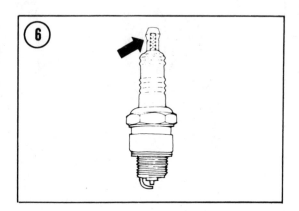

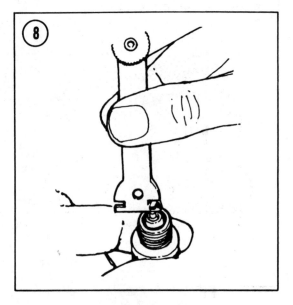

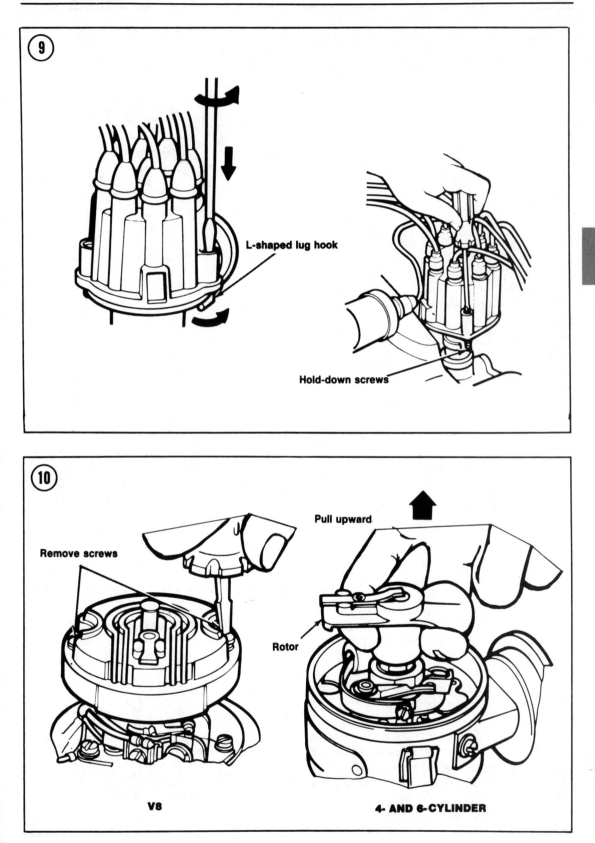

9

L-shaped lug hook

Hold-down screws

10

Remove screws

Pull upward

Rotor

V8

4- AND 6-CYLINDER

4

5. Open breaker points with a screwdriver blade and inspect for pitting or other defects.

CAUTION
Do not touch breaker points with your fingers. The oil from your skin will stick to the points. The breaker point surfaces must remain dry and clean at all times.

6. Wipe inside of distributor cap with a clean cloth. Check the cap electrodes for cracks, carbon tracks and burned, worn or corroded terminals (**Figure 11**). Replace cap and rotor as a set if any of these defects are found.

7. Remove each cap wire with a twisting motion while pulling on the wire boot. Check for damaged or corroded cap towers (**Figure 12**). If the towers are corroded, clean with a wire brush (**Figure 13**).

8. Clean and inspect rotor for damage or deterioration. Replace if necessary.

9. Check spark plug wiring for signs of wear or deterioration. Look for abrasion or heat damage on wires routed near hot exhaust manifolds.

10. Make sure all spark plug wires are installed to the correct plugs. Wires should be positioned properly in their supports to avoid contact with the engine and prevent crossfiring.

11. Tighten all ignition system connections and replace any loose, frayed or damaged wires.

Service

If points are badly pitted or burned, they must be replaced. These conditions are usually caused by improper conditions in other parts of the ignition system or by dirt or other contamination in the distributor. The cause must be corrected when installing new points or the same condition will rapidly develop again.

1. Check breaker point contact surfaces. Points with an even, overall gray color and only slight roughness or pitting need not be replaced. They can be dressed with a clean point file. Do not use sandpaper or emery cloth for dressing points and do not attempt to remove all irregularities–just scale or dirt.

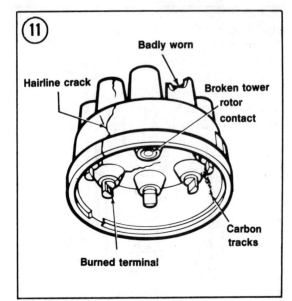

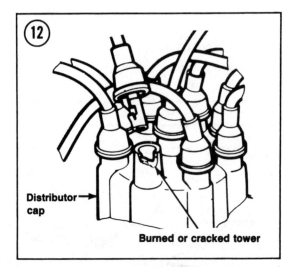

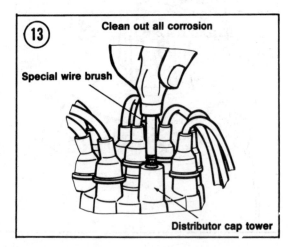

2. Check the alignment of the points and correct as necessary. See **Figure 14**.

3. Clean the distributor cam with cleaning solvent and a clean, lint-free cloth. Rotate cam lubricator wick 1/2 turn or 180°. See **Figure 15**. Replace wick every 24,000 miles.

4. Use a flat feeler gauge and set points to 0.016 in. (used points). Breaker arm rubbing block must be on high point of a distributor cam lobe during adjustment. The setting is correct when the gauge passes through the contact point gap with a slight bit of friction.

5A. If the point gap needs adjustment, loosen the retaining screw on 6- cylinder models. Insert a screwdriver tip into the notch beside the points (**Figure 16**) and twist to open or close the point gap. When adjustment is correct, tighten the retaining screw. Recheck gap to make sure it did not change when the screw was tightened.

5B. On V8 models, insert an Allen wrench in the point set hex screw and adjust the gap.

6. To replace breaker points for a 6-cylinder distributor:

    a. Remove distributor cap by releasing hold-down screws. Move cap out of the way.

    b. Remove rotor.

    c. Remove condenser and primary lead wires from quick disconnect terminal (**Figure 17**).

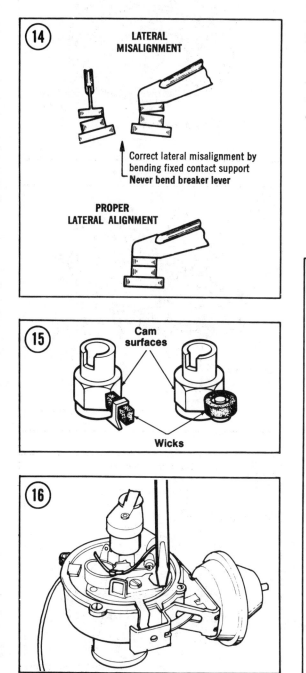

14

LATERAL
MISALIGNMENT

Correct lateral misalignment by
bending fixed contact support
Never bend breaker lever

PROPER
LATERAL ALIGNMENT

15

Cam
surfaces

Wicks

16

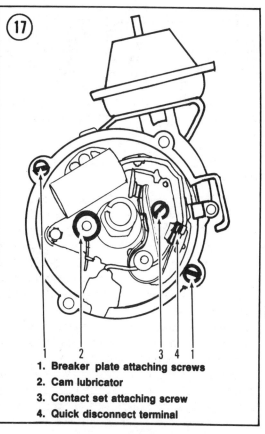

17

1. **Breaker plate attaching screws**
2. **Cam lubricator**
3. **Contact set attaching screw**
4. **Quick disconnect terminal**

d. Remove contact set attaching screw and remove point set.

e. If condenser is to be replaced, remove attaching screw and remove condenser from breaker plate.

f. Use a clean, lint-free cloth to wipe breaker plate free of dirt and grease.

g. Install new point set on breaker plate and attach with screws.

NOTE
Locating lug on point set must engage matching hole in breaker plate. See **Figure 18**.

h. If condenser was removed, install new condenser on breaker plate with attaching screw.

i. Connect primary and condenser lead wires to quick disconnect terminal on point set.

j. Use a spring gauge to measure breaker arm spring tension. Pressure must be between 19 and 23 ounces.

NOTE
Hook spring gauge over the breaker lever (movable arm of the point set) and read tension just as points separate. Spring tension can be adjusted by carefully bending the breaker lever spring. Decrease pressure by carefully pinching the spring. To increase pressure, remove point set from distributor and bend spring away from lever. Avoid excessive distortion of the spring.

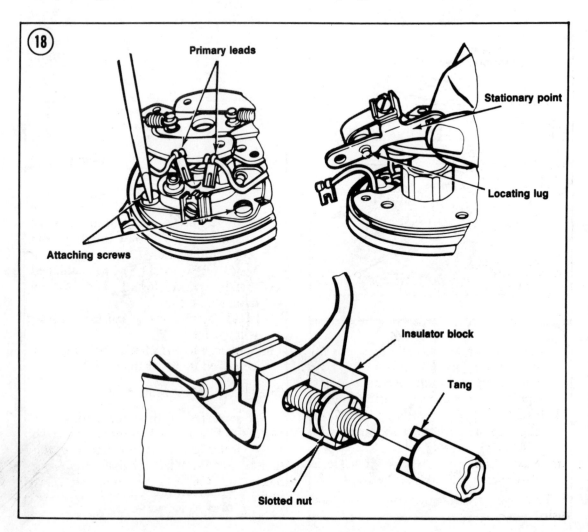

(18)
Primary leads
Stationary point
Locating lug
Attaching screws
Insulator block
Tang
Slotted nut

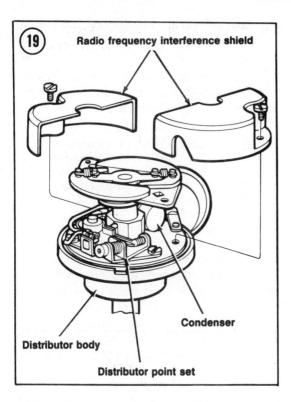

(19) **Radio frequency interference shield**

Condenser

Distributor body

Distributor point set

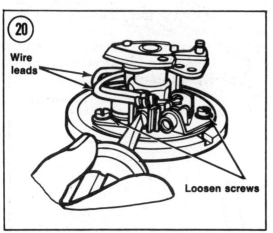

(20)

Wire leads

Loosen screws

NOTE
The contact point set (and condenser on 1974 models) is replaced as a single unit. Breaker lever tension and point gap are preset at the factory and only dwell angle requires adjustment after point replacement.

a. Remove distributor cap by placing a screwdriver blade in the slotted head of each latch screw, pressing down and rotating 1/4 turn in either direction. Move cap out of way.

b. Remove rotor attaching screws, then remove rotor.

c. Remove the 2-piece RFI shield, if so equipped, by removing attaching screws. See **Figure 19**.

d. Loosen the 2 point set assembly attaching screws and remove point set from breaker plate. See **Figure 20**.

e. Remove primary and condenser lead wires from nylon insulated connector in point set.

f. On 1972-1973 distributors, remove attaching screw and remove condenser.

g. Install new condenser with attaching screw on 1972-1973 models.

h. Install new point set with attaching screws.

i. Connect primary and condenser lead wires to nylon insulated connector on point set. Make certain lead wires are routed so they do not interfere with point set operation.

j. Install RFI shield, if so equipped.

k. Install rotor. Install and tighten attaching screws.

l. Install distributor cap and lock in place with latches.

m. Start engine and check dwell angle as described in this chapter.

Dwell Angle Adjustment

The preferred method for setting dwell angle is to first set the breaker point gap with a flat feeler gauge on 6-cylinder engines (points for 8-cylinder engines are factory preset) and then check the setting with a dwell meter. It is very important that breaker points be set to the proper gap. Points set too closely

k. Set the new points to 0.019 in. with a flat feeler gauge. The rubbing block of points must be resting on the highest point of a cam lobe when this adjustment is made.

l. Install rotor and distributor cap. Lock cap to distributor housing with hold-down screws.

m. Start engine and check dwell angle as described in this chapter.

7. To replace breaker points on an 8-cylinder distributor:

tend to burn and pit rapidly. Points with an excessive gap result in a weak spark at high speeds. New points must be set to a wider gap than used points to compensate for wear of the rubbing block while seating to the distributor cam.

6-cylinder engine

1. Set the parking brake and block the front wheels.
2. Connect a dwell meter and tachometer according to the manufacturer's instructions.

> *NOTE*
> *Dwell meters have an adjustment switch for 4-, 6- and 8-cylinder readings. Be sure the switch is set to the 6-cylinder position or the reading will be incorrect.*

3. Disconnect and plug the vacuum advance line at the distributor.
4. Start the engine and let it idle. Read the dwell angle on the meter. It should be 31-34°.

> *NOTE*
> *If dwell angle is not within these limits, reset the point gap. Check for misalignment of points or worn distributor cam lobes.*

5. If the dwell angle was below the specified amount, the breaker point gap is too large; if angle was above specified amount, breaker point gap is too small. Adjust gap according to Step 4 and Step 5 under *Service*.
6. Start engine again and take another dwell reading. Adjust points again if necessary.
7. When dwell is to specifications, increase engine speed to 1,750 rpm. Any variation in dwell angle should not exceed 3°. A greater variation indicates excessive distributor wear or a loose breaker plate.
8. Shut engine off, turn test selector knob to OFF position and disconnect dwell meter. Unplug and reconnect vacuum line to the distributor.

8-cylinder engine

1. After installing breaker point set and reassembling the distributor, start the engine

and let it warm to normal operating temperature (upper radiator hose hot).
2. Disconnect and plug vacuum line at distributor advance.
3. Connect a dwell meter and tachometer according to the manufacturer's instructions.

> *NOTE*
> *Dwell meters have an adjustment switch for 4-, 6- and 8-cylinder readings. Be sure the switch is set to the 8-cylinder position or the reading will be incorrect.*

4. Raise the window in the distributor cap and insert a hex wrench in the adjusting screw head. See **Figure 21**.
5. Turn adjusting screw until a dwell angle of 29-31° (30° preferred) is reached.
6. If a dwell meter is unavailable, turn the adjusting screw clockwise until the engine begins to misfire. Then turn screw 1/2 turn in opposite direction. This method will give an approximate dwell angle setting, but should be used only when a dwell meter is not available.
7. Increase engine speed to 1,750 rpm and check for variation in dwell angle. Any variation in excess of 3° indicates excessive distributor wear or a loose breaker plate.
8. Remove the hex wrench and close the access window in the distributor cap. Unplug and install the vacuum line to the distributor.

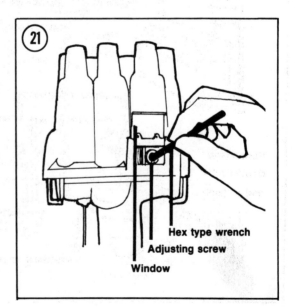

Hex type wrench
Adjusting screw
Window

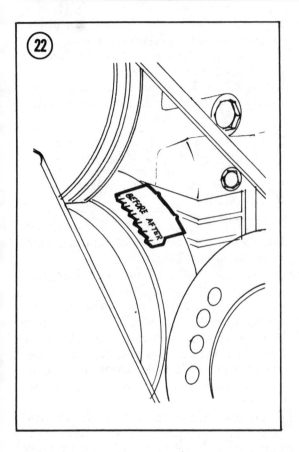

Ignition Timing Adjustment

Ignition timing should be checked and adjusted (if required) after point replacement and dwell angle adjustment have been completed. The cylinder firing order for all engines is:

    a. 4-cylinder, 1-3-4-2.
    b. Inline 6-cylinder, 1-5-3-6-2-4.
    c. V6 engines, 1-6-5-4-3-2.
    d. V8 engines, 1-8-4-3-6-5-7-2.

1. Clean the timing marks with a stiff brush. **Figure 22** shows a typical location.
2. Mark the timing mark and pointer with white paint or chalk for better visibility.
3. Disconnect and plug the distributor vacuum line with a pencil or golf tee. See **Figure 23**.
4. Connect a timing light and tachometer according to manufacturer's instructions. **Figure 23** shows a typical circuit connection.

WARNING
Work carefully from this point. You will be working close to the fan. This can cause damage to the equipment leads and possible personal injury.

4

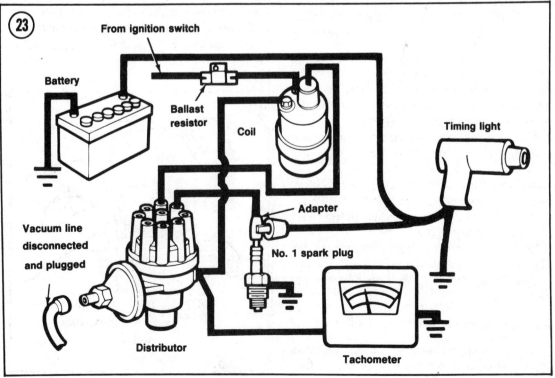

5. Start the engine and run at idle. Check the idle speed and compare to specifications on the VECI decal. If necessary, adjust engine speed to idle specifications (see Chapter Five for procedure). Shut engine off and disconnect tachometer.

6. Restart engine and aim timing light at timing marks. Compare setting of timing marks with specifications on the VECI decal. If the marks are not correctly aligned, shut the engine off and loosen the distributor hold-down clamp bolt one full turn. In some installations, the use of a special distributor wrench is necessary. See **Figure 24**.

7. Restart the engine and turn the distributor body slightly to the right or left as shown in **Figure 25**. As you do this, the timing will change according to which direction and how much you turn the distributor.

8. When the timing marks are properly aligned, shut the engine off and tighten the distributor clamp bolt. Restart the engine and recheck timing.

9. When timing is correct, turn off the engine, disconnect the timing light and make sure the distributor clamp bolt is tight. Reconnect the tachometer and start the engine.

10. Check carburetor idle speed and reset to specifications on VECI decal if necessary. Refer to Chapter Five for procedure. Shut engine off.

11. Disconnect the tachometer. Unplug and reconnect the distributor vacuum line.

HIGH ENERGY IGNITION SYSTEM

The High Energy Ignition (HEI) system initially appeared on certain 1974 models. It is used on all 1975 and later models. Variations incorporate electronic spark timing (HEI-EST), electronic spark control (HEI-ESC) and electronic module retard (HEI-EMR).

All 8-cylinder and some 6-cylinder engines are equipped with a distributor containing all ignition components in one unit. The system used on some 6-cylinder engines is identical in operating theory and uses similar components, but has an externally mounted coil.

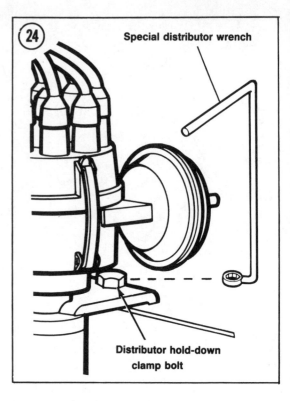

Special distributor wrench

Distributor hold-down clamp bolt

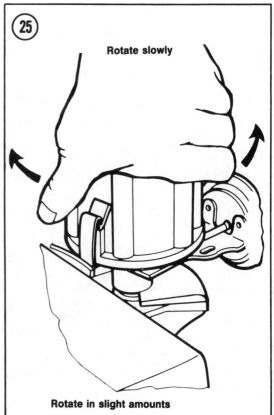

Rotate slowly

Rotate in slight amounts

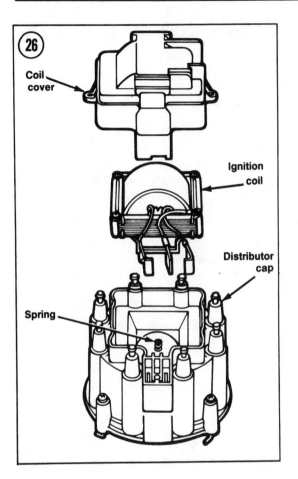

The HEI is a pulse-triggered, transistor controlled, inductive discharge system. Breaker points are not used. Principal system components are the ignition coil, electronic module, magnetic pickup assembly, and the centrifugal and vacuum advance mechanisms.

Ignition Coil

The HEI coil operates in basically the same way as a standard coil, but is smaller in size and generates a higher secondary voltage when the primary circuit is broken. The coil is mounted in the cap of the 8-cylinder and some 6-cylinder distributors (**Figure 26**) and externally mounted in other 6-cylinder applications.

Electronic Module

The electronic module is contained within the distributor housing (**Figure 27**). Circuits within the module perform 5 basic functions: spark triggering, switching, current limiting, dwell control and distributor pickup. Modules used in EST, EMR and ESC distributors also control timing advance and retard under specified conditions.

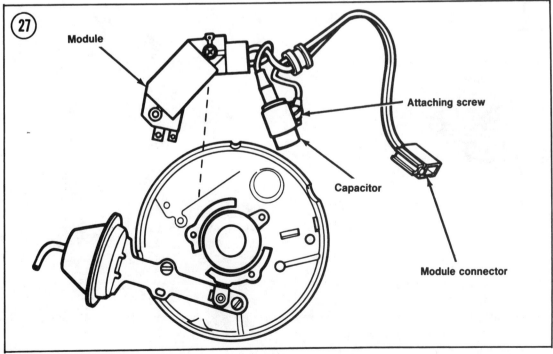

Magnetic Pickup Assembly

The magnetic pickup assembly consists of a rotating timer core with external teeth (one for each cylinder) rotated by the distributor shaft, a stationary pole piece with internal teeth and a pickup coil and magnet located between the pole piece and a bottom plate.

Centrifugal and Vacuum Advance

The centrifugal and vacuum advance mechanisms are basically identical to the units used in breaker point distributors. Distributors used with EST, EMR and ESC variations contain no advance mechanisms, as advance and retard are controlled electronically.

System Operation

As the distributor shaft rotates the timer core teeth out of alignment with the pole piece teeth, a voltage is created in the magnetic field of the pickup coil. The pickup coil sends this voltage to the electronic module, which determines from the rotational speed of the distributor shaft when to start building current in the ignition coil primary windings.

When the timer core teeth are again aligned with the pole piece teeth, the magnetic field is changed, creating a different voltage. This signal is sent to the electronic module by the pickup coil and causes the module to shut off the ignition coil primary circuit. This collapses the coil magnetic field and induces a high secondary voltage to fire one spark plug.

The electronic module limits the 12-volt current to the ignition coil to 5-6 amperes. The module also triggers the opening and closing of the coil primary circuit with zero energy loss. In a breaker point ignition, some energy can be lost due to point arcing and/or capacitor charging time lag (the capacitor shown in **Figure 27** functions only as a radio noise suppressor). The efficiency of the triggering system allows 35,000 volts or more to be delivered through the secondary wiring system to the spark plugs.

The module circuit controlling dwell causes dwell time to increase as engine speed increases.

System Maintenance

Routine maintenance is not required for the HEI system. If parts or components fail, they are serviced by replacement. However, engine timing should be checked and the distributor cap and rotor should be visually inspected every 18 months or 22,500 miles. At the same time, inspect the spark plug wires for burned or cracked insulation or other damage. Distributors with an integral coil use a special plug wire connector to attach the wires to the distributor cap terminals. If it is necessary to replace the wires, depress the 2 spring latches (**Figure 28**) on the plug wire connector with a screwdriver and remove the connector. It will have half the wires attached to it; the other half of the wires will remain attached to the distributor cap (**Figure 29**). Disconnect and replace one

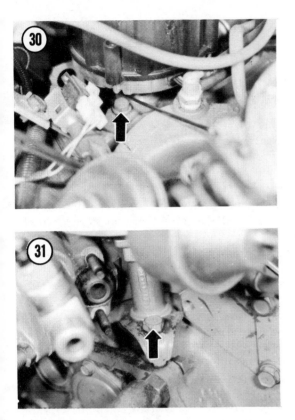

wire at a time. This will prevent any confusion as to which spark plug and distributor cap terminal the wire should connect to.

The HEI system uses large (8 mm) diameter, silicone-insulated spark plug wires. While these are more heat resistant and less vulnerable to deterioration than standard wires, they should not be mistreated. When removing wires from spark plugs, grasp only on the boots. Twist boot 1/2 turn in either direction to break seal, then pull to remove. Use of spark plug wire pliers (**Figure 4**) is recommended for wire removal.

Spark plugs should be replaced at specified intervals.

The only adjustments possible on the HEI ignition system are centrifugal and vacuum advance, both of which should be entrusted to a dealer or automotive ignition system specialist. On models equipped with EST, EMR or ESC, the distributor contains no centrifugal or vacuum advance mechanisms. Distributor advance is electronically controlled by the electronic control module.

Suspected ignition trouble with the HEI ignition system should be referred to a dealer or ignition specialist. Testing of the electronic module requires special equipment and skills and an otherwise good electronic circuit can be damaged by an incorrect test hookup.

Distributor Cap and Rotor

The distributor cap and rotor used with the HEI ignition should be periodically inspected for the same defects as those used with breaker point distributors. Replace the cap and rotor as a set, if necessary.

Ignition Timing Adjustment

To adjust basic timing on engines equipped with the HEI ignition:
1. Clean the timing marks with a stiff brush. **Figure 22** shows a typical location.
2. Mark the timing mark and pointer with white paint or chalk for better visibility.
3. Disconnect and plug the vacuum line at the distributor with a pencil or golf tee.

NOTE
Use only a clamp-on or inductive timing light with the HEI ignition. The distributor cap has a special terminal marked "TACH." Connect one lead of the tachometer to this terminal and the other lead to ground. Some tachometers must connect from the "TACH" terminal to the battery positive post. Check the manufacturer's instructions before making connections.

4. Connect an inductive timing light and tachometer according to manufacturer's instructions.
5. Start engine and allow it to idle normally. Adjust the curb idle speed to specifications, if necessary. See VECI label on engine for specifications and procedure.
6. Aim timing light at timing marks. If the marks are aligned, the timing is satisfactory.
7. If timing marks are not aligned, shut the engine off. Loosen the distributor hold-down clamp bolt. **Figure 30** shows the V8 and **Figure 31** shows the V6 HEI clamp bolts. Rotate the distributor slightly to change

timing. When marks are properly aligned, tighten hold-down clamp bolt.

8. Recheck timing and shut engine off.

9. Disconnect equipment and unplug and reconnect vacuum line to distributor.

Carburetor Adjustments

Refer to Chapter Five for procedures.

DIESEL ENGINE TUNE-UP

Diesel engines do not require a tune-up in the same sense as a gasoline engine, primarily because the diesel engine uses a compression ignition instead of an electrical ignition. Fewer maintenance tasks are thus required on a diesel engine, but the required tasks are just as important, if not more so, then the more extensive gasoline engine maintenance. Owner maintenance on diesel engines should be limited to the tasks described in this chapter and Chapter Three. Tampering by an unskilled mechanic, especially with the injection system, can lead to serious (and expensive) damage.

Idle Speed Adjustment

NOTE
A special tachometer with a magnetic probe (part No. J-26925 or equivalent) must be used on diesel engines. Most tachometers for gasoline engines operate from the electrical ignition pulses and will not work on diesel engines.

1. Connect the tachometer probe to the engine by inserting it in the timing indicator hole. See **Figure 32**.

2. Start the engine and let it reach normal operating temperature (upper radiator hose hot).

3. Set the parking brake and block the rear wheels. Place the transmission selector in DRIVE and make sure the air conditioner, if so equipped, is off.

4. Turn the slow idle speed screw on the injection pump (**Figure 33**) to obtain the slow idle speed listed on the VECI decal.

5A. If the car has an air conditioner, turn it on and disconnect the wires to the air conditioning compressor.

5B. If there is no air conditioner, disconnect the solenoid connector (**Figure 34**). Connect a jumper wire between ground and one of the solenoid terminals. Connect a second jumper wire between the second solenoid terminal and the battery positive terminal to energize the solenoid.

6. Adjust the solenoid plunger (**Figure 34**) to obtain the specified idle speed.

7. Stop the engine, reconnect all wires and connectors to their original locations and remove all test equipment.

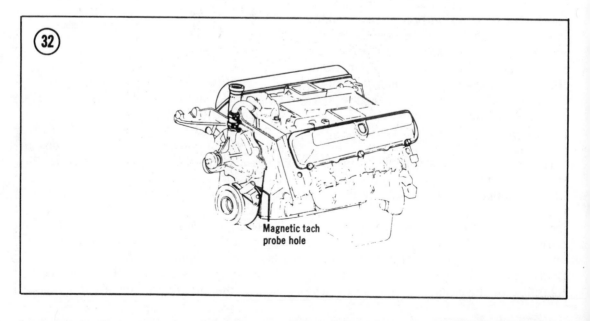

32

Magnetic tach
probe hole

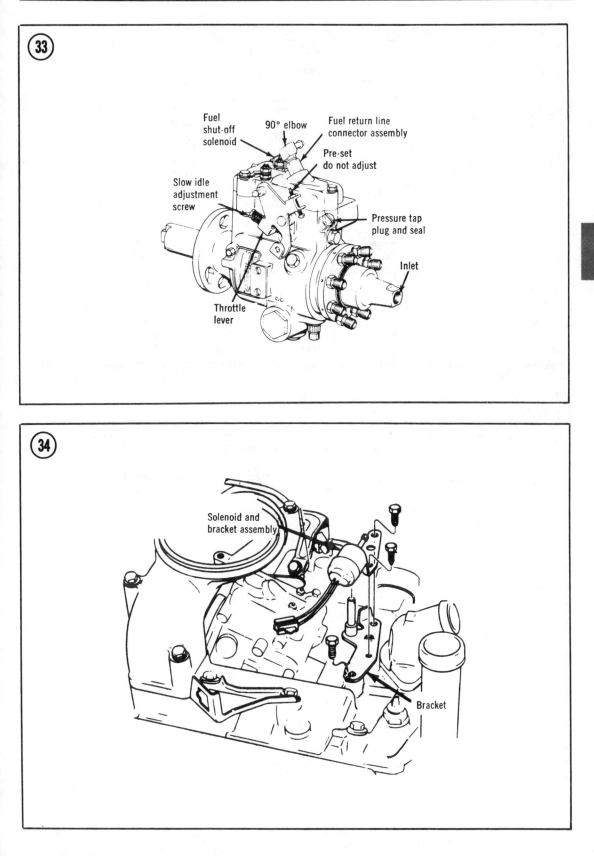

33

Fuel
shut-off
solenoid

90° elbow

Fuel return line
connector assembly

Pre-set
do not adjust

Slow idle
adjustment
screw

Pressure tap
plug and seal

Inlet

Throttle
lever

34

Solenoid and
bracket assembly

Bracket

4

Table 1 TUNE-UP SPECIFICATIONS (BUICK)

1972-1973 Buick				
Engine/Carb./ Trans.[1]	Idle Speeds		AC Spark Plug	
	Curb[2]	Fast[3, 4]	Gap (in.)	No.
350-2 bbl. M	800	800 [5]	0.040	R45TS
350-2 bbl. A	650	700 [5]	0.040	R45TS
350-4 bbl. M	800	820	0.040	R45TS
350-4 bbl. A	650	700	0.040	R45TS
455-4 bbl. M	900	920	0.040	R45TS
455-4 bbl. A	650	700	0.040	R45TS
455-4 bbl. (Stage 1) M	900	920	0.040	R45TS
455-4 bbl. (Stage 1) A	650	700	0.040	R45TS

Engine/Carb./ Trans.[1]	Idle Mixture		Distributor		Timing (Degrees BTDC)[6]
	Before Lean Drop	After Lean Drop	Point Gap (in.)	Dwell Angle	
350-2 bbl. M	850	800	0.016	28-32	4
350-2 bbl. A	700	650	0.016	28-32	4
350-4 bbl. M	850	700	0.016	28-32	4
350-4 bbl. A	700	650	0.016	28-32	4
455-4 bbl. M	950	900	0.016	28-32	4
455-4 bbl. A	700	650	0.016	28-32	4
455-4 bbl. (Stage 1) M	950	900	0.016	28-32	8
455-4 bbl. (Stage 1) A	700	650	0.016	28-32	10

1. M=Manual transmission; A=Automatic transmission.
2. Headlights and air conditioning off; automatic transmission in DRIVE; manual transmission in NEUTRAL.
3. With EGR hose disconnected and plugged and automatic transmission in PARK or NEUTRAL.
4. Requires idle stop solenoid adjustment to 600 rpm for manual transmission and 500 rpm for automatic transmission.
5. Preset on 1972 models.
6. Set at curb idle speed with distributor vacuum advance line disconnected and plugged.

(continued)

Table 1 TUNE-UP SPECIFICATIONS (continued)

1974 Buick				
Engine/Carb. **Trans.**[1]	**Idle Speeds**		**AC Spark Plug**	
	Curb[2]	**Fast**[3, 4]	**Gap (in.)**	**No.**
350-2 bbl. M	800	700	0.040	R45TS
350-2 bbl. A	650	700	0.040	R45TS
350-4 bbl. A	650	700	0.040	R45TS
455-2 bbl. A	650	700	0.040	R45TS
455-4 bbl. A	650	700	0.040	R45TS
455-4 bbl. (Stage 1) A	650	700	0.040	R45TS

Engine/Carb. **Trans.**[1]	**Idle Mixture**		**Distributor**		**Timing (Degrees BTDC)**[5]
	Before **Lean Drop**	**After** **Lean Drop**	**Point** **Gap (in.)**	**Dwell** **Angle**	
350-2 bbl. M	850	800	0.016	28-32	4
350-2 bbl. A	700	650	0.016	28-32	4
350-4 bbl. A	700	650	0.016	28-32	4
455-2 bbl. A	720	650	0.016	28-32	4
455-4 bbl. A	720	650	0.016	28-32	4
455-4 bbl. (Stage 1) A	720	650	0.016	28-32	4

1. M=Manual transmission; A=Automatic transmission.
2. Headlights and air conditioning off; automatic transmission in DRIVE; manual transmission in NEUTRAL.
3. With EGR hose disconnected and plugged and automatic transmission in PARK or NEUTRAL.
4. Requires idle stop solenoid adjustment to 500 rpm.
5. Set at curb idle speed with distributor vacuum advance line disconnected and plugged.

1975 Buick				
Engine/Carb./ **Trans.**[1]	**Idle Speeds**		**AC Spark Plug**	
	Curb[2]	**Fast**[3]	**Gap (in.)**	**No.**
231-2 bbl. M	800[4]	Preset	0.060	R44SX
231-2 bbl. A	650	Preset	0.060	R44SX
350-4 bbl. A	600	1,800	0.060	R45TSX
455-4 bbl. A	600	1,800	0.060	R45TSX

Engine/Carb./ **Trans.**[1]	**Idle Mixture**		**Timing (Degrees BTDC)**[5]
	Before **Lean Drop**	**After** **Lean Drop**	
231-2 bbl. M	1,100	800	12
231-2 bbl. A	730	650	12
350-4 bbl. A	680	600	12
455-4 bbl. A	680	600	12

1. M=Manual transmission; A=Automatic transmission.
2. Headlights and air conditioning off; automatic transmission in DRIVE; manual transmission in NEUTRAL.
3. With EGR hose disconnected and plugged and automatic transmission in PARK or NEUTRAL.
4. Set idle stop solenoid to 600 rpm.
5. Set at curb idle speed with distributor vacuum advance line disconnected and plugged.

(continued)

Table 1 TUNE-UP SPECIFICATIONS (continued)

1976 Buick				
Engine/Carb./ Trans.[1]	**Idle Speeds**		**AC Spark Plug**	
	Curb[2]	**Fast[3]**	**Gap (in.)**	**No.**
231-2 bbl. M	800 [4]	Preset	0.060	R44SX
231-2 bbl. A	600	Preset	0.060	R44SX
350-4 bbl. A	600	1,800	0.060	R45TSX
455-4 bbl. A	600	1,800	0.060	R45TSX
Engine/Carb./ Trans.[1]	**Idle Mixture**		**Timing (Degrees BTDC)[5]**	
	Before Lean Drop	**After Lean Drop**		
231-2 bbl. M	1,100	800	12	
231-2 bbl. A	680	600	12	
350-4 bbl. A	680	600	12	
455-4 bbl. A	680	600	12	

1. M=Manual transmission; A=Automatic transmission.
2. Headlights and air conditioning off; automatic transmission in DRIVE; manual transmission in NEUTRAL.
3. With EGR hose disconnected and plugged and automatic transmission in PARK or NEUTRAL.
4. Set idle stop solenoid to 600 rpm.
5. Set at curb idle speed with distributor vacuum advance line disconnected and plugged.

(continued)

Table 1 TUNE-UP SPECIFICATIONS (continued)

1977 Buick				
Engine/Carb./ Trans.[1]	**Idle Speeds**		**AC Spark Plug**	
	Curb[2]	**Fast[3]**	**Gap (in.)**	**No.**
231-2 bbl. M	800 [4]	Preset	0.060	R46TSX
231-2 bbl. A	600 [5]	Preset	0.060	R46TSX
350-4 bbl. A	500 [6]	1,600	0.060	R45TS
403-4 bbl. A				
Federal	550 [6]	900	0.060	R46SZ
Altitude	600 [6]	1,000	0.060	R46SZ
California	550 [6]	1,000	0.060	R46SZ

Engine/Carb./ Trans.[1]	**Idle Mixture**		**Timing (Degrees BTDC)[7]**
	Before Lean Drop	**After Lean Drop**	
231-2 bbl. M	860	800	12[8]
231-2 bbl. A	610	600	12
350-4 bbl. A	550	500	8
403-4 bbl. A			
Federal	580	550	24 [9]
Altitude	625	600	20 [9]
California	575	550	20 [9]

1. M=Manual transmission; A=Automatic transmission.
2. Headlights and air conditioning off; automatic transmission in DRIVE; manual transmission in NEUTRAL.
3. With EGR hose disconnected and plugged and automatic transmission in PARK or NEUTRAL.
4. Set idle stop solenoid to 500 rpm (Federal) or 600 rpm (California).
5. Set idle speed-up solenoid @ 670 rpm.
6. Set idle speed-up solenoid @ 650 rpm.
7. Set at curb idle speed with distributor vacuum advance line disconnected and plugged.
8. Set @ 600 rpm.
9. Set @ 1,100 rpm.

(continued)

4

Table 1 TUNE-UP SPECIFICATIONS (continued)

Engine/Carb./ Trans.[1]	Idle Speeds		AC Spark Plug	
	Curb[2]	Fast[3]	Gap (in.)	No.
231-2 bbl. M	800[4]	Preset	0.060	R46TSX
231-2 bbl. A	600[5]	Preset	0.060	R46TSX
231-2 bbl. A Turbo	650	Preset	0.060	R44TSX
231-4 bbl. A Turbo	650	2,500	0.060	R44TSX
301-2 bbl. A	550	2,500	0.060	R46TSX
305-2 bbl. A	500[6]	Preset	0.045	R45TS
350-4 bbl. A				
Federal	550[6]	1,550	0.060	R46TSX
Altitude	600[7]	1,600	0.060	R45TS
California	500	1,600	0.045	R45TS
403-4 bbl. A				
Federal	550[7]	900	0.060	R46SZ
Altitude	600[7]	1,000	0.060	R46SZ
California	550[7]	1,000	0.060	R46SZ

1978 BUICK

Engine/Carb./ Trans.[1]	Propane Enriched Idle Speed		Timing (Degrees BTDC)[8]
	Manual	Automatic	
231-2 bbl. M	940[9]	-	15
231-2 bbl. A	-	650[5]	15
231-2 bbl. A Turbo	-	-	15
231-4 bbl. A Turbo	-	-	15
301-2 bbl. A	-	580	12
305-2 bbl. A	-	520/540[10]	4[7]
350-4 bbl. A			
Federal	-	590	15
Altitude	-	630/670	8
California	-	530/570	8
403-4 bbl. A			
Federal	-	625/645	20[11]
Altitude	-	625/645	20[11]
California	-	565-585	20[11]

1. M=Manual transmission; A=Automatic transmission.
2. Headlights and air conditioning off; automatic transmission in DRIVE; manual transmission in NEUTRAL.
3. With EGR hose disconnected and plugged and automatic transmission in PARK or NEUTRAL.
4. Set idle stop solenoid to 500 rpm on Federal and 600 rpm on California engines.
5. Altitude and California, 615 rpm.
6. Set idle speed-up solenoid @ 600 rpm.
7. Set idle speed-up solenoid @ 700 rpm.
8. Set at curb idle speed with distributor vacuum advance line disconnected and plugged.
9. Altitude and California, 880 rpm.
10. Altitude, 620/640 rpm.
11. Set @ 1,100 rpm.

(continued)

Table 1 TUNE-UP SPECIFICATIONS (continued)

1979 Buick				
Engine/Carb./ Trans.[1]	**Idle Speeds**		**AC Spark Plug**	
	Curb[2]	**Fast[3]**	**Gap (in.)**	**No.**
231-2 bbl. M	800[4]	2,200	0.060	R45TSX
231-2 bbl. A	550	2,200	0.060	R45TSX
231-4 bbl. A Turbo	650	2,500	0.040	R44TS
301-2 bbl. A	500	2,000	0.060	R46TSX
305-2 bbl. A	500[5]	1,600	0.045	R45TS
350-4 bbl. A				
Engine code X	550[5]	1,550	0.060	R45TSX
Engine code R	550[5, 6]	900[7]	0.060	R46SZ
Engine code L	500[8]	1,600[9]	0.045	R45TS
403-4 bbl. A				
Federal	550	900	0.060	R46SZ
Altitude	600	1,000	0.060	R46SZ
California	500	1,000	0.060	R46SZ

Engine/Carb./ Trans.[1]	**Propane Enriched Idle Speed**		**Timing (Degrees BTDC)[10]**
	Manual	**Automatic**	
231-2 bbl. M	1,000		15
231-2 bbl. A		575	15
231-4 bbl. A Turbo		-	15
301-2 bbl. A		530	12[11]
305-2 bbl. A		520/540	4[12]
350-4 bbl. A			
Engine code X		590	15
Engine code R		625/640[13]	20[14]
Engine code L		520/560[15]	8
403-4 bbl. A			
Federal		625/645	20[14]
Altitude		590	20[14]
California		565/585	20[14]

1. M=Manual transmission; A=Automatic transmission.
2. Headlights and air conditioning off; automatic transmission in DRIVE; manual transmission in NEUTRAL.
3. With EGR hose disconnected and plugged and automatic transmission in PARK or NEUTRAL.
4. Set idle stop solenoid to 600 rpm on California engines.
5. Set idle speed-up solenoid @ 600 rpm.
6. Altitude, 600 rpm; California, 500 rpm.
7. California, 1,000 rpm.
8. Altitude, 600 rpm.
9. Altitude, 1,750 rpm.
10. Set at curb idle speed with distributor vacuum advance line disconnected and plugged.
11. Set @ 650 rpm.
12. Set @ 600 rpm.
13. Altitude, 590 rpm; California, 565-585 rpm.
14. Set @ 1,100 rpm.
15. Altitude, 630/670 rpm.

(continued)

Table 1 TUNE-UP SPECIFICATIONS (continued)

Engine/Carb./Trans.[1]	Idle Speeds Curb[2]	Fast[3]	AC Spark Plug Gap (in.)	No.
1980 Buick				
231-2 bbl. M	800	2,200	0.060	R45TSX
231-2 bbl. A	550[4]	2,000[5]	0.060	R45TSX
301-4 bbl. A	500[6]	2,500	0.060	R45TSX
350-4 bbl. A				
Engine code X	550[6]	1,850	0.060	R45TSX
Engine code R	550[6]	700[7]	0.080	R46SZ
350 Diesel A	600	750	-	-

Engine/Carb. Trans.[1]	Propane Enriched Idle Speed Manual	Automatic	Timing (Degrees BTDC)[8]
231-2 bbl. M	830		15
231-2 bbl. A		610	15
301-4 bbl. A		550	12
350-4 bbl. A			
Engine code X		590	15
Engine code R		575	18[7]
350 Diesel A	-	-	See note 8

1. M=Manual transmission; A=Automatic transmission.
2. Headlights and air conditioning off; automatic transmission in DRIVE; manual transmission in NEUTRAL.
3. With EGR hose disconnected and plugged and automatic transmission in PARK or NEUTRAL.
4. Set idle speed-up solenoid to 620 rpm on California engines.
5. California, 2,200 rpm.
6. Set idle speed-up solenoid @ 650 rpm.
7. With automatic transmission in DRIVE.
8. Set at curb idle speed with distributor vacuum advance line disconnected and plugged.
9. Crankshaft timing not required. Align timing marks on injector pump and adapter with engine off.

Table 2 TUNE-UP SPECIFICATIONS (CHEVROLET)

1972 Chevrolet				
Engine/Carb./Trans.[1]	Idle Speeds		AC Spark Plug	
	Curb[2,3]	Fast	Gap (in.)	No.
250-1 bbl. M	700	2,400	0.035	R45T
250-1 bbl. A	600	2,400	0.035	R45T
350-2 bbl. M	900	Preset	0.035	R44T
350-2 bbl. A	600	Preset	0.035	R44T
400-2 bbl. M	900	2,200	0.035	R44T
400-2 bbl. A	600	2,200	0.035	R44T
402-4 bbl. M	750	1,350	0.035	R44T
402-4 bbl. A	600	1,500	0.035	R44T
454-4 bbl. M	750	1,350	0.035	R44T
454-4 bbl. A	600	1,500	0.035	R44T

Engine/Carb./Trans.[1]	Idle Mixture		Distributor		Timing (Degrees BTDC)[4]
	Before Lean Drop	After Lean Drop	Point Gap (in.)	Dwell Angle	
250-1 bbl. M	800	700	0.019	31-34	4
250-1 bbl. A	630	600	0.019	31-34	4
350-2 bbl. M	1,050	900	0.019	29-31	6
350-2 bbl. A	650	600	0.019	29-31	6
400-2 bbl. M	900	900	0.019	29-31	2
400-2 bbl. A	650	600	0.019	29-31	6
402-4 bbl. M	800	750	0.019	29-31	8
402-4 bbl. A	650	600	0.019	29-31	8
454-4 bbl. M	-	-	0.019	29-31	8
454-4 bbl. A	-	-	0.019	29-31	8

1. M=Manual transmission; A=Automatic transmission.
2. Headlights and air conditioning off; automatic transmission in DRIVE; manual transmission in NEUTRAL.
3. Requires idle stop solenoid adjustment to 450 rpm.
4. Set at curb idle speed with distributor vacuum advance line disconnected and plugged.

(continued)

Table 2 TUNE-UP SPECIFICATIONS (continued)

1973 CHEVROLET				
Engine/Carb./ Trans.[1]	Idle Speeds		AC Spark Plug	
	Curb[2]	Fast[3]	Gap (in.)	No.
250-1 bbl. M	700[4]	1,800	0.035	R46T
250-1 bbl. A	600[4]	1,800	0.035	R46T
350-2 bbl. M	900[5]	Preset	0.035	R44T
350-2 bbl. A	600[5]	Preset	0.035	R44T
350-4 bbl. M	900[6]	1,300	0.035	R44T
350-4 bbl. A	600[6]	1,600	0.035	R44T
400-2 bbl. A	600[6]	1,600	0.035	R44T
454-4 bbl. M	900[6]	1,300	0.035	R44T
454-4 bbl. A	600[6]	1,600	0.035	R44T

Engine/Carb./ Trans.[1]	Idle Mixture		Distributor		Timing (Degrees BTDC)[7]
	Before Lean Drop	After Lean Drop	Point Gap	Dwell Angle	
250-1 bbl. M	750	700	0.019	31-34	6
250-1 bbl. A	630	600	0.019	31-34	6
350-2 bbl. M	950	900	0.019	29-31	8
350-2 bbl. A	630	600	0.019	29-31	8
350-4 bbl. M	920	900	0.019	29-31	8
350-4 bbl. A	620	600	0.019	29-31	12
400-2 bbl. A	630	600	0.019	29-31	8
454-4 bbl. M	25	900	0.019	29-31	10
454-4 bbl. A	625	600	0.019	29-31	10

1. M=Manual transmission; A=Automatic transmission.
2. Headlights and air conditioning off; automatic transmission in DRIVE; manual transmission in NEUTRAL.
3. With EGR hose disconnected and plugged and automatic transmission in PARK or NEUTRAL.
4. Requires idle stop solenoid adjustment to 450 rpm.
5. Requires idle stop solenoid adjustment to 400 rpm.
6. Requires idle stop solenoid adjustment to 500 rpm.
7. Set at curb idle speed with distributor vacuum advance line disconnected and plugged.

(continued)

Table 2 TUNE-UP SPECIFICATIONS (continued)

1974 Chevrolet				
Engine/Carb./ Trans.[1]	**Idle Speeds**		**AC Spark Plug**	
	Curb[2,3]	**Fast[4,5]**	**Gap (in.)**	**No.**
350-2 bbl. M	900	Preset	0.035	R44T
350-2 bbl. A	600	Preset	0.035	R44T
350-4 bbl. A	600	1,600	0.035	R44T
400-2 bbl. A	600	1,600	0.035	R44T
400-4 bbl. A	600	1,600	0.035	R44T
454-4 bbl. M	800	1,500	0.035	R44T
454-4 bbl. A	600	1,600	0.035	R44T

Engine/Carb./ Trans.[1]	**Idle Mixture**		**Distributor**		**Timing (Degrees BTDC)[6]**
	Before Lean Drop	**After Lean Drop**	**Point Gap**	**Dwell Angle**	
350-2 bbl. M	1,000	900	0.019	29-31	TDC
350-2 bbl. A	650	600	0.019	29-31	8
350-4 bbl. A	630	600	0.019	29-31	8
400-2 bbl. A	650	600	0.019	29-31	8
400-4 bbl. A	650	600	0.019	29-31	8
454-4 bbl. M	850	800	0.019	29-31	10
454-4 bbl. A	630	600	0.019	29-31	10

1. M=Manual transmission; A=Automatic transmission.
2. Headlights and air conditioning off; automatic transmission in DRIVE; manual transmission in NEUTRAL.
3. Requires idle stop solenoid adjustment to 500 rpm.
4. With EGR hose disconnected and plugged and automatic transmission in PARK or NEUTRAL.
5. With distributor spark advance hose disconnected and plugged.
6. Set at curb idle speed with distributor vacuum advance line disconnected and plugged.

(continued)

4

Table 2 TUNE-UP SPECIFICATIONS (continued)

Engine/Carb./ Trans.[1]	Idle Speeds		AC Spark Plug	
	Curb[2]	Fast[3, 4]	Gap (in.)	No.
140-1 bbl. M	1,200	2,000[5]	0.060	R43TSX
140-1 bbl. A	750[6]	2,200	0.060	R43TSX
140-2 bbl. M	700	1,600	0.060	R43TSX
140-2 bbl. A	750[7]	1,600	0.060	R43TSX
140-2 bbl. M California	1,200[8]	1,600	0.060	R43TSX
140-2 bbl. A California	750	1,600	0.060	R43TSX
262-2 bbl. M	800	Preset	0.060	R44TX
262-2 bbl. A	600	Preset	0.060	R44TX
350-2 bbl. A	600	Preset	0.060	R44TX
350-4 bbl. M	800	1,600	0.060	R44TX
350-4 bbl. A	600	1,600	0.060	R44TX
400-4 bbl. A	600	1,600	0.060	R44TX
454-4 bbl. A	600[9]	1,600	0.060	R44TX

Engine/Carb./ Trans.[1]	Idle Mixture		Timing (Degrees BTDC)[10]
	Before Lean Drop	After Lean Drop	
140-1 bbl. M	1,000	900	TDC
140-1 bbl. A	650	600	8
140-2 bbl. M	820	700	10
140-2 bbl. A	830	750	12
140-2 bbl. M California	820[11]	700	10
140-2 bbl. A California	830	750	12
262-2 bbl. M	900	800	8
262-2 bbl. A	630	600	8
350-2 bbl. A	650	600	6
350-4 bbl. M	900	800	6[12]
350-4 bbl. A	650	600	8[13]
400-4 bbl. A	650	600	8
454-4 bbl. A	630	600	16

1. M=Manual transmission; A=Automatic transmission.
2. Headlights and air conditioning off; automatic transmission in DRIVE; manual transmission in NEUTRAL.
3. With EGR hose disconnected and plugged and automatic transmission in PARK or NEUTRAL.
4. With distributor spark advance hose disconnected and plugged.
5. 1,500 rpm without catalytic converter.
6. Requires idle stop solenoid adjustment @ 550 rpm.
7. Requires idle stop solenoid adjustment @ 600 rpm.
8. Requires idle stop solenoid adjustment @ 700 rpm.
9. Requires idle stop solenoid adjustment @ 500 rpm.
10. Set at curb idle speed with distributor vacuum advance line disconnected and plugged.
11. With idle stop solenoid de-energized.
12. California, 4° BTDC.
13. California, 6° BTDC.

(continued)

Table 2 TUNE-UP SPECIFICATIONS (continued)

1976 CHEVROLET				
Engine/Carb./ Trans.[1]	Idle Speeds		AC Spark Plug	
	Curb[2]	Fast[3]	Gap (in.)	No.
140-1 bbl. M	1,200[4]	2,000[5]	0.035	R43TS
140-1 bbl. A	750[6]	2,200	0.035	R43TS
140-2 bbl. M	700[7, 8]	2,200	0.035	R43TS
140-2 bbl. A	750[9]	2,200	0.035	R43TS
262-2 bbl. M	800	Preset	0.045	R45TS
262-2 bbl. A	600[10]	Preset	0.045	R45TS
350-2 bbl. A	600	Preset	0.045	R45TS
350-4 bbl. A	600	1,600[11]	0.045	R45TS
400-4 bbl. A	600	1,600[11]	0.045	R45TS
454-4 bbl. A	550	1,600[11]	0.045	R45TS
Engine/Carb./ Trans.[1]	Idle Mixture		Timing (Degrees BTDC)[12]	
	Before Lean Drop	After Lean Drop		
140-1 bbl. M	875[13]	750	8	
140-1 bbl. A	825	750	10	
140-2 bbl. M	900	700	10	
140-2 bbl. A	830	750	12	
262-2 bbl. M	900	800	6	
262-2 bbl. A	630	600	8	
350-2 bbl. A	650	600	6	
350-4 bbl. A	650	600	8	
400-4 bbl. A	650	600	8	
454-4 bbl. A	580	550	12	

1. M=Manual transmission; A=Automatic transmission.
2. Headlights and air conditioning off; automatic transmission in DRIVE; manual transmission in NEUTRAL.
3. With EGR hose disconnected and plugged and automatic transmission in PARK or NEUTRAL.
4. Set idle stop solenoid to 750 rpm
5. Without catalytic converter, 1,500 rpm.
6. Set idle stop solenoid to 550 rpm.
7. Set idle speed-up solenoid to 1,200 rpm.
8. California, 1,000 rpm with idle stop solenoid adjustment to 700 rpm.
9. Set idle stop solenoid to 700 rpm.
10. Set idle speed-up solenoid to 650 rpm.
11. With distributor spark advance line connected.
12. Set at curb idle speed with distributor vacuum advance line disconnected and plugged.
13. With idle stop solenoid de-energized.

(continued)

4

Table 2 TUNE-UP SPECIFICATIONS (continued)

1977 Chevrolet				
Engine/Carb./ Trans.[1]	Idle Speeds		AC Spark Plug	
	Curb[2]	Fast[2]	Gap (in.)	No.
140-2 bbl. M	700[4]	2,500	0.035	R43TS
140-2 bbl. A	650[4]	2,500	0.035	R43TS
140-2 bbl. M Altitude	800[4]	2,500	0.035	R43TS
140-2 bbl. A Altitude	700[4]	2,500	0.035	R43TS
250-1 bbl. A				
Federal	550[5]	2,000	0.035	R46TS
Altitude	600[5]	2,000	0.035	R46TS
California	550	1,800	0.035	R46TS
305-2 bbl. A	500[6]	Preset	0.045	R45TS
305-2 bbl. A Altitude	600[6]	Preset	0.045	R45TS
350-4 bbl. A	500	1,600	0.045	R45TS
350-4 bbl. A Altitude	600[6]	1,600	0.045	R45TS

Engine/Carb./ Trans.[1]	Idle Mixture		Timing (Degrees BTDC)[7]
	Before Lean Drop	After Lean Drop	
140-2 bbl. M	780	700	TDC
140-2 bbl. A	680	650	2[8]
140-2 bbl. M Altitude	880	800	TDC[9]
140-2 bbl. A Altitude	730	700	2
250-1 bbl. A			
Federal	575	550	8
Altitude	650	600	10
California	640	600	6[10]
305-2 bbl. A	600	500	8[11]
305-2 bbl. A Altitude	650	600	6[12]
350-4 bbl. A	550	500	8
350-4 bbl. A Altitude	650	600	8

1. M=Manual transmission; A=Automatic transmission.
2. Headlights and air conditioning off; automatic transmission in DRIVE; manual transmission in NEUTRAL.
3. With EGR hose disconnected and plugged and automatic transmission in PARK or NEUTRAL.
4. Set idle speed-up solenoid to 1,250 rpm.
5. Set idle stop solenoid to 450 rpm.
6. Set idle speed-up solenoid to 650 rpm.
7. Set at curb idle speed with distributor vacuum advance line disconnected and plugged.
8. California, TDC.
9. California, 2° BTDC.
10. Some engines are timed @ 8° BTDC.
11. California, 8° BTDC.
12. Some engines are timed @ 6° BTDC.

(continued)

Table 2 TUNE-UP SPECIFICATIONS (continued)

1978 Chevrolet				
Engine/Carb./ Trans.[1]	Idle Speeds		AC Spark Plug	
	Curb[2]	Fast[3]	Gap	No.
151-2 bbl. M	1,000[4, 5]	2,200	0.060	R43TSX
151-2 bbl. A	650[5, 6]	2,400	0.060	R43TSX
196-2 bbl. M	800[7]	Preset	0.060	R46TSX
196-2 bbl. A	600	Preset	0.060	R46TSX
231-2 bbl. M	800[7]	Preset	0.060	R46TSX
231-2 bbl. A	600[8]	Preset	0.060	R46TSX
250-1 bbl. A	550[9]	2,100	0.035	R46TS
305-2 bbl. A	600[10]	Preset	0.045	R45TS
305-2 bbl. A Altitude	500[10]	Preset	0.045	R45TS
350-4 bbl. A	500[10]	1,600	0.045	R45TS
350-4 bbl. A Altitude	600[10]	1,600	0.045	R45TS

Engine/Carb./ Trans.[1]	Propane Enriched Idle Speed		Timing (Degrees BTDC)[11]
	Manual	Automatic	
151-2 bbl. M	1,000/1,150		14
151-2 bbl. A		650/690	14
196-2 bbl. M	940		15
196-2 bbl. A		640	15
231-2 bbl. M	880		15
231-2 bbl. A		650	15
250-1 bbl. A		630/650	10
305-2 bbl. A		520/540	6
305-2 bbl. A Altitude		620/640	8
350-4 bbl. A		530/570	6
350-4 bbl. A Altitude		630-670	6[12]

1. M=Manual transmission; A=Automatic transmission.
2. Headlights and air conditioning off; automatic transmission in DRIVE; manual transmission in NEUTRAL.
3. With EGR hose disconnected and plugged and automatic transmission in PARK or NEUTRAL.
4. With air conditioning, set idle speed-up solenoid adjustment to 1,200 rpm.
5. Without air conditioning, set idle stop solenoid adjustment to 500 rpm.
6. With air conditioning, set idle speed-up solenoid adjustment to 850 rpm.
7. Set idle stop solenoid to 600 rpm.
8. Set idle speed-up solenoid to 670 rpm.
9. Set idle stop solenoid to 425 rpm.
10. Set idle speed-up solenoid to 600 rpm.
11. Set at curb idle speed with distributor vacuum advance line disconnected and plugged.
12. With air conditioning, 8° BTDC.

(continued)

Table 2 TUNE-UP SPECIFICATIONS (continued)

1979 Chevrolet				
Engine/Carb./ Trans.[1]	**Idle Speeds**		**AC Spark Plug**	
	Curb[2]	**Fast[3]**	**Gap (in.)**	**No.**
151-2 bbl. M	900	2,200	0.060	R44TSX
151-2 bbl. A	650	2,400	0.060	R44TSX
151-2 bbl. M California	1,000	2,200	0.060	R44TSX
151-2 bbl. A California	650	2,400	0.060	R44TSX
196-2 bbl. M	800	2,200	0.060	R45TSX
196-2 bbl. A	550	2,200	0.060	R45TSX
231-2 bbl. M	800	2,200	0.060	R45TSX
231-2 bbl. A	600	2,200	0.060	R45TSX
250-1 bbl. A	675	2,000	0.035	R46TS
250-1 bbl. A California	600	2,000	0.035	R46TS
305-2 bbl. M	600	1,300	0.045	R45TS
305-2 bbl. A	500	1,600	0.045	R45TS
305-2 bbl. A California	600	1,950	0.045	R45TS
350-4 bbl. A	500	1,600	0.045	R45TS
350-4 bbl. A Altitude	600	1,750	0.045	R45TS
350-4 bbl. A California	500	1,600	0.045	R45TS

Engine/Carb./ Trans.[1]	**Propane Enriched Idle Speed**		**Idle Stop Solenoid (rpm)**	**Speed-up Solenoid (rpm)**	**Timing (Degrees BTDC)[4]**
	Manual	**Automatic**			
151-2 bbl. M	1,040		500	1,250	12
151-2 bbl. A		695	500	1,250	12
151-2 bbl. M California	760		500	1,250	14
151-2 bbl. A California		760	500	1,250	14[5]
196-2 bbl. M	1,000		600		15
196-2 bbl. A		575		670	15
231-2 bbl. M	840		600		15
231-2 bbl. A		615			15
250-1 bbl. A		1,200/1,250	400		8
250-1 bbl. A California		975/1,025	400		6
305-2 bbl. M	710/750			650	4
305-2 bbl. A		520/540		650	4
305-2 bbl. A California		640/660		650	2
350-4 bbl. A		530/570		600	6
350-4 bbl. A Altitude		630/670		600	8
350-4 bbl. A California		520/560		600	8

1. M=Manual transmission; A=Automatic transmission.
2. Headlights and air conditioning off; automatic transmission in DRIVE; manual transmission in NEUTRAL.
3. With EGR hose disconnected and plugged and automatic transmission in PARK or NEUTRAL.
4. Set at curb idle speed with distributor vacuum advance line disconnected and plugged.
5. Set timing @ 1,000 rpm.

(continued)

Table 2 TUNE-UP SPECIFICATIONS (continued)

1980 Chevrolet				
Engine/Carb./ Trans.[1]	**Idle Speeds**		**AC Spark Plug**	
	Curb[2]	**Fast[3]**	**Gap (in.)**	**No.**
151-2 bbl. M	1,000	2,600[4]	0.060	R44TSX
151-2 bbl. A	650	2,600	0.060	R44TSX
229-2 bbl. A	600	1,750	0.045	R45TS
231-2 bbl. M	800	2,200	0.060	R45TSX
231-2 bbl. A	550[5]	2,000	0.060	R45TSX
305-4 bbl. A	500	1,850	0.045	R45TS
305-4 bbl. A California	550	2,200	0.045	R45TS
350-4 bbl. A	500	1,850	0.045	R45TS
350 Diesel	600	750	-	-

Engine/Carb./ Trans.[1]	**Propane Enriched Idle Speed**		**Idle Stop Solenoid (rpm)**	**Speed-up Solenoid (rpm)**	**Timing (Degrees BTDC)[6]**
	Manual	**Automatic**			
151-2 bbl. M	1,150		550	1,250	12
151-2 bbl. A		700	550	1,250	12
229-2 bbl. A		630/650		675	12
231-2 bbl. M	830		600		15
231-2 bbl. A		600	620		15
305-4 bbl. A		550		600	4
305-4 bbl. A California		See note 7		650	4
350-4 bbl. A		550		600	6
350 Diesel					See note 8

1. M=Manual transmission; A=Automatic transmission.
2. Headlights and air conditioning off; automatic transmission in DRIVE; manual transmission in NEUTRAL.
3. With EGR hose disconnected and plugged and automatic transmission in PARK or NEUTRAL.
4. California, 2,400 rpm.
5. Without Electronic Spark Timing, 600 rpm.
6. Set at curb idle speed with distributor vacuum advance line disconnected and plugged.
7. Electronically controlled.
8. Crankshaft timing not required. Align timing marks on injection pump and adapter with engine off.

4

Table 3 TUNE-UP SPECIFICATIONS (OLDSMOBILE)

1972 Oldsmobile				
Engine/Carb./ Trans.[1]	Idle Speeds		AC Spark Plug	
	Curb[2]	Fast	Gap (in.)	No.
350-2 bbl. A	650[3]	900	0.040	R46S
350-4 bbl. A	600	1,100	0.040	R45S
455-4 bbl. A	600[3]	1.100	0.040	R46S
Engine/Carb./ Trans.[1]	Distributor		Timing (Degrees BTDC)[4]	
	Point Gap (in.)	Dwell Angle		
350-2 bbl. A	0.016	28-32	8[5]	
350-4 bbl. A	0.016	28-32	12[5]	
455-4 bbl. A	0.016	28-32	8[5]	

1. M=Manual transmission; A=Automatic transmission.
2. Headlights and air conditioning off; automatic transmission in DRIVE; manual transmission in NEUTRAL.
3. Set idle stop solenoid to 550 rpm.
4. Set at curb idle speed with distributor vacuum advance line disconnected and plugged.
5. Set timing @ 1,100 rpm.

1973 Oldsmobile				
Engine/Carb./ Trans.[1]	Idle Speeds		AC Spark Plug	
	Curb[2]	Fast[3]	Gap (in.)	No.
350-2 bbl. A	700	900	0.040	R46S
350-4 bbl. A	650[4]	1,100	0.040	R46S
455-4 bbl. A	650[4]	1,100	0.040	R46S
Engine/Carb./ Trans.[1]	Distributor		Timing (Degrees BTDC)[5, 6]	
	Point Gap (in.)	Dwell Angle		
350-2 bbl. A	0.016	28-32	12	
350-4 bbl. A	0.016	28-32	12	
455-4 bbl. A	0.016	28-32	8	

1. M=Manual transmission; A=Automatic transmission.
2. Headlights and air conditioning off; automatic transmission in DRIVE; manual transmission in NEUTRAL.
3. With EGR line disconnected and plugged and automatic transmission in PARK.
4. Set idle stop solenoid @ 550 rpm.
5. Set at curb idle speed with distributor vacuum advance line disconnected and plugged.
6. Set timing @ 1,100 rpm.

(continued)

Table 3 TUNE-UP SPECIFICATIONS (continued)

1974 Oldsmobile				
Engine/Carb./ Trans.[1]	**Idle Speeds**		**AC Spark Plug**	
	Curb[2]	**Fast[3], [4]**	**Gap (in.)**	**No.**
350-4 bbl. A	650	1,000	0.040	R46S
455-4 bbl. A	650	1,000	0.040	R46S

Engine/Carb./ Trans.[1]	**Idle Mixture**		**Distributor**		**Timing (Degrees BTDC)[4], [5]**
	Before Lean Drop	**After Lean Drop**	**Point Gap (in.)**	**Dwell Angle**	
350-4 bbl. A	680	650	0.016	28-32	12
455-4 bbl. A	680	650	0.016	28-32	8

1. M=Manual transmission; A=Automatic transmission.
2. Headlights and air conditioning off; automatic transmission in DRIVE; manual transmission in NEUTRAL.
3. With EGR hose disconnected and plugged and automatic transmission in PARK or NEUTRAL.
4. Set idle stop solenoid to 550 rpm.
5. Set at curb idle speed with distributor vacuum advance line disconnected and plugged.
6. Set timing @ 1,100 rpm.

1975 Oldsmobile				
Engine/Carb./ Trans.[1]	**Idle Speeds**		**AC Spark Plug**	
	Curb[2]	**Fast[3]**	**Gap (in.)**	**No.**
231-2 bbl. M	800	1,800	0.060	R44SX
231-2 bbl. A	650	1,800	0.060	R44SX
350-4 bbl. A	550	900	0.060	R46SX
350-4 bbl. A California	600	1,000	0.060	R46SX
400-2 bbl. A	650	Preset	0.060	R46TSX
455-4 bbl. A	550	900	0.060	R46SX
455-4 bbl. A California	600	800	0.060	R46SX

Engine/Carb./ Trans.[1]	**Idle Mixture**		**Idle Stop Solenoid (rpm)**	**Idle Speed-up Solenoid (rpm)**	**Timing (Degrees BTDC)[4]**
	Before Lean Drop	**After Lean Drop**			
231-2 bbl. M	880	800	600		12
231-2 bbl. A	730	650	500		12
350-4 bbl. A	580	550		650	20[5]
350-4 bbl. A California	630	600		650	20[5]
400-2 bbl. A	630	650			16
455-4 bbl. A	580	550		650	16[5]
455-4 bbl. A California	630	600		650	16[5]

1. M=Manual transmission; A=Automatic transmission.
2. Headlights and air conditioning off; automatic transmission in DRIVE; manual transmission in NEUTRAL.
3. With EGR hose disconnected and plugged and automatic transmission in PARK or NEUTRAL.
4. Set at curb idle speed with distributor vacuum advance line disconnected and plugged.
5. Set timing @ 1,100 rpm.

(continued)

Table 3 TUNE-UP SPECIFICATIONS (continued)

| Engine/Carb./ Trans.[1] | Idle Speeds | | AC Spark Plug | |
	Curb[2]	Fast[3]	Gap (in.)	No.
140-2 bbl. M	700[4]	2,200[5]	0.035	R43TS
140-2 bbl. A	750	2,200[5]	0.035	R43TS
231-2 bbl. M	800	1,800	0.060	R44SX
231-2 bbl. A	600	1,800	0.060	R44SX
350-4 bbl. A	550	900	0.080	R46SX
350-4 bbl. A California	600	1,000	0.080	R46SX
455-4 bbl. A	550	900	0.080	R46SX
455-4 bbl. A California	600	800	0.080	R46SX

| Engine/Carb./ Trans.[1] | Idle Mixture | | Idle Stop Solenoid (rpm) | Idle Speed-up Solenoid (rpm) | Timing (Degrees BTDC)[6] |
	Before Lean Drop	After Lean Drop			
140-2 bbl. M	900	700	700		10
140-2 bbl. A	830	750	600[7]		12
231-2 bbl. M	1,100	800	600		12
231-2 bbl. A	680	600			12
350-4 bbl. A	580	550		650	20[8]
350-4 bbl. A California	625	600		650	20[8]
455-4 bbl. A	580	550		650	16[8]
455-4 bbl. A California	625	600		650	14[8]

1. M=Manual transmission; A=Automatic transmission.
2. Headlights and air conditioning off; automatic transmission in DRIVE; manual transmission in NEUTRAL.
3. With EGR hose disconnected and plugged and automatic transmission in PARK or NEUTRAL.
4. California, 1,000 rpm.
5. With distributor vacuum line connected.
6. Set at curb idle speed with distributor vacuum advance line disconnected and plugged.
7. California, 700 rpm.
8. Set timing @ 1,100 rpm.

(continued)

Table 3 TUNE-UP SPECIFICATIONS (continued)

1977 Oldsmobile				
Engine/Carb./ Trans.[1]	Idle Speeds		AC Spark Plug	
	Curb[2]	Fast[3]	Gap (in.)	No.
140-2 bbl. M	700	2,500	0.035	R43TS
140-2 bbl. A	650	2,500	0.035	R43TS
140-2 bbl. M Altitude	800	2,500	0.035	R43TS
140-2 bbl. A Altitude	700	2,500	0.035	R43TS
231-2 bbl. M	800	Preset	0.060	R46TSX
231-2 bbl. A	600	Preset	0.060	R46TSX
350-4 bbl. A				
Federal	550	900	0.060	R46SZ
Altitude	600	1,000	0.060	R46SZ
California	550	1,000	0.060	R46SZ
403-4 bbl. A	550	900	0.060	R46SZ
Altitude	600	1,000	0.060	R46SZ
California	575	550	0.060	R46SZ

Engine/Carb./ Trans.[1]	Idle Mixture		Idle Stop Solenoid (rpm)	Idle Speed-up Solenoid (rpm)	Timing (Degrees BTDC)[6]
	Before Lean Drop	After Lean Drop			
140-2 bbl. M	780	700		1,250	TDC
140-2 bbl. A	680	650		850	2[5]
140-2 bbl. M Altitude	880	800		1,250	TDC[6]
140-2 bbl. A Altitude	730	700		850	2
231-2 bbl. M	860[7]	800	600		12
231-2 bbl. A	640[8]	600		670	12
350-4 bbl. A					
Federal	580	550		700	20[9]
Altitude	625	600		700	20[9]
California	575	550		700	18[9]
403-4 bbl. A	580	550		650	20[9]
Altitude	625	600		650	20[9]
California	575	550		650	20[9]

1. M=Manual transmission; A=Automatic transmission.
2. Headlights and air conditioning off; automatic transmission in DRIVE; manual transmission in NEUTRAL.
3. With EGR hose disconnected and plugged and automatic transmission in PARK or NEUTRAL.
4. Set at curb idle speed with distributor vacuum advance line disconnected and plugged.
5. California, TDC.
6. Set timing @ 700 rpm.
7. California, 810 rpm.
8. Altitude and California, 610 rpm.
9. Set timing @ 1,100 rpm.

(continued)

4

Table 3 TUNE-UP SPECIFICATIONS (continued)

1978 Oldsmobile				
Engine/Carb./ Trans.[1]	**Idle Speeds**		**AC Spark Plug**	
	Curb[2]	**Fast**[3]	**Gap (in.)**	**No.**
151-2 bbl. M	1,000	2,200	0.060	R43TSX
151-2 bbl. A	650	2,400	0.060	R43TSX
231-2 bbl. M	800	1,850	0.060	R46TSX
231-2 bbl. A	600	1,850	0.060	R46TSX
260-2 bbl. M	650	750	0.060	R46SZ
260-2 bbl. A				
Federal	500	800	0.060	R46SZ
Altitude	550	900	0.060	R46SZ
California	500	800	0.060	R46SZ
305-2 bbl. M	600	1,600	0.045	R45TS
305-2 bbl. A	500	1,600	0.045	R45TS
305-2 bbl. A Altitude	600	1,600	0.045	R45TS
350-4 bbl. A				
Federal	550	900	0.060	R46SZ
Altitude	600	1,000	0.060	R46SZ
California	550	1,000	0.060	R46SZ
350 Diesel	575	650		
403-4 bbl. A				
Federal	550	900	0.060	R46SZ
Altitude	600	1,000	0.060	R46SZ
California	550	1,000	0.060	R46SZ

Engine/Carb./ Trans.[1]	**Propane Enriched Idle Speed**		**Idle Stop Solenoid (rpm)**	**Idle Speed-up Solenoid (rpm)**	**Timing (Degrees BTDC)**[4]
	Manual	**Automatic**			
151-2 bbl. M	1,150	680/700	500	1,200	14
151-2 bbl. A			500	1,200	14
231-2 bbl. M	940	650[5]	600		15
231-2 bbl. A				670	15
260-2 bbl. M	780/800			800	18[6]
260-2 bbl. A		560/580			
Federal		615		625	20[6]
Altitude		615			20
California				625	18[6]
305-2 bbl. M	700/740	520/540		650	4
305-2 bbl. A		630/670		650	4[7]
305-2 bbl. A Altitude				650	8
350-4 bbl. A		625/645			
Federal		590		650	20[6]
Altitude		565/585		700	20[6]
California				650	20[6]
350 Diesel					See note 8
403-4 bbl. A		625/645			
Federal		630/670		650	18[6]
Altitude		565/585		700	20[6]
California				650	20[6]

1. M=Manual transmission; A=Automatic transmission.
2. Headlights and air conditioning off; automatic transmission in DRIVE; manual transmission in NEUTRAL.
3. With EGR hose disconnected and plugged and automatic transmission in PARK or NEUTRAL.
4. Set at curb idle speed with distributor vacuum advance line disconnected and plugged.
5. Altitude and California, 615 rpm.
6. Set timing @ 1,100 rpm.
7. California, 6° BTDC.
8. Crankshaft timing is not required. Align injector pump and adapter timing marks with engine off.

(continued)

Table 3 TUNE-UP SPECIFICATIONS (continued)

1979 Oldsmobile				
Engine/Carb./ Trans.[1]	Idle Speeds Curb[2]	Fast[3]	AC Spark Plug Gap (in.)	No.
151-2 bbl. M	900[4]	2,200	0.060	R44TSX
151-2 bbl. A	650	2,400	0.060	R44TSX
231-2 bbl. M	800	2,200	0.060	R45TSX
231-2 bbl. A	550[5]	2,200	0.060	R45TSX
260-2 bbl. A	500	800	0.060	R46SZ
305-2 bbl. M	600	1,300	0.045	R45TS
305-2 bbl. A	500	1,600	0.045	R45TS
305-2 bbl. A California	600	1,950	0.045	R45TS
350-4 bbl. A	550	900	0.060	R46SZ
350-4 bbl. A California	500	1,000	0.060	R46SZ
350 Diesel	575	650		
403-4 bbl. A	550	900	0.060	R46SZ
403-4 bbl. A California	500	1,000	0.060	R46SZ

Engine/Carb./ Trans.[1]	Propane Enriched Idle Speed Manual	Automatic	Idle Stop Solenoid (rpm)	Idle Speed-up Solenoid (rpm)	Timing (Degrees BTDC)[6]
151-2 bbl. M	1,040		500	1,250	12
151-2 bbl. A		695	500	850	12
231-2 bbl. M	1,000[7]		600		15
231-2 bbl. A		550[8]		670	15
260-2 bbl. A		560/580		625	20[9]
305-2 bbl. M		710/750		700	4
305-2 bbl. A		520/540		700	4
305-2 bbl. A California		640/660		650	2
350-4 bbl. A		625/645[10]		650	20[9]
350-4 bbl. A California		565/585		600	20[9]
350 Diesel					See note 11
403-4 bbl. A		625/645[10]		650	20[9]
403-4 bbl. A California		565/585		600	20[9]

1. M=Manual transmission; A=Automatic transmission.
2. Headlights and air conditioning off; automatic transmission in DRIVE; manual transmission in NEUTRAL.
3. With EGR hose disconnected and plugged and automatic transmission in PARK or NEUTRAL.
4. California, 1,000 rpm.
5. Altitude and California, 600 rpm.
6. Set at curb idle speed with distributor vacuum advance line disconnected and plugged.
7. California, 840 rpm.
8. Altitude and California, 615 rpm.
9. Set timing @ 1,100 rpm.
10. Altitude, 590 rpm.
11. Crankshaft timing not required. Align injector pump and adapter marks with engine off.

(continued)

Table 3 TUNE-UP SPECIFICATIONS (continued)

1980 Oldsmobile				
Engine/Carb./ Trans.[1]	**Idle Speeds**		**AC Spark Plug**	
	Curb[2]	**Fast[3]**	**Gap (in.)**	**No.**
151-2 bbl. M	1,000	2,600[4]	0.060	R44TSX
151-2 bbl. A	650	2,600	0.060	R44TSX
231-2 bbl. M	800	2,200	0.060	R45TSX
231-2 bbl. A	550	2,000	0.060	R45TSX
265-2 bbl. A	550	2,200	0.060	R45TSX
307-4 bbl. A	500	700[5]	0.080	R46SX
350-4 bbl. A	500	700[5]	0.045	R46SX
350 Diesel	575	650		

Engine/Carb./ Trans.[1]	**Propane Enriched Idle Speed[6]**		**Idle Stop Solenoid (rpm)**	**Idle Speed-up Solenoid (rpm)**	**Timing (Degrees BTDC)[7]**
	Manual	**Automatic**			
151-2 bbl. M	1,150		500	1,200	12
151-2 bbl. A		700	500	850	12
231-2 bbl. M	830		600		15
231-2 bbl. A		600		670[8]	15
265-2 bbl. A		580/590			10
307-4 bbl. A		530		600	20[9]
350-4 bbl. A		565-585		600	18[9]
350 Diesel					See note 10

1. M=Manual transmission; A=Automatic transmission.
2. Headlights and air conditioning off; automatic transmission in DRIVE; manual transmission in NEUTRAL.
3. With EGR hose disconnected and plugged and automatic transmission in PARK or NEUTRAL.
4. California, 2,400 rpm.
5. Set with transmission in DRIVE.
6. Electronically controlled on California models.
7. Set at curb idle speed with distributor vacuum advance line disconnected and plugged.
8. California, 620 rpm.
9. Set timing @ 1,100 rpm.
10. Crankshaft timing not required. Align injector pump and adapter marks with the engine off.

Table 4 TUNE-UP SPECIFICATIONS (PONTIAC)

Engine/Carb./ Trans.[1]	Idle Speeds		AC Spark Plug	
	Curb[2]	Fast[3]	Gap (in.)	No.
1972 Pontiac				
400-2 bbl. A	625	Preset	0.040	R46TS
400-4 bbl. A	700[4]	1,500	0.040	R45TS
455-2 bbl. A	625	Preset	0.040	R45TS
455-4 bbl. A	650[4]	1,500	0.040	R45TS

Engine/Carb./ Trans.[1]	Idle Mixture		Distributor		Timing (Degrees BTDC)[5]
	Before Lean Drop	After Lean Drop	Point Gap (in.)	Dwell	
400-2 bbl. A	700	600	0.019	28-32	10[6]
400-4 bbl. A	775	700	0.019	28-32	10
455-2 bbl. A	700	625	0.019	28-32	10[6]
455-4 bbl. A	725	650	0.019	28-32	10[6]

1. M=Manual transmission; A=Automatic transmission.
2. Headlights and air conditioning off; automatic transmission in DRIVE; manual transmission in NEUTRAL.
3. With automatic transmission in PARK or NEUTRAL.
4. Set idle stop solenoid to 500 rpm.
5. Set at curb idle speed with distributor vacuum advance line disconnected and plugged.
6. With some late models, 12° BTDC.

Engine/Carb./ Trans.[1]	Idle Speeds		AC Spark Plug	
	Curb[2]	Fast[3]	Gap (in.)	No.
1973 Pontiac				
350-2 bbl. A	650	Preset	0.040	R46TS
400-2 bbl. A	650	Preset	0.040	R46TS
400-4 bbl. A	650	1,500	0.040	R45TS
455-4 bbl. A	650	1,500	0.040	R45TS

Engine/Carb./ Trans.[1]	Idle Mixture		Distributor		Timing (Degrees BTDC)[4]
	Before Lean Drop	After Lean Drop	Point Gap (in.)	Dwell	
350-2 bbl. A	700	650	0.019	28-32	12
400-2 bbl. A	700	650	0.019	28-32	12
400-4 bbl. A	700	650	0.019	28-32	12
455-4 bbl. A	700	650	0.019	28-32	12

1. M=Manual transmission; A=Automatic transmission.
2. Headlights and air conditioning off; automatic transmission in DRIVE; manual transmission in NEUTRAL.
3. With EGR line disconnected and plugged and automatic transmission in PARK or NEUTRAL.
4. Set at curb idle speed with distributor vacuum advance line disconnected and plugged.

(continued)

4

Table 4 TUNE-UP SPECIFICATIONS (continued)

1974 Pontiac				
Engine/Carb./ Trans.[1]	**Idle Speeds**		**AC Spark Plug**	
	Curb[2]	**Fast[3]**	**Gap (in.)**	**No.**
400-2 bbl. A	650	Preset	0.040	R46TS
400-2 bbl. A California	625	Preset	0.040	R46TS
400-4 bbl. A	650	1,500	0.040	R45TS
455-4 bbl. A	650	1,500	0.040	R45TS
455-4 bbl. A California	625	1,500	0.040	R45TS

	Idle Mixture		**Distributor**		**Timing**
Engine/Carb./ Trans.[1]	**Before Lean Drop**	**After Lean Drop**	**Point Gap (in.)**	**Dwell**	**(Degrees BTDC)[4]**
400-2 bbl. A	720	650	0.019	28-32	12
400-2 bbl. A California	690	625	0.019	28-32	10
400-4 bbl. A	720	650	0.019	28-32	12
455-4 bbl. A	680	650	0.019	28-32	12
455-4 bbl. A California	675	625	0.019	28-32	10

1. M=Manual transmission; A=Automatic transmission.
2. Headlights and air conditioning off; automatic transmission in DRIVE; manual transmission in NEUTRAL.
3. With EGR line disconnected and plugged and automatic transmission in PARK or NEUTRAL.
4. Set at curb idle speed with distributor vacuum advance line disconnected and plugged.

1975 Pontiac				
Engine/Carb./ Trans.[1]	**Idle Speeds**		**AC Spark Plug**	
	Curb[2]	**Fast[3]**	**Gap (in.)**	**No.**
400-2 bbl. A	650	Preset	0.060	R46TSX
400-4 bbl. A	650	1,800	0.060	R45TSX
400-4 bbl. A California	600	1,800	0.060	R46TSX
455-4 bbl. A	650	1,800	0.060	R45TSX

	Idle Mixture		**Timing**
Engine/Carb./ Trans.[1]	**Before Lean Drop**	**After Lean Drop**	**(Degrees BTDC)[4]**
400-2 bbl. A	730	650	16[5]
400-4 bbl. A	690[6]	650[6]	16
400-4 bbl. A California	660	600	12
455-4 bbl. A	720	650	16

1. M=Manual transmission; A=Automatic transmission.
2. Headlights and air conditioning off; automatic transmission in DRIVE; manual transmission in NEUTRAL.
3. With EGR line disconnected and plugged and automatic transmission in PARK or NEUTRAL.
4. Set at curb idle speed with distributor vacuum advance line disconnected and plugged.
5. California, 12° BTDC.
6. Catalina/Safari wagons, 665-625 rpm.

(continued)

Table 4 TUNE-UP SPECIFICATIONS (continued)

1976 Pontiac				
Engine/Carb./ Trans.[1]	Idle Speeds		AC Spark Plug	
	Curb[2]	Fast[3]	Gap (in.)	No.
140-1 bbl. M	1,200	1,500	0.035	R43TS
140-1 bbl. A	750	2,200	0.035	R43TS
140-2 bbl. M	700[4]	2,200	0.035	R43TS
140-2 bbl. A	750	2,200	0.035	R43TS
231-2 bbl. M	800	Preset	0.060	R44SX
231-2 bbl. A	600	Preset	0.060	R44SX
400-2 bbl. A	550	Preset	0.060	R45TSX
400-4 bbl. A	575	1,800	0.060	R45TSX
455-4 bbl. A	550	1,800	0.060	R45TSX
455-4 bbl. A California	600	1,800	0.060	R45TSX

Engine/Carb./ Trans.[1]	Idle Mixture		Idle Stop Solenoid (rpm)	Idle Speed-up Solenoid (rpm)	Timing (Degrees BTDC)[5]
	Before Lean Drop	After Lean Drop			
140-1 bbl. M	875	750	750		8
140-1 bbl. A	850	750	550		10
140-2 bbl. M	820	700	See note 6		10
140-2 bbl. A	830	750	600		12
231-2 bbl. M	1,100	800	600		12
231-2 bbl. A	680	600			12
400-2 bbl. A	640	550		650	16
400-4 bbl. A	640	575		650	16
455-4 bbl. A	640	550		650	16
455-4 bbl. A California	640	600		650	12

1. M=Manual transmission; A=Automatic transmission.
2. Headlights and air conditioning off; automatic transmission in DRIVE; manual transmission in NEUTRAL.
3. With EGR line disconnected and plugged and automatic transmission in PARK or NEUTRAL.
4. California, 1,000 rpm.
5. Set at curb idle speed with distributor vacuum advance line disconnected and plugged.
6. California, 700 rpm.

(continued)

Table 4 TUNE-UP SPECIFICATIONS (continued)

1977 Pontiac				
Engine/Carb./ Trans.[1]	Idle Speeds		AC Spark Plug	
	Curb[2]	Fast[3]	Gap (in.)	No.
140-2 bbl. M	700	2,500	0.035	R43TS
140-2 bbl. A	650	2,500	0.035	R43TS
140-2 bbl. M Altitude/Ca.	800	2,500	0.035	R43TS
140-2 bbl. A Altitude	700	2,500	0.035	R43TS
151-2 bbl. M	1,000	2,400	0.060	R44TSX
151-2 bbl. A	650	2,400	0.060	R44TSX
231-2 bbl. M	800	Preset	0.060	R46TSX
231-2 bbl. A	600	Preset	0.060	R46TSX
301-2 bbl. A	550	1,750	0.045	R45TS
350-4 bbl. A				
Engine code P	575	1,800	0.060	R45TSX
Engine code R	550	900	0.060	R45TSX
Altitude	600	1,000	0.060	R45TSX
California	550	1,000	0.060	R45TSX
403-4 bbl. A				
Federal	550	900	0.060	R46SZ
Altitude	600	1,000	0.060	R46SZ
California	550	1,000	0.060	R46SZ

Engine/Carb./ Trans.[1]	Idle Mixture		Idle Stop Solenoid (rpm)	Idle Speed-up Solenoid (rpm)	Timing (Degrees BTDC)[4]
	Before Lean Drop	After Lean Drop			
140-2 bbl. M	780	700		1,250	TDC
140-2 bbl. A	680	650		850	2
140-2 bbl. M Altitude/Ca.	880	800		1,250	TDC[5]
140-2 bbl. A Altitude	2730	700		850	2
151-2 bbl. M	1,250	1,000	600	1,200	14
151-2 bbl. A	685	650	500	850	14[6]
231-2 bbl. M	860[7]	800	600		12
231-2 bbl. A	640[8]	600		670	12
301-2 bbl. A	590	550		650	12
350-4 bbl. A					
Engine code P	600	575		650	16
Engine code R	580	550		650	20[9]
Altitude	625	600		650	20[9]
California	575	600		650	20[9]
403-4 bbl. A					
Federal	580	550		650	22[9]
Altitude	625	600		650	20[9]
California	575	550		650	10[9]

1. M=Manual transmission; A=Automatic transmission.
2. Headlights and air conditioning off; automatic transmission in DRIVE; manual transmission in NEUTRAL.
3. With EGR line disconnected and plugged and automatic transmission in PARK or NEUTRAL.
4. Set at curb idle speed with distributor vacuum advance line disconnected and plugged.
5. California, 2° ATDC.
6. California, 12° BTDC.
7. California, 810 rpm.
8. Altitude and California, 610 rpm.
9. Set timing @ 1,100 rpm.

(continued)

Table 4 TUNE-UP SPECIFICATIONS (continued)

1978 Pontiac				
Engine/Carb./ Trans.[1]	**Idle Speeds**		**AC Spark Plug**	
	Curb[2]	**Fast[3]**	**Gap (in.)**	**No.**
151-2 bbl. M	1,000	2,200	0.060	R43TSX
151-2 bbl. A	650	2,400	0.060	R43TSX
231-2 bbl. M	800	Preset	0.060	R46TSX
231-2 bbl. A	600	Preset	0.060	R46TSX
301-2 bbl. A	550	2,200	0.060	R45TSX
301-4 bbl. A	550	2,300	0.060	R45TSX
350-4 bbl. A				
Federal	550	1,550	0.060	R46TSX
Altitude	550	900	0.060	R46SZ
California	550	1,000	0.060	R46SZ
403-4 bbl. A				
Federal	575	1,800	0.060	R45TSX
Altitude	600	1,000	0.060	R46SZ
California	550	1,000	0.060	R46SZ

Engine/Carb./ Trans.[1]	**Propane Enriched Idle Speed**		**Idle Stop Solenoid (rpm)**	**Idle Speed-up Solenoid (rpm)**	**Timing (Degrees BTDC)[4]**
	Manual	**Automatic**			
151-2 bbl. M	1,150[5]		500		14
151-2 bbl. A		680/700[5]	500	850	12[6]
231-2 bbl. M	940[7]		600		15
231-2 bbl. A		650[8]		670[9]	15
301-2 bbl. A		680		650	12
301-4 bbl. A		590		650	12
350-4 bbl. A					
Federal		590			15
Altitude		590		650	20[10]
California		565/585		600	20[10]
403-4 bbl. A					
Federal		615		650	16
Altitude		630/670		700	20
California		565/685		650	20

1. M=Manual transmission; A=Automatic transmission.
2. Headlights and air conditioning off; automatic transmission in DRIVE; manual transmission in NEUTRAL.
3. With EGR line disconnected and plugged and automatic transmission in PARK or NEUTRAL.
4. Set at curb idle speed with distributor vacuum advance line disconnected and plugged.
5. California, 760 rpm.
6. California, 14° BTDC.
7. California, 880 rpm.
8. Altitude and California, 615 rpm.
9. California, 620 rpm.
10. Set timing @ 1,100 rpm.

(continued)

Table 4 TUNE-UP SPECIFICATIONS (continued)

1979 Pontiac				
Engine/Carb./ Trans.[1]	**Idle Speeds** Curb[2]	**Fast[3]**	**AC Spark Plug** Gap (in.)	**No.**
151-2 bbl. M	900[4]	2,200	0.060	R44TSX
151-2 bbl. A	650	2,400	0.060	R44TSX
231-2 bbl. M	800	2,200	0.060	R44TSX
231-2 bbl. A	550	2,200	0.060	R45TSX
231-2 bbl. A Altitude/Ca.	600[5]	2,200	0.060	R45TSX
301-2 bbl. A	500	2,000	0.060	R46TSX
301-4 bbl. A	500	2,200	0.060	R46TSX
305-2 bbl. A	600	1,950	0.045	R45TS
350-4 bbl. A				
Federal	550	1,550	0.060	R45TSX
Altitude	550	900	0.060	R45TSX
California	500	1,000	0.060	R45TSX
403-4 bbl. A	550	900	0.060	R46SZ
403-4 bbl. A California	500	1,000	0.060	R46SZ

Engine/Carb./ Trans.[1]	**Propane Enriched Idle Speed** Manual	Automatic	**Idle Stop Solenoid** (rpm)	**Idle Speed-up Solenoid** (rpm)	**Timing (Degrees BTDC)[6]**
151-2 bbl. M	1,040		500	1,200	12[7]
151-2 bbl. A		695[8]	500	850	12[7, 9]
231-2 bbl. M	1,000		600		15
231-2 bbl. A		575		670	15
231-2 bbl. A Altitude/Ca.		615			15
301-2 bbl. A		530		650	12[10]
301-4 bbl. A		640		650	12[10]
305-2 bbl. A		640/660		650	2
350-4 bbl. A					
Federal		590			15
Altitude		590		650	20[11]
California		625/645		650	20[11]
403-4 bbl. A		625/645[12]		650	18[11]
403-4 bbl. A California		565/585		600	20[11]

1. M=Manual transmission; A=Automatic transmission.
2. Headlights and air conditioning off; automatic transmission in DRIVE; manual transmission in NEUTRAL.
3. With EGR line disconnected and plugged and automatic transmission in PARK or NEUTRAL.
4. California, 1,000 rpm.
5. With C-4 emission system, 580 rpm. Set idle speed-up solenoid to 670 rpm.
6. Set at curb idle speed with distributor vacuum advance line disconnected and plugged.
7. California, 14° BTDC.
8. California, 760 rpm.
9. Set timing @ 1,000 rpm.
10. Set timing @ 650 rpm.
11. Set timing @ 1,100 rpm.
12. Altitude, 590 rpm.

(continued)

Table 4 TUNE-UP SPECIFICATIONS (continued)

1980 Pontiac				
Engine/Carb./ Trans.[1]	**Idle Speeds**		**AC Spark Plug**	
	Curb[2]	**Fast[3]**	**Gap (in.)**	**No.**
151-2 bbl. M	1,000	2,600[4]	0.060	R44TSX
151-2 bbl. A	650	2,600	0.060	R44TSX
231-2 bbl. M	800	2,000	0.060	R45TSX
231-2 bbl. A	550	2,000	0.060	R45TSX
265-2 bbl. A	550	2,200	0.060	R45TSX
301-2 bbl. A	500	2,500	0.060	R46TSX
350-4 bbl. A	550	1,850	0.060	R45TSX
350 Diesel	600	750		

Engine/Carb./ Trans.[1]	**Propane Enriched Idle Speed[5]**		**Idle Stop Solenoid (rpm)**	**Idle Speed-up Solenoid (rpm)**	**Timing (Degrees BTDC)[6]**
	Manual	**Automatic**			
151-2 bbl. M	1,150		500	1,200	12
151-2 bbl. A		700	500	850	12
231-2 bbl. M	830			670	15
231-2 bbl. A		610		670[7]	15
265-2 bbl. A		580/590		650	10
301-2 bbl. A		540/550		650	12
350-4 bbl. A		590		650	15
350 Diesel					See note 8

1. M=Manual transmission; A=Automatic transmission.
2. Headlights and air conditioning off; automatic transmission in DRIVE; manual transmission in NEUTRAL.
3. With EGR line disconnected and plugged and automatic transmission in PARK or NEUTRAL.
4. California, 2,400 rpm.
5. Electronically controlled on California models.
6. Set at curb idle speed with distributor vacuum advance line disconnected and plugged.
7. California, 620 rpm.
8. Crankshaft timing not required. Align injector pump and adapter marks with engine off.

4

Table 5 CYLINDER HEAD BOLT TORQUES

Engine	Year	ft.-lb.	N·m
		Buick	
231	1975-1976	75	102
	1977-on	65-75	88-102
252	All	80	108
260	1976	85	115
301	1977-1980	90	122
305	1977-1982	65	88
307	1981	85	115
350 gasoline	1972	75	102
	1973-1977	80	108
	1977-1979[1]	65	88
	1977-1980[2]	130	176
350 diesel	All	130[3]	176[3]
403	1977-1979	130	176
455	1972-1976	100	136
		Chevrolet	
140	1975-1977	60	81
151	1978-1980	95	129
196	1978-1979	60-70	81-95
229	1980-on	60-70	81-95
231	1978-on	80	108
250	1972-1979	95	129
260 diesel	1982-on	See Note 4	See Note 4
262	1975-1976	60-70	81-95
262	1985	65	88
267	1980-on	65	88
305	1977-on	60-70	81-95
350 gasoline	1972-1981	60-70	81-95
350 diesel	All	130[3]	180[3]
400	1972-1976	60-70	81-95
402[5]	1972	80	108
454[5]	1972-1976	80	108
		Oldsmobile	
140	1976-1977	60	81
151	1978-1980	85	115
231	1975-1976	85	115
	1977-on	80	108
260	1978-1982	85	115
265	1980	95	129
301	1979	95	129
305	1979	65	88
307	1980-1981	130	176
	1982-on	125	160
350	1972-1974	80-85	108-115
	1975-1976	85	115
	1977-1979[1]	65	88
	1977-1980[2]	130	176
350 Diesel	All	130[3]	176[3]
400	1975	95	129
403	1977-1979	130	176
455	1972-1976	85	115

(continued)

Table 5 CYLINDER HEAD BOLT TORQUES (continued)

Engine	Year	ft.-lb.	N•m
	Pontiac		
140	1976-1977	60	81
151	1977-1978	85	115
229	1983-on	65	88
231	1976	85	115
	1977-1981	80	108
265	1980-1981	85	115
301	1977-1978	85	115
	1979-1980	95	129
305	1981-on	65	88
350 gasoline	1973	95	129
	1977-1978[2]	130	176
	1978-1980[6]	80	108
350 diesel	All	130[3]	180[3]
400	1972-1976	95	129
403	1978-1979	130	176
455	1972-1977	95	129

1. Engine code L.
2. Engine code R.
3. Wipe bolt threads with oil before installation.
4. All except No. 5, 6, 11, 12, 13 and 14: 142 ft.-lb. (193 N•m). No. 5, 6, 11, 12, 13 and 14: 59 ft.-lb. (80 N•m).
5. If aluminum bolts are used, torque long bolts to 75 ft.-lb. (102 N•m) and short bolts to 65 ft.-lb. (88 N•m).
6. Engine code X.

4

CHAPTER FIVE

FUEL SYSTEM

This chapter contains procedures for air cleaner service, carburetor adjustment and replacement and fuel pump testing/replacement for all General Motors passenger cars covered in this manual.

Illustrations and procedures in this chapter are general in nature. During the years covered, the various General Motors models used many types of carburetors. Most of the carburetor types were produced in a number of variations to fit the individual requirements of the various engine-transmission-vehicle combinations and emission control laws. For this reason, 2 carburetors which look alike may not be interchangeable.

AIR CLEANER REMOVAL/INSTALLATION

4-cylinder Engine

Figure 1 shows a typical air cleaner assembly used on Monza, Starfire and Sunbird 4-cylinder engines. The air cleaner assembly is a one-piece welded unit which is discarded at 50,000 mile intervals.

1. Remove 2 wing nuts from top of air cleaner assembly.
2. Disconnect air cleaner assembly from snorkel.

3. Remove air cleaner from carburetor air horn and discard.
4. Installation is the reverse of removal. Check air horn gasket for damage and replace as required. Tighten wing nuts securely.

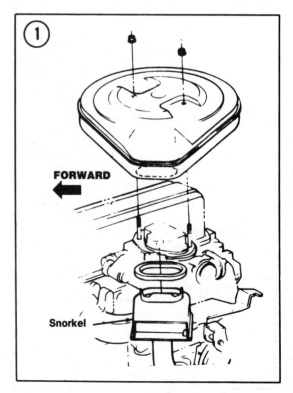

FORWARD

Snorkel

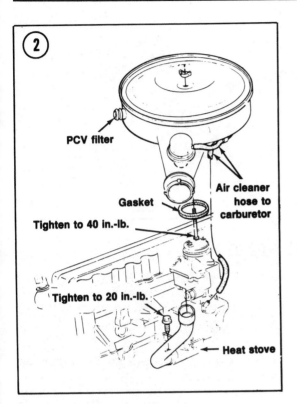

(2)

PCV filter

Gasket

Tighten to 40 in.-lb.

Tighten to 20 in.-lb.

Air cleaner hose to carburetor

Heat stove

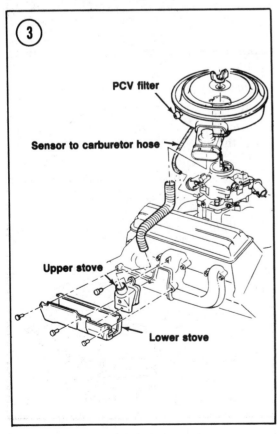

(3)

PCV filter

Sensor to carburetor hose

Upper stove

Lower stove

6-cylinder and V8 Engines

Refer to **Figure 2** (6-cylinder) and **Figure 3** (V8) for typical air cleaner assemblies used on General Motors passenger cars.

1. Disconnect the crankcase ventilation or PCV filter line at the air cleaner housing.

2. Disconnect any vacuum lines attached to the side of the air cleaner housing.

3. Disconnect the cold air intake tube at the flexible duct and the heat riser tube at the heat stove.

4. Remove the air cleaner cover wing nut.

5. Lift the air cleaner housing from the carburetor and disconnect the vacuum line from the plastic tee underneath the housing.

6. Remove the air cleaner housing from the engine compartment.

7. Check the air cleaner-to-carburetor air horn mounting gasket for damage and replace as necessary.

8. Wipe the air cleaner housing and cover with a cloth moistened in solvent. Wipe the housing and cover dry, then inspect for damage or distortion at the gasket mating surfaces.

9. Installation is the reverse of removal. Install a new filter element and/or crankcase ventilation filter pack if required. Make sure the filter element is properly positioned.

CARBURETOR FUNDAMENTALS

A gasoline engine must receive fuel and air mixed in a precise proportion in order to operate efficiently at various speeds. At sea level, under normal conditions, the ratio is 14.7:1 at high speed and 12:1 at low speeds. Carburetors are designed to maintain these ratios while providing for sudden acceleration or increased loads.

A mixture with an excess of fuel is said to be "rich." One with a deficiency of fuel is said to be "lean."

The choke valve in a carburetor produces a richer than normal mixture of fuel and air until the engine warms up.

The throat of a carburetor is often called a "barrel." A single-barrel carburetor has only one throat. Two-barrel carburetors have 2 throats and 2 complete sets of metering

5

devices, but only one float bowl and float. A 4-barrel carburetor has 4 throats, 4 complete sets of metering devices and 2 floats.

Figures 4-6 show typical 1-barrel, 2-barrel and 4-barrel carburetors used on vehicles covered in this manual.

CARBURETOR ADJUSTMENTS

All carburetors manufactured for use on 1972-1978 models are equipped with factory preset idle mixture screws. These screws are capped with plastic limiter caps that allow only a limited adjustment. Under normal conditions, a satisfactory idle can be obtained without removing the caps. If the carburetor is overhauled or if emissions levels are excessively high, limiter cap removal may be necessary to achieve the desired idle.

The idle mixture screw has been made "tamperproof" on 1979 and later carburetors in accordance with Federal law to prevent unauthorized adjustment. The idle mixture screw is encased inside a locking plug cast in the carburetor throttle body and is covered by a hardened steel plug. See **Figure 7** for an exploded view. The plug is to be removed only if the carburetor cannot be made to run correctly after an overhaul.

The following procedure can be used with 1972-1978 models. Refer to the Vehicle Control Information (VECI) label in the engine compartment for 1979-on procedures.

Curb Idle Speed

Precautions

1. Some 1972-1973 6-cylinder engines use a Combined Emission Control (CEC) solenoid. This looks like an idle solenoid but it is not. Do not use this solenoid to set curb idle. It should only be adjusted as explained under *CEC Solenoid Adjustment* in this chapter.
2. If the car is equipped with a Hydro-Boost power brake system, the brake pedal should not be depressed while setting the idle speed, as brake application causes the engine speed to decrease.
3. If equipped with air conditioning, adjust the idle speed with the system off.

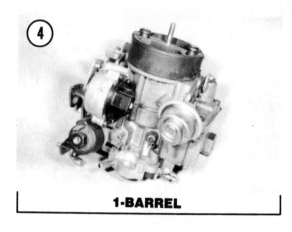

1-BARREL

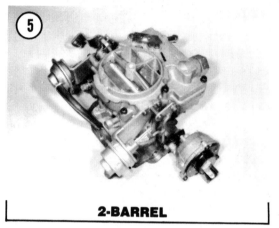

2-BARREL

Preliminary procedure

1. Warm the engine to normal operating temperature (upper radiator hose hot). Make sure the choke is fully open and the air conditioner is off.
2. Set the parking brake and block the drive wheels.
3. Connect a tachometer according to the manufacturer's instructions.
4. Refer to the Vehicle Emission Control Information (VECI) decal in the engine compartment and disconnect/plug the specified vacuum hoses. These generally include:
   a. 1972-1974 distributor vacuum advance line.
   b. 1972 Pontiac speed control spark system line from carburetor to vacuum solenoid.
   c. Automatic parking brake line at vacuum release cylinder (if so equipped).

d. Automatic level ride control line at air cleaner (if so equipped).

e. Evaporative emission control hoses at vapor canister.

Refer to **Table 1** for specific engine/hose if VECI label is damaged or missing.

5. The air cleaner should be left installed for all final idle readings. If necessary to remove

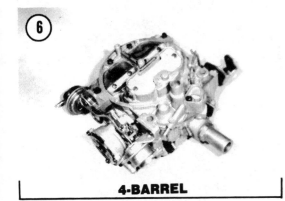

4-BARREL

it for access to the adjusting screws, plug all vacuum lines to the intake manifold or carburetor on 1972-1976 models. Leave all vacuum lines attached to the air cleaner on 1977 models.

6. Disconnect and plug the distributor vacuum advance line, then set ignition timing at the specified rpm with the transmission in the specified gear.

7. Reconnect the vacuum advance line on all except 1972-1974 models.

Adjustment (1972-1977)

Refer to the Vehicle Emission Control Information decal located in the engine compartment for the correct idle speeds for your car. Use the tune-up specifications provided in Chapter Four only if the decal has been defaced or otherwise damaged.

5

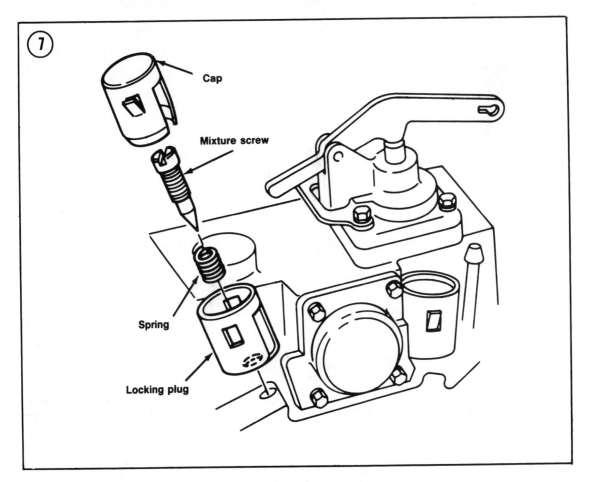

Cap

Mixture screw

Spring

Locking plug

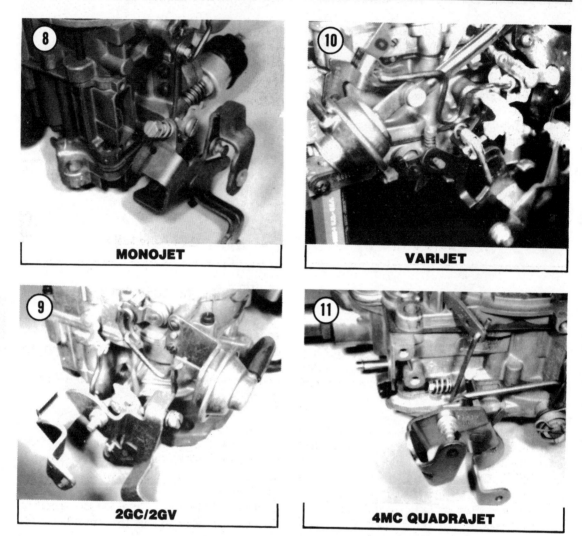

MONOJET

VARIJET

2GC/2GV

4MC QUADRAJET

Figures 8-11 show idle speed screw locations on the Monojet, 2GC/2GV, Varijet and 4MC Quadrajet carburetors.

1. Check carburetor and determine if an idle solenoid is used.

2A. If no idle solenoid is used, adjust the idle speed screw to the specified rpm.

2B. If an idle stop solenoid is used, the throttle plates are closed in 2 stages to prevent dieseling after the engine is turned off. Use of this type of solenoid requires that the idle be adjusted to 2 different levels–a higher curb idle speed and a lower base idle speed. Idle stop solenoids may use a 1/8 in. Allen-head hex in one end or a hex nut on the end of the plunger screw for adjustment. Adjust as follows:

a. Curb idle rpm–with the engine on and the transmission in NEUTRAL, momentarily open/close the throttle plates by hand to let the solenoid plunger fully extend. If equipped with an automatic transmission, shift into DRIVE and adjust the curb idle speed to specifications by adjusting the plunger screw or turning the complete solenoid assembly (Allen-head type).

b. Base idle rpm–disconnect electrical lead to de-energize solenoid. Set base idle speed to specifications by adjusting the plunger screw or turning the Allen-head hex on the solenoid end.

3. If an idle speed-up solenoid is used, a higher idle speed-up rpm must be set in

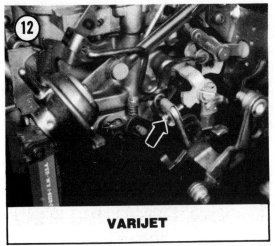

VARIJET

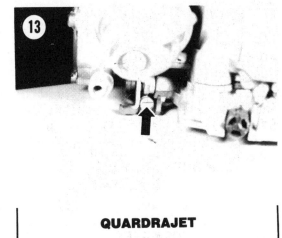

QUARDRAJET

addition to the normal idle to accommodate use of the air conditioner. Adjust as follows:

a. Curb idle rpm–with the engine on, air conditioner off and the automatic transmission in DRIVE, adjust idle speed to specifications with the carburetor idle speed screw.

b. Idle speed-up rpm–turn air conditioner on. Disconnect elecrical connector at the compressor. Place transmission in NEUTRAL and momentarily open/close the throttle plates to let the solenoid plunger fully extend. Shift the transmission back into DRIVE and set idle speed-up rpm to specifications by adjusting the plunger screw or turning the complete solenoid assembly (Allen-head type).

4. Reconnect all vacuum lines and recheck the idle speed.

Fast Idle Speed Adjustment

The fast idle speed is checked/adjusted after setting the curb idle speed. On Rochester 1MV/1ME 1-barrel and 2GC/2GV 2-barrel carburetors, fast idle speed is controlled by curb idle speed and choke rod adjustment. Fast idle speed on these carburetors is thus preset and no adjustment is required. **Figure 12** shows the Varijet fast idle screw. See

Figure 13 for the 4MV/4MC Quadrajet fast idle screw location.

1. Perform the *Preliminary Procedure* described in this chapter. Make sure air conditioner is off.
2. Disconnect and plug the vacuum line at the EGR valve on 1973-1977 engines.
3. If equipped with a CEC solenoid, disconnect the electrical connector from the temperature switch on the bulkhead and ground the wire to energize the CEC valve.
4. Place automatic transmissions in PARK or NEUTRAL.
5. Refer to the VECI decal for the specified fast idle cam step and set the cam follower or screw on that step.
6. Adjust the fast idle screw to obtain the specified fast idle rpm.
7. Reconnect all vacuum lines and electrical connectors. Recheck fast idle speed.

**Idle Mixture Adjustment
(Except 1972 Chevrolet with AIR)**

All 1972-1977 carburetors (except 1972 Chevrolet models equipped with an air pump system) are adjusted by the lean drop procedure. The propane enrichment method is used on 1978 and later carburetors. Since propane enrichment requires the use of special tools and skills, carburetor adjustment on 1978 and later models should be left to a

5

dealer. See **Figure 14** for Monojet, **Figure 15** for 2GV/2GC and **Figure 16** for 4MV/4MC Quadrajet idle mixture screw location.

1. Perform the *Preliminary Procedure* described in this chapter.

2. On 1972-1973 and 1977 carburetors, carefully pry the limiter cap(s) from the idle mixture screws.

3. On 1974-1976 carburetors, cut off idle limiter tab stop from the cap(s) with a pair of side-cutter pliers.

4. Turn the screw(s) clockwise until they lightly seat, then back them out the number of turns specified on the VECI decal.

NOTE
*If decal is defaced or otherwise damaged, refer to **Table 2**. If your engine is not listed, back the screw(s) out just enough so the engine will continue to run.*

5. Place automatic transmission in DRIVE.

6. If idle mixture screw(s) were backed out just enough to let engine run, continue backing them out 1/8 turn at a time until the maximum idle speed is obtained.

7. Adjust idle speed to "Before Lean Drop" rpm with idle speed screw or solenoid, as required.

8. Repeat Step 6 and Step 7 to make sure the correct idle speed is obtained.

9. Turn the idle mixture screw(s) clockwise 1/8 turn at a time until the idle speed reaches the "After Lean Drop" rpm.

10. Reset idle speed to specifications. This may differ from the rpm shown under "After Lean Drop."

11. Check and adjust fast idle speed, if necessary.

12. Reconnect vacuum lines. Install air cleaner, if removed. Recheck idle speed and reset to specifications, if necessary.

Idle Mixture Adjustment
(1972 Chevrolet with AIR)

Idle mixture on these engines is set with the lean roll procedure.

1. Disconnect and plug the distributor vacuum advance line.

MONOJET

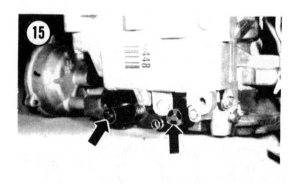

2GV/2GC

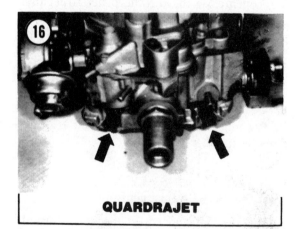

QUARDRAJET

2. Disconnect and plug the vapor canister hose leading to the fuel tank.

3. Warm the engine to normal operating temperature (upper radiator hose hot).

4. Place automatic transmission in DRIVE. Make sure the air conditioner is off.

5. Adjust idle speed screw or idle stop solenoid to obtain specified curb idle speed.

6. Adjust idle mixture screw(s) to obtain the highest and smoothest idle speed possible.

7. Reset curb idle speed to specifications.

8. Turn idle mixture screw clockwise until engine speed drops by 20 rpm (lean roll point).

9. Back idle mixture screw out 1/4 turn.

10. Repeat Step 8 and Step 9 for second idle mixture screw on multi-barrel carburetors.

11. Reset curb idle speed to specifications.

CEC Solenoid Valve Adjustment

A Combined Emission Control or CEC solenoid is used with 1972-1973 Chevrolet 6-cylinder engines. This solenoid combines the functions of a transmission controlled spark solenoid and a throttle return check device, providing an intermediate fast idle

speed during deceleration as a means of reducing exhaust emissions.

The CEC solenoid looks like an idle stop solenoid, but must not be used to adjust curb idle on engines so equipped or a decrease in engine braking effort may result.

Under normal conditions, the CEC solenoid requires adjustment only after it has been replaced, or the carburetor has been overhauled. Follow the instructions on the VECI decal before adjusting the CEC solenoid.

1. Turn air conditioner off.

2. Disconnect and plug the distributor vacuum advance line.

3. Disconnect and plug the canister hose marked "Fuel."

4. With the engine at normal operating temperature (upper radiator hose hot) and the automatic transmission in DRIVE, extend the CEC solenoid plunger until it touches the throttle lever.

5. Adjust the plunger to obtain an idle speed of 850 rpm (manual transmission) or 650 rpm (automatic transmission).

6. Reconnect the canister hose and vacuum line. Shut the engine off.

Automatic Choke Adjustment

Two types of chokes are used on 1972 and later carburetors: a remote choke or an integral choke. The remote choke (**Figure 17**) contains a thermostatic spring mounted in a well on the intake manifold. This spring is connected to the choke by a rod. The integral choke (**Figure 18**) contains a thermostatic spring mounted in a cap attached to the carburetor choke housing.

Remote choke

A remote choke pushes upward to obtain more choking action and pulls downward to provide less choking action. The connecting rod is bent to make it longer and increase tension for more choking action. To reduce choking action, the rod is bent to make it shorter.

Integral choke

An automatic choke reacts to engine temperature. By loosening the clamp screws which hold the thermostatic spring cover to the choke housing on 1972-1979 carburetors so equipped, the spring tension can be increased or decreased to change the adjustment.

Starting with 1980 carburetors, the choke cover is riveted in place to prevent unauthorized adjustment. Choke adjustment on these carburetors is thus restricted to those adjustments (if any) required by an overhaul.

On 1972-1979 carburetors, turning the choke housing cover clockwise will require a higher spring temperature (cold weather) to fully open the choke plate. Turning the cover counterclockwise will cause the choke plate to fully open at a lower temperature (hot weather).

Refer to the VECI label for the specified choke setting. Refer to **Figure 19** for this procedure.

1. Remove the air cleaner assembly.
2. Place the idle speed screw on the high step of the fast idle cam.
3. Loosen the choke cover retaining clamp screws (**Figure 19**). Set the choke cover index mark to the specified mark on the choke housing. See **Figure 18** or **Figure 19**. Tighten clamp screws.
4. Install the air cleaner.

Carburetor Service Removal

Flooding, stumbling on acceleration and general lack of performance may be caused by dirt, water or foreign matter in the carburetor. To verify the condition, the carburetor should be carefully removed from the engine without removing the fuel from the fuel bowl(s). Examine the fuel for contamination and disassemble the carburetor for cleaning.

Figures 20-22 show typical carburetor installations.

1. Remove the air cleaner and gasket.
2. Label and disconnect all vacuum lines and electrical connectors at the carburetor.

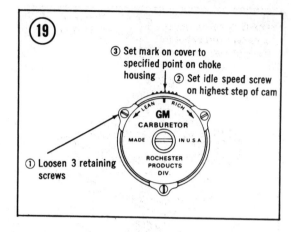

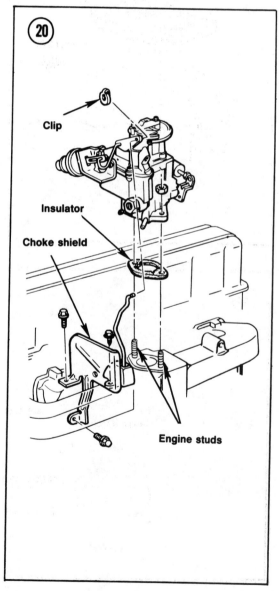

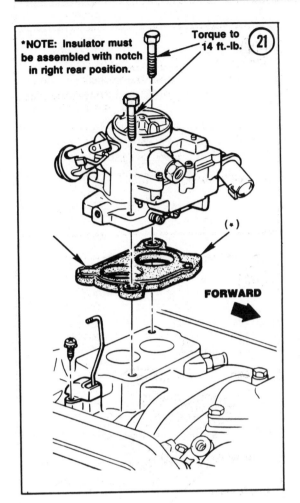

*NOTE: Insulator must be assembled with notch in right rear position.

Torque to 14 ft.-lb. (21)

(•)

FORWARD

3A. If equipped with a remote choke, remove the circlip holding the choke coil rod to the carburetor.

3B. Disconnect the fresh air and choke pipes from integral chokes, if so equipped.

4. Disconnect the throttle rod and return spring from the throttle lever (**Figure 23**).

5. Disconnect the cruise control linkage and automatic transmission downshift cable, if so equipped.

6. Disconnect the fuel line at the fuel inlet nut. Plug the line to prevent fuel leakage.

7. Disconnect any other lines or hoses that might obstruct carburetor removal.

(23)

5

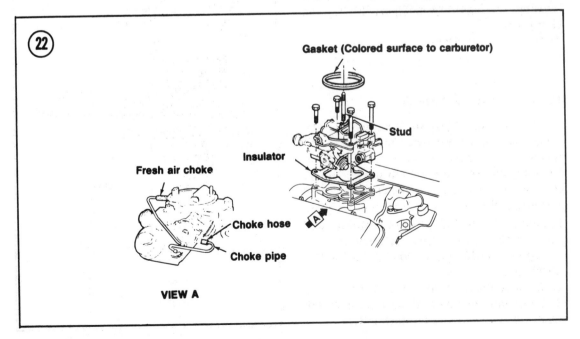

(22)

Gasket (Colored surface to carburetor)

Stud

Insulator

Fresh air choke

Choke hose

Choke pipe

A

VIEW A

8. Remove the carburetor retaining nuts/bolts. Remove the carburetor.

9. Remove the insulator or gasket from the intake manifold flange.

10. Stuff a clean cloth into the intake manifold opening to prevent small parts and contamination from falling inside.

Inspection and Overhaul

Dirt, varnish, water or carbon contamination in or on the carburetor are often the cause of unsatisfactory performance. Gaskets and accelerating pump diaphragms may leak, resulting in carburetion problems. Efficient carburetion depends upon careful cleaning, inspection and proper installation of new parts.

The carburetor model identification (**Figure 24**) is stamped on the float bowl of all carburetors used on 1972 and later engines. The model identification is necessary to obtain the proper carburetor overhaul kit.

The new gaskets and parts included in a carburetor overhaul kit should be installed when the carburetor is assembled and the old parts discarded. Although a complete teardown of each carburetor is beyond the scope of this manual, an exploded view of each carburetor is furnished with the appropriate overhaul kit.

Wash all parts except the choke cap, diaphragms, dashpots, solenoids and other vacuum/electrically operated assist devices in fresh commercial carburetor cleaning solvent. This can be obtained from any auto parts store.

Rinse all parts in kerosene to remove traces of the cleaning solvent, then dry with compressed air. Wipe all parts which cannot be immersed in solvent with a clean, dry soft cloth.

Force compressed air through all passages of the carburetor.

> *CAUTION*
> *Do not use a wire brush to clean any part. Do not use a drill or wire to clean out any opening or passage in the carburetor. A drill or wire may enlarge the hole or passage and change the calibration.*

Check the choke shaft for grooves, wear or excessive looseness or binding. Inspect the choke plate for nicked edges and ease of operation. Make sure all carbon and foreign material has been removed from the automatic choke housing on integral choke models.

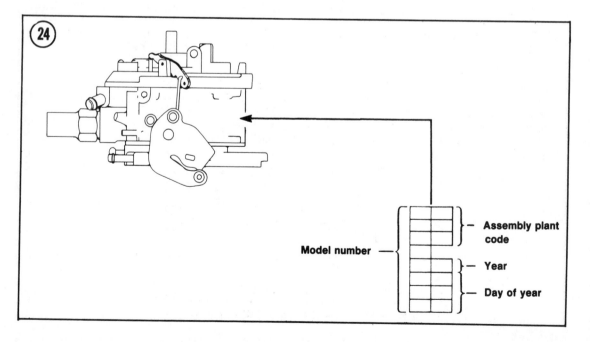

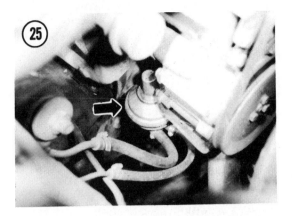

Check the throttle shafts in their bores for excessive looseness or binding. Check the throttle plates for burrs which prevent proper closure.

Inspect all components for cracks or warpage. Check brass floats for leaks by holding them under water which has been heated to 200° F. Bubbles will appear if there is a leak. Check composition floats for fuel absorption by gently squeezing and applying fingernail pressure. If moisture appears, replace the float.

Replace the float if the arm needle contact surface is grooved. If the floats are serviceable, gently polish the needle contact surface of the arm with crocus cloth or steel wool. Replace the float is the shaft is worn.

Replace all screws and nuts that have stripped threads. Replace all distorted or broken springs. Inspect all gasket mating surfaces for nicks and burrs.

Reassemble all parts carefully. It should not be necessary to apply force to any parts. If force seems to be required, you are doing something wrong. Stop and refer to the exploded drawing for your carburetor included with the overhaul kit.

Installation

NOTE
For ease in starting, fill the carburetor bowl before installing the carburetor. Operate the throttle lever several times and verify that fuel discharges from the pump jets prior to installation.

Refer to **Figures 20-22** as appropriate for this procedure.
1. Remove the cloth from the intake manifold opening and clean the manifold gasket mounting surfaces.
2. Install a new gasket or insulator.
3. Install the carburetor on the gasket or spacer. Install mounting nuts/bolts. To prevent warpage of the carburetor base, snug the nuts/bolts, then alternately tighten each nut/bolt in a crisscross pattern until tight. If a torque wrench is available, tighten to 14-17 ft.-lb. (19-23 N•m).
4. Connect the fuel line and all linkage rods.
5. Connect the remote choke rod or integral choke pipes, as appropriate.
6. Connect all vacuum lines and electrical connectors.
7. Adjust the engine idle speed, idle fuel mixture, fast idle speed and solenoid settings (if so equipped).
8. Install the air cleaner.

Float Level Adjustment

When the carburetor is disassembled for cleaning, do not disassemble the linkage. The only internal adjustment that should be necessary is the float level. Follow the procedure specified on the instruction sheet provided with the carburetor overhaul kit.

FUEL PUMP
(GASOLINE ENGINES)

All models use a mechanical fuel pump bolted to the front side of the engine and mechanically operated by a camshaft eccentric. **Figure 25** shows a typical V8 fuel pump; the 4- and 6-cylinder fuel pump is similar.

The 4- and 6-cylinder pump rocker arm rides against the eccentric to provide the up and down motion of the diaphragm. V6 and V8 pumps use a pushrod between the pump arm and camshaft eccentric. The pump is non-repairable and must be replaced if defective.

In addition, Monza, Skyhawk, Starfire and Sunbird models use an electric fuel pump

5

located in the fuel tank as a part of the fuel gauge/filter assembly. See **Figure 26**.

The 2 most common fuel pump problems are incorrect pressure and low volume. Low pressure results in a too-lean mixture and too little fuel at high speeds. High pressure will cause carburetor flooding and result in poor mileage. Low volume also results in too little fuel at high speeds.

If a fuel system problem is suspected, check the fuel filter first. See Chapter Three. If the filter is not clogged or dirty, test the fuel pump.

Fuel Pump Pressure Test
(Mechanical and Electric Pumps)

Refer to **Figure 27** for this procedure.
1. Remove the air cleaner.
2. Disconnect the fuel line at the fuel filter inlet.
3. Connect a pressure gauge and a flexible hose with a restrictor clamp between the fuel line and fuel inlet.
4. Place the end of the hose in a graduated container of at least one quart capacity.
5. If fuel pump is equipped with a vapor return line, pinch off the return line.

6. Start the engine and let it idle. Open the hose restrictor for approximately 5 seconds to vent the system.
7. Close the restrictor and let the pressure stabilize. Read the gauge and compare to **Table 3** according to engine.
8. Slowly increase the idle speed and watch the gauge. The pressure should not vary materially at different engine speeds.
9. If the pump pressure is not within specifications in Step 7 or if it varies materially in Step 8, replace the pump. If the pressure is within specifications, perform a fuel capacity test.

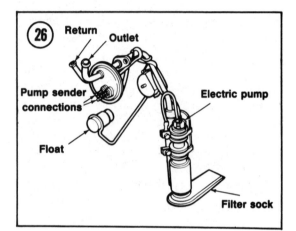

26 Return Outlet
Pump sender connections
Electric pump
Float
Filter sock

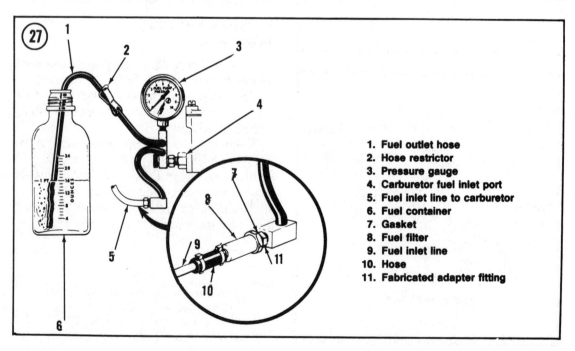

27

1. Fuel outlet hose
2. Hose restrictor
3. Pressure gauge
4. Carburetor fuel inlet port
5. Fuel inlet line to carburetor
6. Fuel container
7. Gasket
8. Fuel filter
9. Fuel inlet line
10. Hose
11. Fabricated adapter fitting

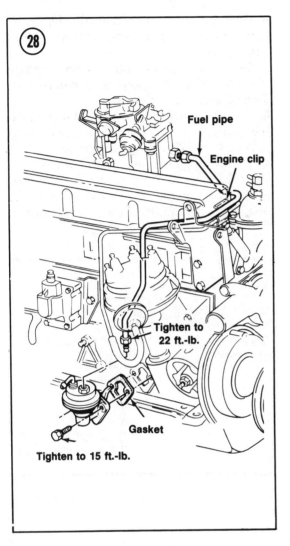

(28)

Fuel pipe

Engine clip

Tighten to
22 ft.-lb.

Gasket

Tighten to 15 ft.-lb.

Fuel Pump Capacity Test
(Mechanical and Electric Pumps)

1. Disconnect the fuel line at the fuel filter inlet.
2. Place the end of the line in a graduated container of at least one quart capacity.
3. Run the engine at idle and time how long it takes to pump one pint of fuel into the container. If it takes more than 30 seconds to pump one pint of fuel, look for a restriction in the fuel line or a dirty fuel filter. If none is found, replace the pump.

Electric Fuel Pump
Voltage Test

Disconnect the 3-wire connector to the fuel pump located in the trunk area. Turn the ignition key ON and check the voltage to the pump at the 3-wire connector with a voltmeter. If the voltmeter reading is 12 volts or more but pump pressure is low, check the pump ground connection near the trunk lid lock striker. If the ground connection is clean and tight, return the car to a dealer and have the electric pump replaced.

If the voltmeter reading is less than 12 volts, make sure the battery is fully charged. If it is, return the car to a dealer and have the fuel pump electrical circuit serviced.

5

Mechanical Fuel Pump
Replacement

Refer to **Figure 28** (4- and 6-cylinder) and **Figure 29** (V6 and V8) for this procedure.
1. Disconnect the inlet and outlet lines from the pump. Plug both lines to prevent vapor and fluid leakage.
2. Remove the pump attaching bolts. Carefully lift the pump from the engine.
3. Remove the gasket (4- and 6-cylinder) or gaskets and spacer plate (V6 and V8).
4. Clean all gasket residue from the pump and the mounting pad on the engine.

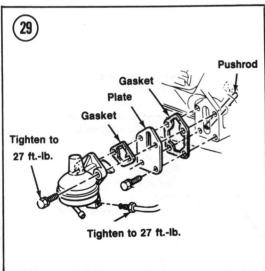

(29)

Pushrod

Gasket

Plate

Gasket

Tighten to
27 ft.-lb.

Tighten to 27 ft.-lb.

NOTE
Prior to pump installation, rotate engine until low point of pump cam lobe contacts the pump arm. This is done by holding the pump loosely in

position and rotating the crankshaft until pressure on the pump lever arm is at a minimum.

4. Installation is the reverse of removal. Use new gasket(s) coated on both sides with oil-resistant gasket sealer. Alternately tighten mounting bolts to 15 ft.-lb. (20 N•m) for 4- and 6-cylinder pumps and 27 ft.-lb. (37 N•m) for V6 and V8 pumps. Tighten fuel line fittings to 22 ft.-lb. (28 N•m).

5. Start the engine and check for leaks.

FUEL FILTER

All gasoline engine fuel filters are located in the carburetor fuel inlet. Filter elements are installed in the inlet with the gasket surface facing outward. Diesel engine fuel filters are installed in a line between the fuel pump and injection pump. Refer to Chapter Three for filter replacement.

Table 1 EVAPORATIVE EMISSION CONTROL LINES

Engine	Year	Disconnect canister hose to
Buick V8	1972-1978	Air cleaner
Chevrolet 4-cyl.	1975	Fuel
	1976-1978	PCV valve
Chevrolet 6-cyl.	1972-1978	Fuel
Chevrolet V8	1972-1978	Fuel
Oldsmobile 4-cyl.	1976-1978	PCV valve
Oldsmobile V6	1976-1978	Air cleaner
Oldsmobile V8	1972-1978	Carburetor
Pontiac 4-cyl.	1976-1978	PCV valve
Pontiac V6	1976-1978	Air cleaner
Pontiac V8	1972	Evaporative
	1973-1978	Carburetor

Table 2 IDLE SCREW MIXTURE ADJUSTMENT

Division	Year	Engine	Number of Turns
Buick	1976	260 cid	5
Chevrolet	1972-1973	All	4
Oldsmobile	1972-1973	All	4
	1974	V8	4 (then best idle)
	1975	V8	3 (then best idle)
Pontiac	1972	All	3 1/2
	1973-1974	All	6
	1975-1976	All	5

Table 3 FUEL PUMP PRESSURE SPECIFICATIONS

Engine	psi
Inline 4-cyl.	3.5-4.5
Inline 6-cyl.	3.5-4.5
V6	
1978-1979 231 cid	3 (minimum)
1980 231 cid, 1979 260 cid	4.5-6
V8	
1972-1975	5-8.5
1976-on	7.5-9

NOTE: If you own a 1985 model, first check the Supplement at the back of the book for any new service information.

CHAPTER SIX

ELECTRICAL SYSTEM

General Motors passenger cars are equipped with a 12-volt, negative-ground electrical system. This chapter includes service procedures for the battery, charging system, starter, fuses and lighting system.

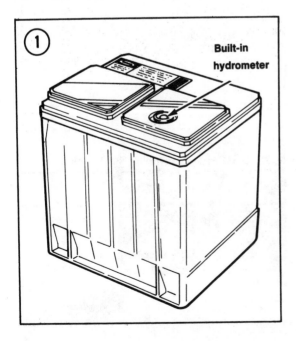

Built-in hydrometer

Use Chapter Two to help isolate any problem that develops in the electrical system. Many electrical problems can be traced to a simple cause such as a blown fuse, a loose or corroded connection, a loose alternator drive belt or a frayed wire. While these are easily corrected problems which may not appear important, they can quickly lead to serious difficulty if allowed to go uncorrected.

Repairing electrical components such as the alternator or starter motor is usually beyond the capability of the inexperienced mechanic and household tool box. Such repairs are best left to the specialized mechanic who is equipped with the necessary experience and tools.

It is often faster and more economical to replace defective parts instead of having them repaired. Make certain, however, that the new or rebuilt part to be installed is an exact replacement for the defective one removed. Also, make sure to isolate and correct the cause of the failure before installing a replacement. For example, an uncorrected short in a alternator circuit will most likely burn out a new alternator as quickly as it damaged the old one. If in doubt, always consult an expert.

BATTERY

The battery is perhaps the single most important component in the automotive electrical system. It is also the one most commonly neglected. In addition to checking and correcting the battery electrolyte level on a weekly basis (Chapter Three), the battery should be cleaned and inspected at periodic intervals.

All GM cars covered in this manual are factory-equipped with a Freedom II maintenance-free battery which incorporates a visual test indicator (**Figure 1**). This test indicator is a built-in hydrometer in one cell. It provides visual information of battery condition for testing only and should not be used as a basis of determining whether the battery is properly charged or discharged, good or bad.

Using the Test Indicator

Refer to **Figure 2**. Make sure the battery is level and the test indicator sight glass is clean. A penlight is useful under dim lighting conditions to determine the indicator color. Look down into the sight glass. If the dot appears green in color, the battery has a sufficient charge for testing. If it appears dark or black, charge the battery before testing. A clear or light yellow appearance indicates that the battery should be replaced and the charging system checked.

Cleaning and Inspection

1. Disconnect both battery cables (**Figure 3**)–negative first, then positive. Remove the battery hold-down clamp (**Figure 4**, typical).
2. Attach a battery carry strap to the terminal posts (**Figure 5**). Remove the battery from the engine compartment.

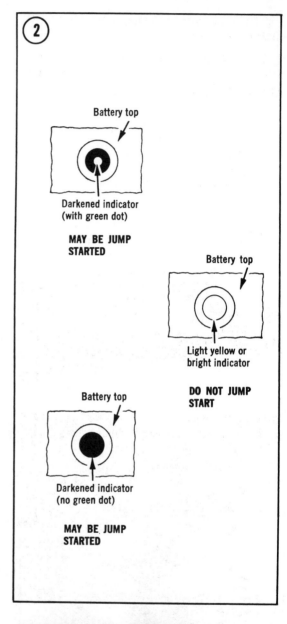

(2)

Battery top

Darkened indicator
(with green dot)

MAY BE JUMP STARTED

Battery top

Light yellow or
bright indicator

DO NOT JUMP START

Battery top

Darkened indicator
(no green dot)

MAY BE JUMP STARTED

(3)

Delco
Freedom
Battery

3. Check the entire battery case for cracks, chafing or other damage.

4. If the battery has individual removable filler caps, cover the vent holes in each cap with a small piece of masking tape.

NOTE
Keep cleaning solution out of the battery cells in Step 5 or the electrolyte will be seriously weakened.

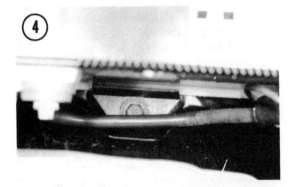

5. Clean the top of the battery with a stiff bristle brush using a baking soda and water solution. Rinse the battery case with clear water and wipe dry with a clean cloth or paper towel.

6. Inspect the battery tray in the engine compartment for corrosion and clean, if necessary, with the baking soda/water solution. Rinse tray with clear water and wipe dry.

7. Remove the masking tape from the filler cap vent holes. Position the battery on the battery tray and install the hold-down clamp (**Figure 6**). Tighten the clamp bolt sufficiently to hold the battery from moving.

8. Clean the battery cable clamps with a stiff wire brush or one of the many tools made for this purpose (**Figure 7**). The same tool is used for cleaning the battery posts (**Figure 8**).

10. Reconnect the positive battery cable, then the negative cable.

6

Be sure the battery cables are connected to their proper terminals. Connecting the battery backwards will reverse the polarity and can damage the alternator.

11. Tighten the battery connections and coat with a petroleum jelly such as Vaseline or a light mineral grease.

12. Check the electrolyte level on unsealed batteries. It should touch the bottom of the vent well in each cell. See **Figure 9**. Top up with distilled water, if necessary.

Testing

NOTE
This test procedure applies only to unsealed batteries. A capacity and rate-of-charge test using special equipment is required in testing Delco Freedom II and other maintenance-free batteries. These tests should be performed by your dealer or an automotive electrical shop.

Hydrometer testing is the best way to check battery condition. Use a temperature-compensated hydrometer with numbered gradations from 1.100-1.300 rather than one with just color-coded bands. To use the hydrometer, squeeze the rubber ball, insert the tip in a cell and release the ball.

Draw enough electrolyte to float the weighted float inside the hydrometer. Note the number in line with the surface of the electrolyte (**Figure 10**). This is the specific gravity for the cell. Return the electrolyte to the cell from which it came. If the specific gravity is less than that indicated in **Table 1** and if the differences in specific gravity from one cell to another are close (less than 0.050), the battery requires a charge.

NOTE
If a temperature-compensated hydrometer is not used, add 0.004 to the specific gravity reading for every 10° above 80° F (25° C). For every 10° below 80° F (25° C), subtract 0.004.

If the difference in specific gravity from one cell to another is greater than 0.050, one or more cells may be sulfated or otherwise poor. In such case, replace the battery before it causes trouble.

Charging

The battery does not have to be removed from the car for charging. Just make certain that the area is well-ventilated and that there is no chance of sparks or flames occurring near the battery.

WARNING
Charging batteries give off highly explosive hydrogen gas. If this explodes, it may spray battery acid over a wide area.

Disconnect the negative battery cable first, then the positive cable. Remove the vent caps and top up each cell with distilled water if necessary. Place a folded paper towel over the vent openings to catch any electrolyte that may spew as the battery charges.

Thread a set of screw-in battery post adapters into the battery terminals to assure

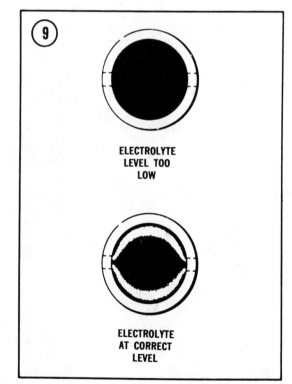

ELECTROLYTE
LEVEL TOO
LOW

ELECTROLYTE
AT CORRECT
LEVEL

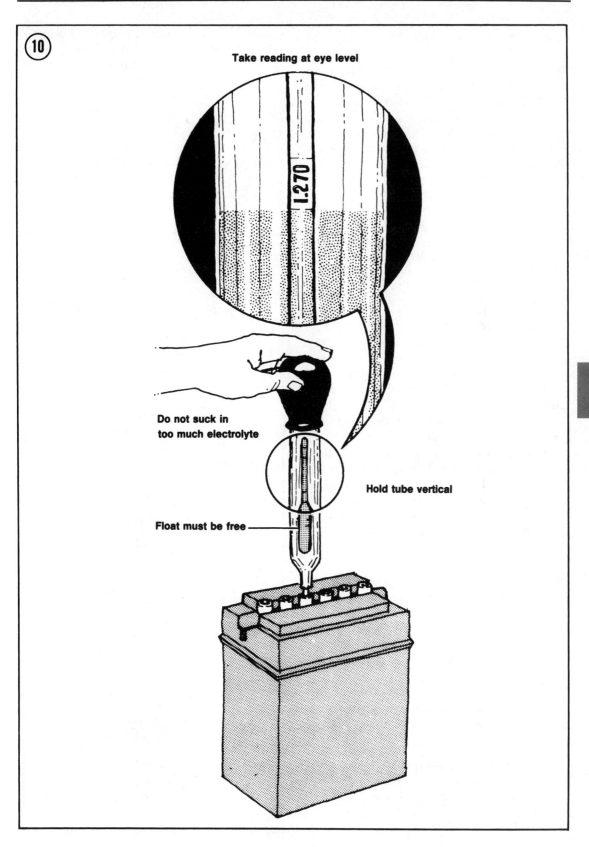

good contact. See **Figure 11**. Connect the charger to the battery (negative to negative, positive to positive). See **Figure 12**. If the charger output is variable, select a low setting (5-10 amps), set the voltage regulator to 12 volts and plug the charger in. If the battery is severely discharged (specific gravity below 1.125), allow it to charge for at least 8 hours. Batteries that are not as badly discharged require less charging time.

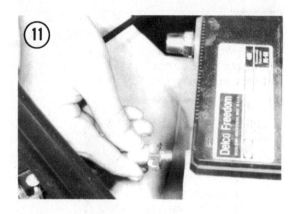

NOTE
*If time permits, charge at the lower rate and for a long period of time. If there is not sufficient time for slow charging, follow the high-rate charging times and rates shown in **Table 2**.*

After the battery has charged for a suitable period of time, unplug the charger and disconnect it from the battery. Be extremely careful about sparks. Test the condition of each cell with a hydrometer as described above and compare the results with **Table 1**.

If the specific gravity indicates that the battery is fully charged, and if the readings remain the same after one hour, the battery can be considered to be in good condition and fully charged. Check the electrolyte level and add distilled water, if necessary, and install the vent caps. Reconnect the negative battery cable, then the positive battery cable.

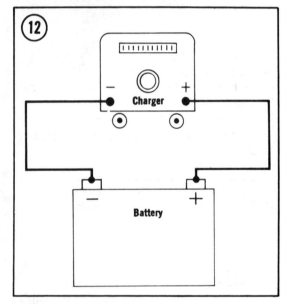

Jump Starting

If the battery becomes severely discharged on the road, it is possible to start and run a vehicle by jump starting it from another battery. If the proper procedure is not followed, jump starting can be dangerous. Check the electrolyte level before jump starting any vehicle. If it is not visible or if it appears to be frozen, do not attempt to jump start the battery. Do not jump start maintenance-free batteries when the temperature is 32° F (0° C) or lower.

WARNING
Use extreme caution when connecting a booster battery to one that is discharged to avoid personal injury or damage to the vehicle.

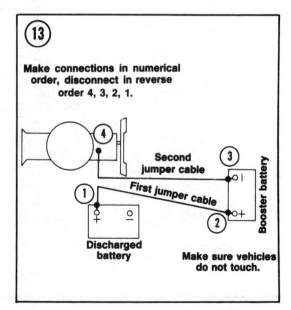

1. Position the 2 cars so that the jumper cables will reach between the batteries, but the cars do not touch.

2. Connect the jumper cables in the order and sequence shown in **Figure 13**.

WARNING
An electrical arc may occur when the final connection is made. This could cause an explosion if it occurs near the battery. For this reason, the final connection should be made to the alternator mounting bracket and not the battery itself.

3. Check that all jumper cables are out of the way of moving parts on both engines.

4. Start the car with the good battery and run the engine at a moderate speed.

5. Start the car with the discharged battery. Once the engine starts, run it at a moderate speed.

CAUTION
Racing the engine may cause damage to the electrical system.

6. Remove the jumper cables in the exact reverse order shown in **Figure 13**. Begin at point No. 4, then 3, 2 and 1.

CHARGING SYSTEM

The charging system consists of the battery, alternator, voltage regulator, charge indicator light or ammeter and wiring. **Figure 14** shows a typical circuit.

Four alternators are used: the 10-SI, 12-SI, 15-SI and 27-SI. They differ primarily in output rating. The output rating is stamped on the alternator frame.

All alternators covered in this manual use an integral solid-state voltage regulator. The regulator is serviced only by replacement.

6

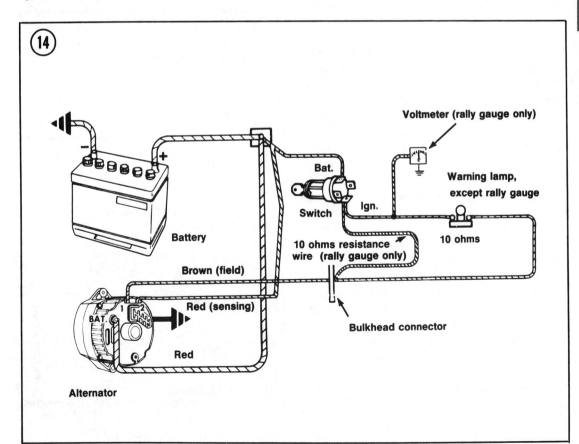

Alternator

The alternator is a self-rectifying, 3-phase current generator consisting of a stationary armature (stator), a rotating field (rotor) and a 3-phase rectifying bridge of silicon diodes. The alternator generates alternating current which is converted to direct current by the silicon diodes for use in the vehicle's electrical circuits. The alternator output is regulated by a voltage regulator to keep the battery charged. The alternator is mounted on the front of the engine and is belt-driven by the crankshaft pulley. **Figure 15** shows a typical alternator installation.

Make sure the connections are not reversed when working on the alternator. Current flow in the wrong direction will damage the diodes and render the alternator unserviceable. When charging the battery in the vehicle, disconnect the battery leads before connecting the charger. This is a precaution against incorrect current bias and heat reaching the alternator.

Troubleshooting

The first indication of charging system trouble is usually a slow engine cranking speed during starting. This will often occur long before the charge warning light or ammeter indicates that there is a potential problem. When charging system trouble is first suspected, have it carefully tested, either by a dealer or an automotive electrical shop. Before having the system tested, however, the following checks should be made to make sure something else is not the cause of what seems to be trouble in the charging system.
1. Check the alternator drive belt for correct tension (Chapter Seven).
2. Check the battery to make sure it is in satisfactory condition, fully charged and that the connections are clean and tight.
3. Check all connections between the engine and alternator to make sure they are clean and tight.

If there are still indications that the charging system is not performing as it should after each of the above points has been carefully checked and any unsatisfactory conditions corrected, perform a charging system test.

Charging System Test

A voltmeter with a 0-20 volt scale and an engine tachometer are required for an accurate charging system test.
1. Connect the positive voltmeter lead to the positive battery cable clamp. Connect the negative voltmeter lead to the negative battery cable clamp. Make sure the ignition and all accessories are off.
2. Record the battery voltage displayed on the voltmeter scale. This is the base voltage.
3. Connect a tachometer to the engine according to the manufacturer's instructions.
4. Start the engine and bring its speed up to about 1,500 rpm. The voltmeter reading should increase from that recorded in Step 2, but not by more than 2 volts.
5. If the voltage does not increase, perform the *Undercharge Test*. If the voltage increase is greater than 2 volts, remove the alternator and have it checked by a dealer or an automotive electrical shop for grounded or shorted field windings.

Undercharge test

A voltmeter with a 0-20 volt scale, an ammeter and a carbon pile are required for this procedure. Refer to **Figure 16** for this procedure.

1. Turn the ignition switch ON. Make sure all electrical harness leads are properly connected.

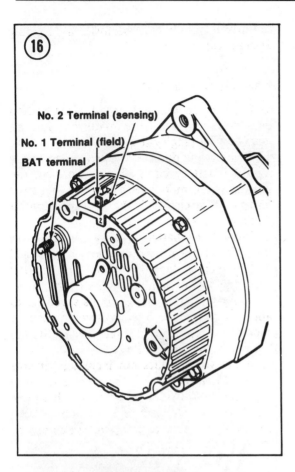

No. 2 Terminal (sensing)

No. 1 Terminal (field)

BAT terminal

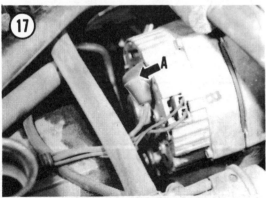

2. Connect the negative voltmeter lead to a good engine ground. Connect the positive voltmeter lead in turn to the:

   a. BAT terminal.

   b. No. 1 terminal.

   c. No. 2 terminal.

3. Read the voltmeter as each connection in Step 2 is made. A zero reading at any of the connections indicates an open circuit.

CAUTION
An open in the No. 2 lead circuit will cause uncontrolled voltage, battery overcharge and possible damage to the battery and accessories. The alternators covered in this manual have a built-in feature to prevent overcharge and accessory damage by preventing the unit from turning on if there is an open in the No. 2 lead circuit. Such an open could occur between terminals, at the crimp between the harness wire or terminal or in the wire itself.

4. Disconnect the voltmeter. Disconnect the negative battery cable.

5. Disconnect the wiring connector at the BAT terminal (A, **Figure 17**). Connect an ammeter between the BAT terminal and the wiring connector.

6. Reconnect the negative battery cable. Turn on all accessories.

7. Connect a carbon pile across the battery posts.

8. Start the engine and run at 2,000 rpm. Adjust the carbon pile to obtain the maximum current output.

9. If the alternator reading is within 10 amps of the unit's rated output, it is satisfactory.

10. If the ammeter reading is not within 10 amps of the rated output, remove the alternator and have it checked by your dealer or an automotive electrical shop.

Regulator Test

An approved regulator tester (GM part No. CTW-1170 or equivalent) is required to determine whether the regulator is functioning properly. Since this test may require disassembly of the alternator and requires the use of special test equipment, have it performed by your dealer or an automotive electrical shop.

Alternator Removal/Installation

This procedure is generalized to cover all applications. On some vehicles, the alternator is mounted low on the engine under other accessory units and can only be reached from underneath the car. Access to the alternator is

6

quite limited in some engine compartments and care should be taken to avoid personal injury during this procedure.

1. Disconnect the negative battery cable.
2. Unplug the connectors from the rear of the alternator. See **Figure 17**.
3. Loosen the belt tension adjuster at the alternator (**Figure 18**).

NOTE
The adjusting bolt is installed from the rear of the bracket on some alternators. On some installations, it may also be necessary to unbolt a brace or bracket.

4. Move the alternator toward the engine and remove the drive belt from the pulley.
5. Unscrew the adjuster bolt. Remove the pivot bolt (A, **Figure 15**). Remove the alternator.
6. Installation is the reverse of removal. Make sure the alternator connectors are properly installed before connecting the negative battery cable.
7. Adjust the drive belt tension (Chapter Seven).

Charge Indicator Lamp

If the alternator and voltage regulator are operating satisfactorily and the charge indicator warning lamp remains on, the charge indicator relay located inside the voltage regulator may be defective. To determine the cause of the problem, perform the following procedure.

1. *Switch OFF, lamp on*–Disconnect leads from alternator No. 1 and No. 2 terminals. If lamp remains on, there is a short circuit between the 2 leads. If the lamp goes out, the rectifier bridge is faulty and must be replaced, as this condition will result in an undercharged battery.
2. *Switch ON, lamp off, engine stopped*–This defect can be caused by the conditions listed in Step 1, by reversal of the No. 1 and No. 2 leads at these 2 terminals or by an open circuit. To determine where the open exists, proceed as follows:

   a. Connect voltmeter between alternator No. 2 terminal and ground. If reading is obtained, proceed to next step. If

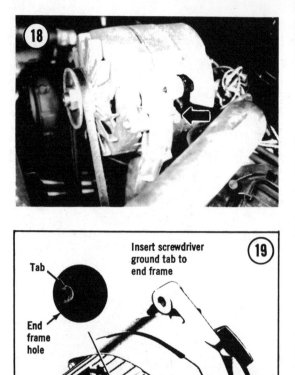

reading is zero, repair open circuit between No. 2 terminal and battery. If lamp comes on, no further check is required.

   b. Disconnect leads from No. 1 and No. 2 terminals on alternator. Turn ignition switch ON and momentarily ground No. 1 terminal.

CAUTION
Do not ground No. 2 lead.

   c. If lamp does not come on, check for blown fuse or fusible link, burned-out lamp bulb, defective bulb socket or open

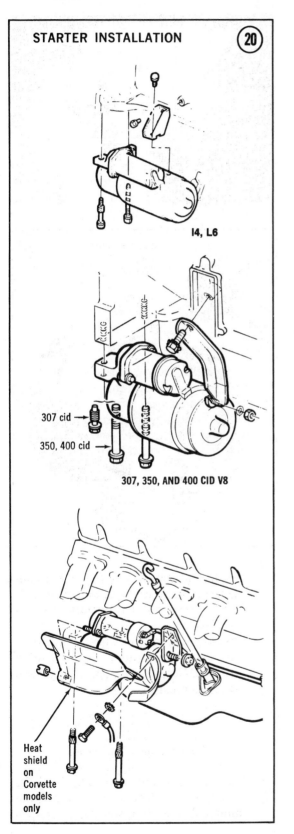

STARTER INSTALLATION 20

I4, L6

307 cid →
350, 400 cid →

307, 350, AND 400 CID V8

Heat
shield
on
Corvette
models
only

in No. 1 lead circuit between alternator and ignition switch.

d. If the lamp lights, remove ground at No. 1 terminal and reconnect No. 1 and No. 2 wires to alternator. Insert a screwdriver in test hole (**Figure 19**) to ground wiring.

e. If lamp does not go on, check connection between wiring harness and alternator No. 1 terminal. If wiring is okay, have alternator brushes, slip rings and field winding checked.

f. If lamp lights, repeat voltmeter check in previous step. If reading is obtained, have regulator replaced.

3. *Switch on, lamp on, engine running*—Possible causes are improper belt tension, a defective or discharged battery, faulty wiring or an open circuit between the alternator and battery.

STARTER

Four Delco starter motors are used with 1972-on engines. The Delco 5MT and 10MT starters are used with gasoline engines; the Delco 15MT/GR and 20MT are used with diesel engines. The starter solenoid is enclosed in the drive housing to protect it from exposure to dirt and adverse weather conditions.

Starter service requires experience and special tools. Diagnostic procedures for troubleshooting the starter motor are given in Chapter Two. If these procedures indicate that the starter and/or solenoid are defective, remove the unit from the engine and have it checked by a dealer or automotive electrical shop.

Removal/Installation

Refer to **Figure 20** for typical starter installations.

1. Disconnect the negative battery cable.
2. Set the parking brake and place the transmission in PARK or first gear.
3. Raise the front of the car with a jack and place it on jackstands.
4. Disconnect all wires at the solenoid terminals.

6

NOTE
Reinstall each nut as wire is removed.
Thread sizes are different and stripped
threads could result if nuts become
mixed up.

5. Loosen starter front bracket (nuts on some models; bolts on others) and remove mounting bolts.
6. Remove the front bracket bolt or nut and rotate bracket clear of work area.
7. Lower starter from engine, front end first.
8. Installation is the reverse of removal. Reinstall any shims that were removed to assure proper pinion-to-flywheel mesh. Tighten mounting bolts to 25-30 ft.-lb. (35-42 N•m), then tighten bracket nut or bolt to same torque. Make sure all electrical connections are tight.

ELECTRICAL CIRCUIT PROTECTION

Electrical circuits are protected by a variety of devices: fuses, circuit breakers and fusible links.

Fuses

A fuse is a "safety valve" installed in an electrical circuit which "blows" (opens the circuit) when excessive current flows in the circuit. This protects the circuit and electrical components, such as the alternator, from being damaged.

Early model fuses look like glass capsules with a thin metal link running through the center. It is this link that burns in half under a heavy electrical load. If this happens, the fuse may appear black and/or the break can be seen in the metal link. All General Motor divisions changed to the use of mini-fuses with the 1978 models. The mini-fuse is a flat design with 2 blades connected by a metal link and encapsulated in plastic. The plastic is color-coded according to amperage value. The mini-fuse functions in the same way as the older glass fuse, but is more reliable and easier to replace.

Whenever a failure occurs in any part of the electrical system, always check the fuse to see if it is blown. Usually the trouble can be traced to a short circuit in the wiring connected to the blown fuse. This may be caused by worn insulation or by a wire which has worked loose and shorted to ground. Occasionally, the electrical overload which causes a fuse to blow may occur in a switch or motor.

A blown fuse should be treated as more than a minor annoyance; it should serve as a warning that something is wrong in the electrical system. Before replacing a fuse, determine what caused it to blow and correct the trouble. Never replace a fuse with one of higher amperage rating than that specified for use. With glass fuses, never use foil or other metallic material to bridge the fuse terminals. Failure to follow these basic rules could result in heat or fire damage to major parts or loss of the entire vehicle.

Fuse Replacement

To replace a glass fuse, carefully pry it out of its holder with the end of a pencil or similar non-metallic probe and snap a new one of the same amperage rating into place.

To replace a mini-fuse, grasp its plastic covered top and pull it from the fuse box. Insert a new fuse of the same amperage rating (color) in place.

Circuit Breakers

Some circuits are protected by circuit breakers mounted either in the fuse block or the circuit itself. A circuit breaker conducts current through an arm made of 2 different types of metal connected together. If too much current passes through this bimetal arm, it heats up and expands. One metal expands faster than the other, causing the arm to move and open the contacts to break the flow of current. As the arm cools down, the metal contracts and the arm closes the contacts, allowing current to pass. Cycling inline circuit breakers will repeat this sequence as long as power is applied or until the condition is corrected. Non-cycling circuit breakers use a coil around the bimetal arm to hold it in an open position until power is shut off or the condition corrected.

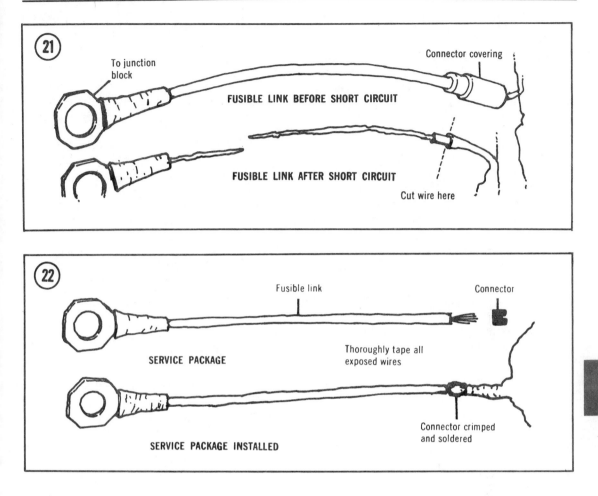

21

To junction block

Connector covering

FUSIBLE LINK BEFORE SHORT CIRCUIT

FUSIBLE LINK AFTER SHORT CIRCUIT

Cut wire here

22

Fusible link

Connector

SERVICE PACKAGE

Thoroughly tape all exposed wires

SERVICE PACKAGE INSTALLED

Connector crimped and soldered

6

Fusible Links

Fusible links are different than fuses. A fusible link is a short length of insulated wire several gauges smaller than the circuit it protects. When heavy current flows through the circuit, the fusible link burns out, protecting the wiring and circuit components.

Fusible Link Replacement

Factory-installed fusible links are color-coded according to the link rating and are covered with heavy insulation. The gauge size is plainly marked on the insulation. If a link burns out, isolate and correct the cause, then splice a new link into the circuit.

1. Obtain the proper service fusible link. Make sure the replacement link is a duplicate of the one removed regarding wire gauge, length and insulation. Do not substitute any other type of gauge or wire.

2. Disconnect the negative battery cable.

3. Disconnect the fusible link and/or eyelet terminal from the component to which it is attached.

4. Cut the harness behind the connector **(Figure 21)** and remove the damaged fusible link.

5. Strip the harness wire insulation approximately 1/2 inch.

6. Position the connector clip around the ends of the new fusible link **(Figure 22)** and harness wire. Crimp connector clip so that both wires are securely fastened.

7. Solder the connection with rosin core solder. Use sufficient heat to obtain a good solder joint, but do not overheat.

8. Tape all exposed wires with insulating tape.

9. Connect the fusible link to the component from which it was removed.

10. Reconnect negative battery cable.

LIGHTS

All lighting elements, with the exception of instrument illumination bulbs, are easily replaced. Individual replacement procedures vary slightly, but can be accomplished with the following procedures.

Headlight Replacement

The headlights are replaceable sealed-beam or halogen units. On single headlight installations, the high- and low-beam circuits and filaments are included in one unit. With dual headlight installations, one bulb on each side is a combination high- and low-beam unit marked 2 or 2A. The other bulb is a high-beam only unit marked 1 or 1A. Mounting tabs on this bulb permit its use only in the inboard or lower headlight support frame. Failure of one circuit in a combination lamp requires replacement of the entire lamp.

CAUTION
Do not interchange halogen and standard sealed beam lamps as their

circuit requirements are different. Use of standard sealed beam lamps in a halogen lamp circuit can cause circuit problems.

Refer to **Figure 23** for typical round and **Figure 24** for typical rectangular headlight installations.

NOTE
If both filaments in a dual beam lamp fail at the same time, it is possible that there is a short in the wiring to that particular lamp. Check the fuse to make sure it is the correct amperage rating and replace if it is not. Carefully inspect the wiring and connector for chafing or damage and correct any breaks in the insulation.

1. Remove the screws holding the headlight bezel and/or trim ring in place. Remove the ring.
2. Loosen the headlight retaining screws, turn the light unit counterclockwise to align the large cutouts with the screws and remove the

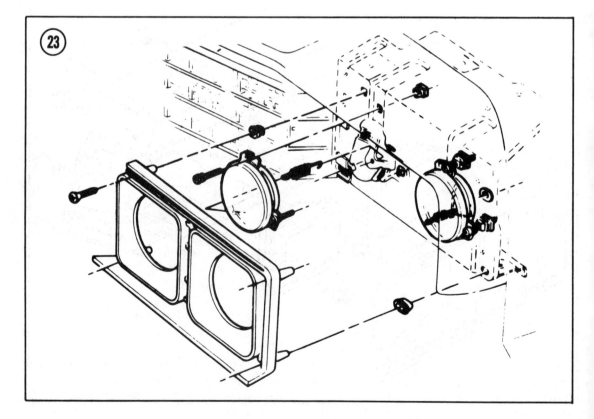

23

unit. Unplug the connector from the rear of the light.

> *NOTE*
> *Do not turn the headlight beam adjusting screws. This will disturb the setting and the headlight beam will require adjustment.*

3. Installation is the reverse of removal. Be sure the connector is firmly seated before installing the unit. Set the light in place; make sure the lugs on the light engage the recesses in the lamp holder. Set the retainer ring in place and turn it clockwise until the small end of each cutout engages a screw. Tighten the screws and install the outer bezel and/or trim ring.

Taillight/Parking/Turn Indicator Bulb Replacement

Because of the large number of models produced during the period covered by this book, it is not possible to provide individual procedures to cover all types of lamp installations. Close examination will usually reveal the approach to be taken for bulb replacement. Some installations require the removal of the lamp lens (held in place by 2 or more screws through the lens faces) for access to the bulb and socket. In other cases, nuts must be removed from the rear of the lamp unit to release the lens. The most common, however, is the twist-out socket removed from the rear of the housing. This type can be serviced with the following procedure.

1. Remove the twist-lock socket from the rear of the lamp housing.
2. Depress bulb and rotate counterclockwise in socket. Remove bulb.
3. Press a new bulb into the socket and turn it clockwise to lock it in place.
4. Install socket in the lamp housing.

6

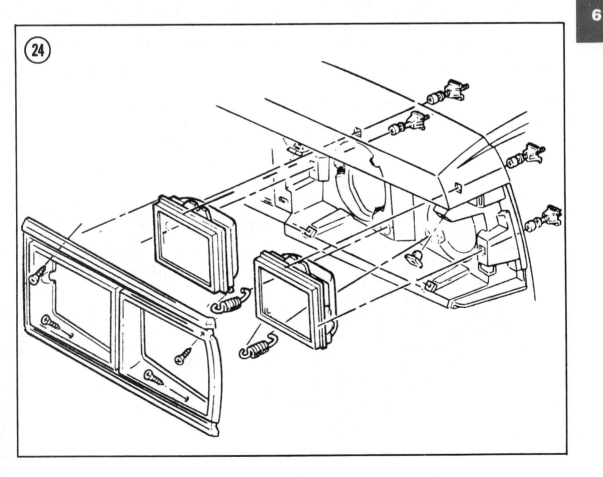

Table 1   ELECTROLYTE SPECIFIC GRAVITY

	Permissible Value	Full Charge Value at 68°F
Moderate climate	Over 1.20	1.26
Cold climate	Over 1.22	1.28
Warm climate	Over 1.18	1.23

Table 2   HIGH-RATE CHARGING TIMES

Specific Gravity Reading	Charge Rate Amperes	Battery Capacity — Ampere Hours				
		45	55	70	80	85
1.125 — 1.150 ①	35	65 min.	80 min.	100 min.	115 min.	125 min.
1.150 — 1.175	35	50 min.	65 min.	80 min.	95 min.	105 min.
1.175 — 1.200	35	40 min.	50 min.	60 min.	70 min.	75 min.
1.200 — 1.225	35	30 min.	35 min.	45 min.	50 min.	55 min.
Above 1.225	5	②	②	②	②	②

① If the specific gravity is below 1.125, use the indicated high rate of charge for the 1.125 specific gravity, then charge at 5 amperes until the specific gravity reaches 1.250 at 80°F.

② Charge at 5 ampere rate only until the specific gravity reaches 1.250 at 80°F.

Warning: At no time during the charging operation should the electrolyte temperature exceed 130°F.

CHAPTER SEVEN

COOLING SYSTEM

All General Motors passenger cars covered in this manual use a pressurized cooling system sealed with a pressure-type radiator cap. The higher operating pressure of the system raises the boiling point of the coolant. This increases the efficiency of the radiator. **Figure 1** shows a typical cooling system.

A crossflow radiator (**Figure 2**) is used on all models. The crossflow radiator is constructed in a tube and slit-fin-core arrangement with the tubes positioned horizontally between the header tanks for crossflow of the coolant. The header tanks on each side of the radiator provide uniform

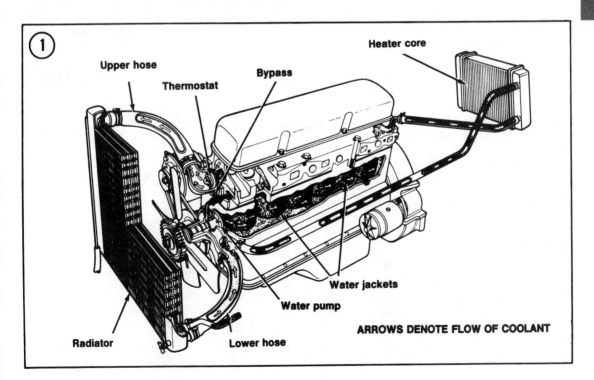

① Heater core

Upper hose

Thermostat

Bypass

Water jackets

Water pump

Radiator

Lower hose

ARROWS DENOTE FLOW OF COOLANT

distribution of the coolant to the crossflow tubes. One header tank contains the transmission oil cooler on automatic transmission models.

Some General Motors vehicles are equipped with a coolant recovery system. This consists of a plastic overflow reservoir connected to the radiator filler neck by a hose (**Figure 3**).

When coolant in the radiator expands to the overflow point, it passes through the filler neck and into the plastic reservoir. Once the coolant remaining in the radiator cools down, it contracts. The vacuum created pulls coolant from the reservoir back into the radiator. This system prevents the radiator from boiling over. By remaining filled to capacity, cooling efficiency is maintained at all times.

GM cooling systems consist of the radiator, coolant recovery tank (if so equipped), pressure cap, water pump, thermostat, fan, thermostatic fan clutch (if so equipped), drive belt(s) and connecting hoses.

Table 1 (approximate cooling system capacities) and **Table 2** (drive belt tension specifications) are at the end of the chapter.

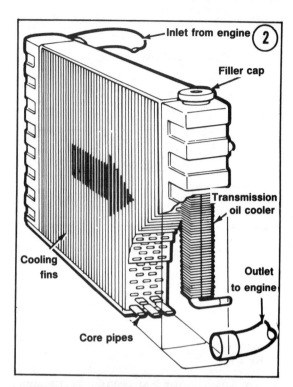

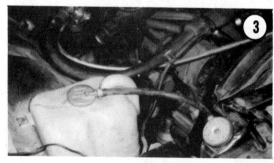

COOLING SYSTEM CHECKS

1. Visually inspect the cooling system and heater hoses for signs of cracking, checking, excessive swelling or leakage.
2. Check that all supporting brackets for hoses are properly positioned (if used) and that the hoses are correctly installed in the brackets.
3. Inspect the front and rear of the radiator core and tanks, all seams and the radiator drain valve for signs of seepage or leaks. See **Figure 4**.
4. Make sure all hose connections are tight and in good condition. Check the hoses carefully at their clamps for cuts or weakness. Overtightening strap-type clamps can cut the outer surface of a hose and weaken it.
5. Remove the radiator pressure cap. Check the rubber cap seal surfaces for tears or cracks

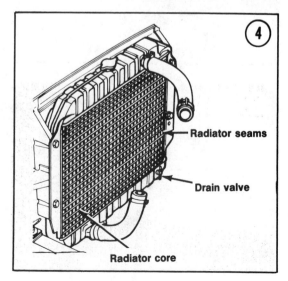

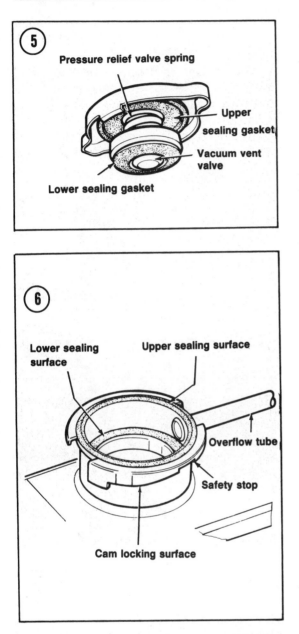

⑤

Pressure relief valve spring

Upper sealing gasket

Vacuum vent valve

Lower sealing gasket

⑥

Lower sealing surface

Upper sealing surface

Overflow tube

Safety stop

Cam locking surface

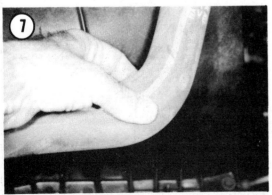

⑦

(**Figure 5**). Check for a bent or distorted cap. Raise the vacuum valve and rubber seal and rinse the cap under warm tap water to flush away any loose rust or dirt particles.

6. Inspect the filler neck seat and sealing surface (**Figure 6**) for nicks, dents, distortion or contamination. Wipe the sealing surface with a clean cloth to remove any rust or dirt. Install the cap properly.

7. Start the engine and warm to normal operating temperature. Shut the engine off and carefully feel the radiator. Crossflow radiators should be hot along the left side and warm along the right side with an even temperature rise from right to left. Cold spots indicate obstructed or clogged radiator sections.

8. Restart the engine and squeeze the upper radiator hose (**Figure 7**) to check water pump operation. If a pressure surge is felt, the water pump is functioning properly. If not, check for a plugged vent hole in the pump.

9. Visually check the area underneath the water pump for signs of leakage or corrosion. A defective water pump will usually leak through the vent hole at the bottom of the pump.

10. Check the crankcase oil dipstick for signs of coolant in the engine oil. On automatic transmission models, check the coolant for signs of transmission fluid leaking from the oil cooler. Check the transmission lines which connect to the oil cooler (**Figure 8**).

7

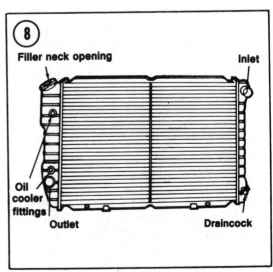

⑧

Filler neck opening

Inlet

Oil cooler fittings

Outlet

Draincock

PRESSURE CHECK

If the cooling system requires frequent topping up, it probably has a leak. Small leaks in a cooling system are not easy to locate, as the hot coolant evaporates as fast as it leaks out, preventing the formation of tell-tale rusty or grayish-white stains.

A pressure test of the cooling system will usually help to pinpoint the source of the leak. The cooling system and the pressure cap should both be tested by a dealer or qualified radiator repair shop.

If the cooling system passes a pressure test but continues to lose coolant, check for an exhaust leak into the cooling system. Drain the coolant until the level is just above the top of the cylinder head. Disconnect the upper radiator hose and remove the thermostat and water pump drive belt. Add sufficient coolant to bring the level to within 1/2 in. of the top of the thermostat housing. Start the engine and open the throttle several times while observing the coolant. If the level rises or if bubbles appear in the coolant, exhaust gases are probably leaking into the cooling system.

> *CAUTION*
> *Do not run the engine with the water pump drive belt disconnected for more than 30 seconds or the engine may overheat.*

COOLANT LEVEL CHECK

Always check coolant level with the engine and radiator cold. Coolant expands as it is heated and checking a hot or warm system will not give a true level reading.

> *WARNING*
> *Never remove the cap from a hot radiator while the engine is running. Severe scalding could result.*

Non-recovery Cooling System

1. Check hose clamps for tightness. Be sure radiator drain valve is closed. **Figure 9** shows a typical drain valve location.

2. Depress the radiator cap, rotate counterclockwise and remove from the filler neck.

3. The coolant level should be maintained about 3 in. below the pressure cap seat in the filler neck when the radiator is cold. See **Figure 10**.

4. If the coolant level is low, top up with a 50/50 mixture of ethylene glycol antifreeze and water.

> *NOTE*
> *To avoid the possibility of chemical damage to the cooling system, do not mix different brands of antifreeze.*

5. Install the radiator cap.

6. Start the engine and warm to normal operating temperature (upper radiator hose hot).

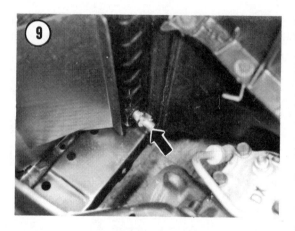

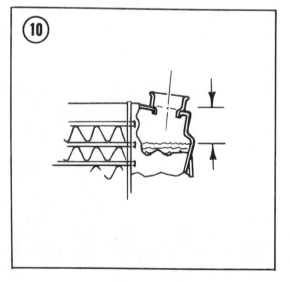

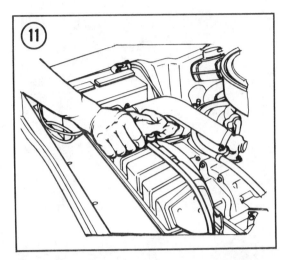

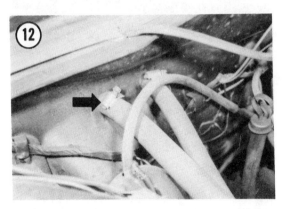

7. Shut the engine off. Cover the radiator cap with a thick cloth and carefully remove it to recheck the coolant level. See **Figure 11**. If necessary, add sufficient coolant to bring the level to the point specified in Step 3.

8. Install the radiator cap.

Coolant Recovery System

Cooling systems equipped with a coolant recovery feature are checked at the reservoir instead of the radiator. Remove the reservoir cap. Add coolant as required to bring the level in the reservoir to the "HOT FULL" or "COLD FULL" mark on the side of the reservoir, according to engine temperature. Install the reservoir cap.

NOTE
Coolant level in radiators with a recovery system should be maintained at the top of the filler neck and the reservoir at its appropriate mark.

CHANGING ENGINE COOLANT

A 50 percent concentration of antifreeze in the coolant should be maintained even if you live in a climate that does not require this degree of freeze protection. Antifreeze is a good corrosion inhibitor and raises the boiling point of the coolant.

The cooling system should be inspected at regular intervals (Chapter Three). If the coolant appears dirty or rusty, the system should be drained, flushed with clean water and refilled. Severe corrosion may require pressure flushing, a job for a dealer or radiator shop. Regardless of appearance, the coolant should be replaced and the system backflushed every 2 years or 24,000 miles.

Flushing

1. Coolant can stain concrete and harm plants. Park the car over a gutter or similar area.

2. Place the heater temperature lever on the instrument panel to its maximum heat position.

3. Open the drain valve at the bottom of the radiator (**Figure 9**).

4. Remove the radiator cap and let the cooling system drain. Close the drain valve.

5. Remove the thermostat as described in this chapter. Temporarily reinstall the thermostat housing.

6. Disconnect the top radiator hose from the radiator. Disconnect the bottom hose from the water pump inlet.

7. Disconnect the heater core outlet hose at the heater core pipe (**Figure 12**). Disconnect the heater core inlet hose at the engine block fitting.

8. Connect a garden hose to the heater core outlet fitting. This does not have to be a positive fit, as long as most of the water enters the heater core. Run water into the heater core until clear water flows from the heater core inlet hose.

9. Insert the garden hose into the hose fitting at the bottom of the radiator. Run water into the radiator until clear water flows from the top fitting. Turn off the water.

7

10. If equipped with a coolant recovery tank, disconnect the tank hose (**Figure 13**). Remove and empty the tank. Flush the recovery tank first with soapy water, then clean water. Drain and reinstall the tank. Connect the hose.

11. Reinstall the thermostat. Use a new thermostat housing gasket coated on each side with water-resistant sealer.

12. Connect the radiator and heater hoses.

Refilling

1. Make sure all hoses are properly connected and their connections are tight.

2. Make sure the radiator drain valve is closed.

3. Fill the system with a 50/50 mixture of ethylene glycol antifreeze and water.

4. Refer to **Table 1** for approximate cooling system capacity for your car. Divide the capacity in half and pour that amount of antifreeze into the radiator. Add the same amount of water. This should bring the coolant level to approximately 3 in. below the filler neck seat. If it does not, add a 50/50 mixture of antifreeze and water to bring the coolant to the specified level.

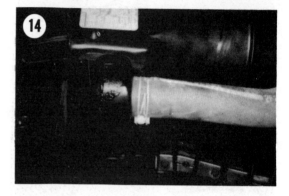

RADIATOR HOSES

Replace any hoses that are cracked, brittle, mildewed or very soft and spongy. If a hose is in doubtful condition, but not definitely bad, replace it to be on the safe side. This will avoid the inconvenience of a roadside repair.

Always replace a radiator hose with the same type removed. Plain or pleated rubber hoses do not have the same strength as reinforced molded hoses. Check the hose clamp condition and, if necessary, install new clamps with a new hose.

5. If equipped with a coolant recovery tank, add enough coolant to the reservoir to bring its level up to the "COLD LEVEL" mark. Install the recovery tank cap.

6. Start the engine (radiator cap off) and warm to normal operating temperature (upper radiator hose hot).

7. Check the coolant level with the engine idling. Add sufficient coolant to bring the level to the bottom of the filler neck seat.

8. If equipped with a coolant recovery tank, add coolant to bring the level to the "HOT FULL" mark on the tank.

9. Install the radiator and/or recovery tank cap.

Replacement

1. Place a clean container under the radiator drain valve. Remove the radiator cap and open the drain valve. Drain about one quart of coolant when replacing an upper hose. Completely drain the coolant to replace a lower hose. If the coolant is clean, save it for reuse.

2. Loosen the clamp (**Figure 14**) at each end of the hose to be removed. Grasp the hose

NOTE
If the radiator cap has an arrow embossed on it, the arrow should align with the overflow hose when the cap is properly installed.

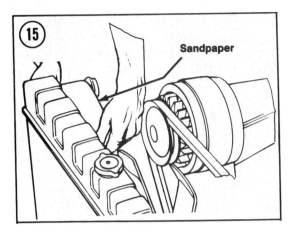

Sandpaper

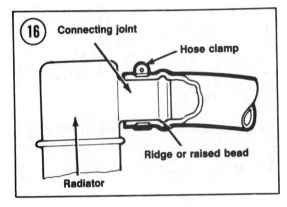

Connecting joint

Hose clamp

Ridge or raised bead

Radiator

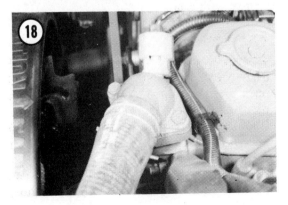

and twist it off the connection with a pulling motion.

3. If the hose is corroded to the fitting, cut it off with a sharp knife about one inch beyond the end of the fitting. Remove the clamp and slit the remaining piece of hose lengthwise, then peel it off the fitting.

4. Clean all corrosion from the fitting with sandpaper (**Figure 15**), then rinse the fitting to remove any particles.

5. Position the clamps at least 1/4 in. from each end of the new hose. Wipe the inside diameter of the hose and the outside of the fitting with dishwasher liquid. Install the hose end on the fitting with a twisting motion.

6. Position the clamps for easy access as shown in **Figure 16**. Tighten each clamp snugly with a screwdriver or nut driver. Recheck them for tightness after operating the car for a few days.

7. Fill the radiator with the coolant removed in Step 1. Start the engine and operate it for a few minutes, checking for signs of leakage around the connections.

THERMOSTAT

The thermostat is located in an elbow housing at the cylinder head water outlet above the water pump. It connects to the upper radiator hose on 6-cylinder and V8 engines (**Figure 17**) and 4-cylinder engines (**Figure 18**).

The thermostat is designed to open and close at predetermined temperatures. It blocks coolant flow to the radiator when the engine is cold. As the engine warms up, the thermostat gradually opens, allowing coolant to circulate through the radiator. Check the thermostat when removed to determine its opening point; the heat range should be stamped on the thermostat valve. When replacing a thermostat, always use one with the same temperature rating.

Removal

1. Make sure the engine is cool. Disconnect the negative battery cable.

2. Place a clean container under the radiator drain valve. Remove the radiator cap and open the drain valve. Drain about one quart

7

of coolant from the radiator. If the coolant is clean, save it for reuse.

NOTE
On some V6 installations, it may be necessary to remove the distributor cap, rotor and vacuum advance diaphragm to provide access for housing removal.

3. If clearance is limited, disconnect the upper radiator hose at the thermostat housing.

NOTE
On some installations, it will be necessary to remove the alternator attaching brace before attempting Step 4.

4. Remove the thermostat housing retaining bolts.
5. Pull the housing away from the cylinder head or manifold far enough to gain access to the thermostat.
6. Remove the thermostat. Remove the gasket.

Testing

1. Place the thermostat in a 33 percent glycol solution heated 25° F above the temperature stamped on the thermostat valve.
2. Submerge the thermostat and agitate the solution. Replace the thermostat if the valve does not open fully.
3. Remove the thermostat and place in another 33 percent glycol solution heated to 10° F under the temperature stamped on the valve.
4. Submerge the thermostat and agitate the solution. Replace the thermostat if the valve does not close fully.
5. Check the thermostat for leakage by cooling to room temperature and holding it up to a bright light. Light leakage around the thermostat valve indicates a defective thermostat.

Installation

1. Stuff a clean shop cloth in the cylinder head or manifold to prevent gasket residue from entering the engine. Clean all gasket or RTV sealant residue from the thermostat housing flange and cylinder head or manifold gasket surfaces with a putty knife. See **Figure 19**.
2. Coat a new gasket with water-resistant sealer and install it on the cylinder head or intake manifold.

NOTE
If RTV sealant is used instead of a gasket, run a 1/8 in. (3 mm) bead of seal around the thermostat housing sealing surface on the intake manifold or cylinder head.

3. Install the thermostat as shown in **Figure 20**.

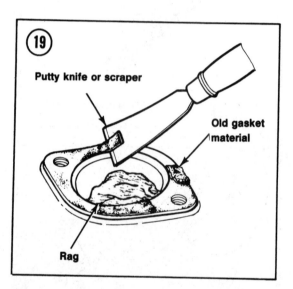

Putty knife or scraper
Old gasket material
Rag

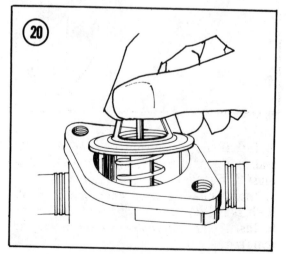

21

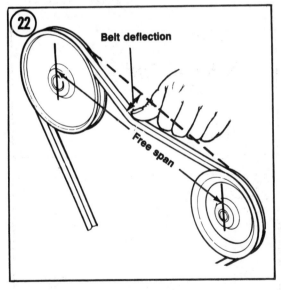

22

Belt deflection

Free span

4. Install the thermostat housing. If RTV sealant is used instead of a gasket, the housing must be installed while the sealant is wet.

5. Install housing bolts and tighten to 30 ft.-lb. (41 N•m).

6. Install the alternator upper brace, if removed.

7. Install the distributor vacuum advance diaphragm, rotor and cap if removed.

8. Connect the upper radiator hose and tighten the clamp securely.

9. Connect the negative battery cable.

10. Fill the cooling system with the coolant removed in Step 2 of *Removal* procedure. Start the engine and run with radiator cap removed for several minutes. Check for leaks and proper coolant level.

DRIVE BELTS

Standard V-belts are used on General Motors vehicles covered in this manual. Drive belts should be correctly adjusted at all times. A loose belt will cause improper accessory operation. A belt that is too tight will put a severe strain on the accessory bearings.

Inspection

Inspect all engine drive belts for wear and damage at each oil change period. Belts which show signs of wear, cracks, glazing or frayed/broken cords should be replaced.

Tension Adjustment

General Motors recommends the use of a belt tension gauge (**Figure 21**) whenever possible as the most accurate means of setting belt tension. If access to the drive belt is limited, tension may be established by the deflection method.

Deflection method

Depress the belt at a point midway between the pulleys. If the free span is less than 12 inches, the belt should deflect 1/8-1/4 in. Deflection should be 1/8-3/8 in. on belts with a free span greater than 12 inches. See **Figure 22**.

Tension gauge method

1. Install the belt tension gauge on the drive belt (**Figure 21**) and check tension according to the gauge manufacturer's instructions.

2. If adjustment is required, loosen the accessory unit's mounting and adjusting

7

bracket bolts. **Figure 23** shows a typical V6 alternator installation with the adjusting bracket bolt head facing in the opposite direction from the pivot and bracket bolts.

3. Move accessory unit toward or away from engine until correct tension is obtained (**Table 2**).

4. Tighten mounting and adjusting bolts, then recheck tension with the gauge.

Belt Removal

When equipped with air conditioning, its drive belt may be located in the first track of the crankshaft pulley and will not have to be removed for fan belt replacement. Cars equipped with power steering and/or an Air Injection Reactor air pump may require removal of their drive belt(s) before the fan drive belt can be removed.

> *NOTE*
> *Depending upon the positioning of the accessory units, it may be necessary to perform Step 1 and/or Step 2 of this procedure from underneath the vehicle on some cars.*

1. On a car equipped with power steering, loosen the power steering pump at its mounting bracket. **Figure 24** shows a typical V8 installation; others are similar. Move the pump toward the engine and remove the drive belt.

> *NOTE*
> *The AIR air pump may be driven by the power steering pump belt. If so, Step 2 is required only on vehicles not equipped with power steering.*

A. Pivot bolt	B. Adjustment bolt

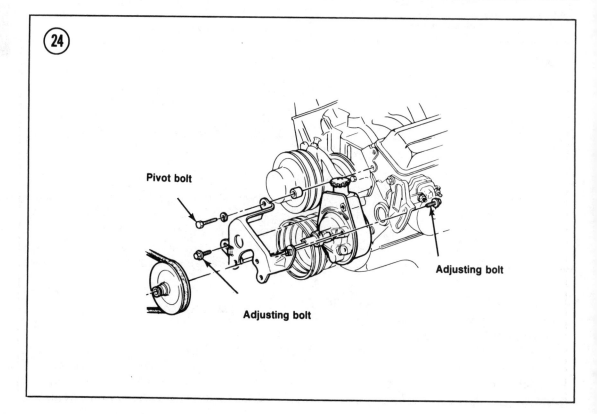

Pivot bolt

Adjusting bolt

Adjusting bolt

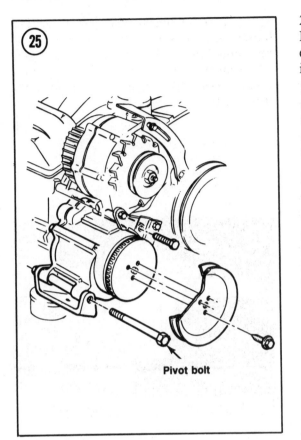

Pivot bolt

2. Repeat Step 1 to remove the Air Injection Reactor (AIR) air pump drive belt, if so equipped. **Figure 25** shows a typical V8 installation; others are similar.

3. Loosen the alternator mounting and adjusting arm bolts. Move the alternator toward the engine. Remove belt(s) from the alternator and crankshaft pulleys and lift them over the fan.

Belt Installation

1. Place belt(s) over fan. Install belt(s) in water pump pulley, crankshaft pulley and alternator pulley grooves. Adjust belt tension as described in this chapter.

2. On cars equipped with power steering, install power steering pump drive belt. Tighten pump at mounting bracket and adjust drive belt.

3. If the AIR pump uses a separate belt, install the belt. Tighten pump at mounting bracket and adjust drive belt tension.

COOLING FAN

Fixed drive fans may mate directly to the water pump hub (**Figure 26**) or use a spacer

7

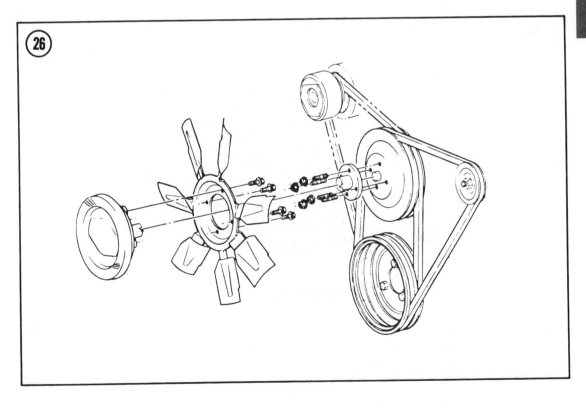

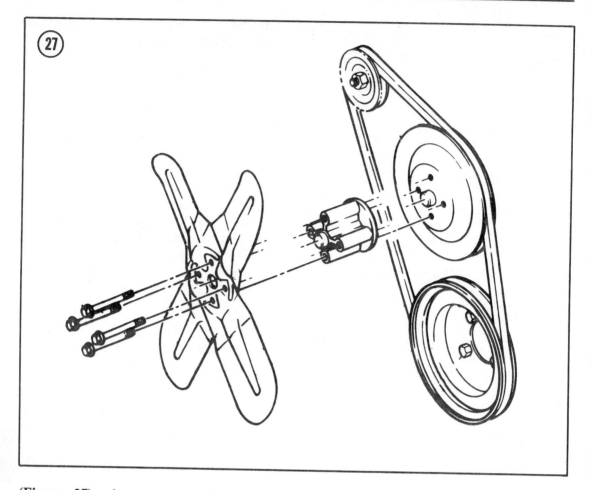

(**Figure 27**). A car equipped with air conditioning or an extra-cooling radiator may use a fan drive clutch (**Figure 28**). This uses a temperature-controlled fluid coupling that permits use of a powerful fan without great power loss or noise. The fan speed is regulated according to the temperature of the air passing through the radiator core.

CAUTION
Bent or damaged fans should not be reused, as any distortion will affect fan balance and operation. Damaged fans cannot be properly repaired and should be replaced.

WARNING
General Motors has indicated that some 1978 Buick, Oldsmobile and Pontiac models covered in this manual may have a defective cooling fan hub which can break under excessive stress conditions. Return the vehicle to a dealer to have the fan hub inspected, if you have not already done so.

Removal/Installation (Fixed Drive Fan)

1. Disconnect the negative battery cable.
2. Loosen the fan belt.
3. Remove the capscrews and lockwashers holding the fan to the water pump hub.
4. Remove the fan and spacer.
5. Installation is the reverse of removal. Tighten capscrews to 20 ft.-lb. (27 N•m). Adjust fan belt as described in this chapter.

Removal/Installation (Fan Drive Clutch)

1. Disconnect the negative battery cable.
2. Remove the upper radiator support and/or upper fan shroud as necessary.

3. Loosen and remove the accessory drive belts.

4. Scribe balance marks on fan clutch and water pump hub for proper alignment during installation.

5. Remove the attaching bolts or nuts holding the fan clutch hub to the water pump hub.

6. Remove the fan clutch assembly.

7. Remove the capscrews and lockwashers holding fan to drive coupling. Separate the fan and coupling.

NOTE
When fan clutch is removed from water pump hub, support it so the clutch disc remains vertical to prevent silicone fluid leakage.

8. Installation is the reverse of removal. Check fan drive clutch flange-to-water pump hub for proper mating. Align balance marks made in Step 4. Tighten attaching bolts or nuts to 20 ft.-lb. (27 N•m). Adjust drive belts as described in this chapter.

RADIATOR REMOVAL/ INSTALLATION

1. Disconnect the negative battery cable.

2. Place a clean container under the radiator. Remove the radiator cap and open the drain valve. Drain the coolant.

3. Remove screws holding radiator upper support or upper shroud, as required.

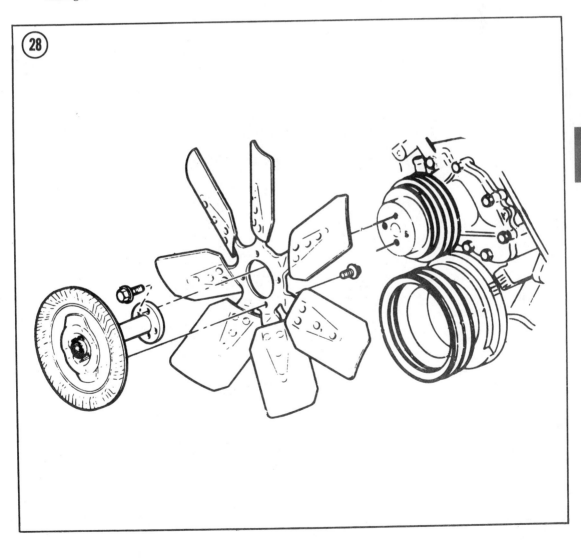

4. On automatic transmission cars, disconnect the transmission cooler lines at the radiator. Plug the lines to prevent fluid leakage.

5. Disconnect the upper and lower radiator hoses at the radiator.

6. Remove the radiator mounting bolts. Remove the radiator.

7. Installation is the reverse of removal. Make sure the radiator is properly seated in its mounting pads. Refill the cooling system. Start engine and run with radiator cap off until upper radiator hose is hot. Add coolant with engine idling until level reaches bottom of filler neck. Install cap and check for leaks. Shut engine off.

Table 1 APPROXIMATE COOLING SYSTEM CAPACITIES

Engine	Year	Quarts
Buick Centurion, Estate Wagon, La Sabre, Riviera		
455	1972-1976	19.5
403	1977-1978	15.5
400	1972-1975	23.5
350 gasoline	1972-1976	17.0
350 gasoline	1977-1980	14.5
350 diesel	1981-on	18.0
305	1978	16.6
301	1977-1978	18.2
301	1979-1980	21.0
252	All	12.0
231	1976-on	13.0
Buick Skylark		
All	1975	13.0
All	1976	14.0
All	1977	11.5
All	1978-1980	12.5
Chevrolet Bel Air, Biscayne, Caprice, Impala		
454	1972-1976	18.0
400	1972-1976	18.0
350	1972-1977	18.0
350	1978-1979	16.5
350 gasoline	1980-1981	16.0
350 diesel	1981-on	18.5
305	1982	15.5
267	1980-1981	16.5
267	1982-on	17.0
262 diesel	1982-on	13.4
250	1977	15.0
250	1978-1979	14.0
231	1980-1981	11.5
231	1982-on	12.0
229	1980-on	14.0
Chevrolet Monza		
305	1977-1979	16.0
262	1975-1976	18.5
231	1980	12.0
200	1978	12.0
196	1978-1979	12.0
151	1978-1980	11.5
140	1975	8.5
140	1976-1977	8.5
(continued)		

Table 1 APPROXIMATE COOLING SYSTEM CAPACITIES (continued)

Engine	Year	Quarts
Oldsmobile 88, Custom Cruiser		
455	1972-1976	21.0
403	1977-1979	15.8
350 gasoline	1972-1976	20.0
350 gasoline	1977-1980	14.5
350 diesel	1980-on	18.0
307	1980-on	15.6
265	1980	19.0
260	1979	16.0
260	1981-on	16.5
231	1975-on	13.0
Oldsmobile Starfire		
All	1975	13.0
All	1976	13.5
140	1977	8.0
151	1978-1980	11.0
231	1977-1980	12.0
305	1977-1980	16.5
Pontiac Bonneville, Catalina, Grande Ville, Parisienne, Safari		
455	1972	18.0
455	1973	21.2
455	1974	19.8
455	1975	18.0
455	1976	22.0
403	1977	16.1
403	1978	17.7
403	1979	16.7
400	1972	19.8
400	1973-1974	21.7
400	1975	18.6
400	1976	21.6
400	1977	19.8
400	1978	20.3
350 gasoline	1972	20.2
350 gasoline	1973-1974	21.9
350 gasoline	1977-1979	16.5
350 diesel	1981-1982	17.0
350 diesel	1983-on	18.3
305	1983-on	15.5
265	1980-1981	19.0
231	1983-on	14.2
Pontiac Sunbird		
305	1978	17.2
305	1979	15.5
231	1977-1980	12.5
151	1977-1978	11.2
151	1979	12.8
151	1980	12.0
140	1977	8.9

7

Table 2 DRIVE BELT TENSION SPECIFICATIONS

| | Tension in lbs. | |
	New Belt	Used Belt[1]
All 4-, 6-cylinder and gasoline V8 (except 231 cid V6)		
Alternator (except 80 amp)	125[2]	75
Alternator (80 amp)	145	100
AIR pump/power steering pump	125[3]	75
Air conditioning compressor	145	65-95
231 cid V6		
Alternator	145	80
Power steering pump, air conditioning compressor	165	100
350 cid diesel		
Alternator, power steering pump, AIR pump (non-air conditioned)	125	70-80
Air conditioning compressor, AIR pump	150	85-95

1. A belt is considered used after one complete revolution on the engine pulleys.
2. 1983-on, 138 lbs.
3. 1983-on, 145 lbs.

BRAKES AND WHEEL BEARINGS

A combination of self-adjusting drum and disc brakes are used on 1972 and later models. Front wheel disc brakes were optional through 1974. They became standard equipment in 1975 on all models.

All models use a Delco-Moraine single piston, sliding caliper disc brake (**Figure 1**) and duo-servo rear drum brakes. Rear drum brakes have a star and screw adjusting mechanism on full-size models (**Figure 2**),

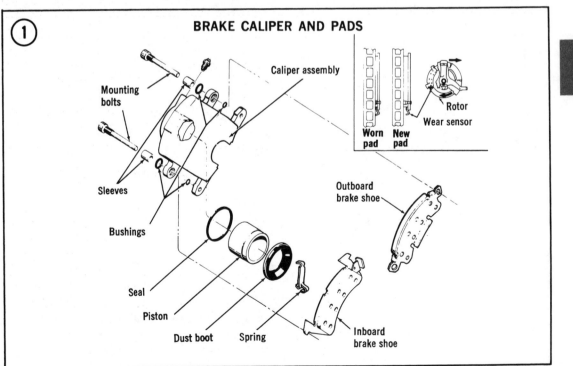

BRAKE CALIPER AND PADS

(1)

Mounting bolts

Caliper assembly

Worn pad   New pad

Rotor

Wear sensor

Sleeves

Outboard brake shoe

Bushings

Seal

Piston

Dust boot   Spring

Inboard brake shoe

8

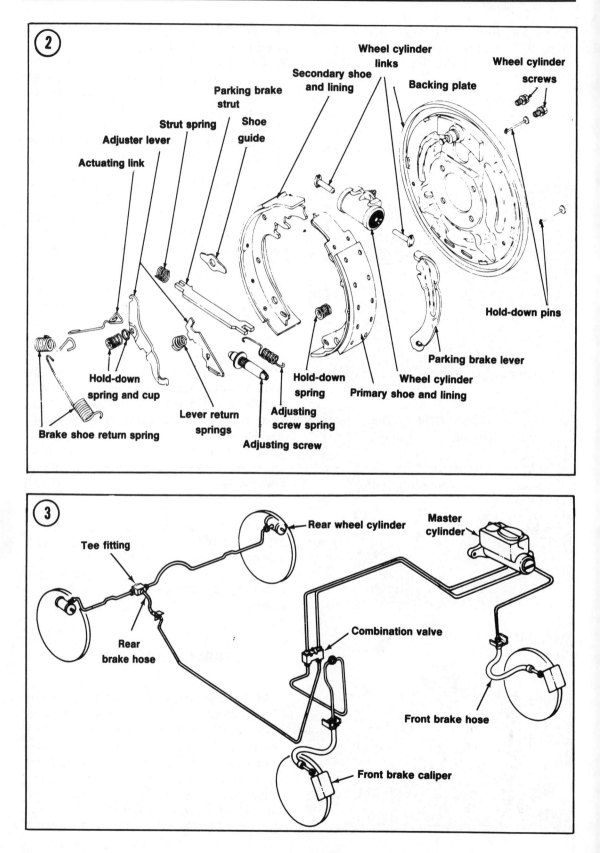

(2)

Wheel cylinder
links

Secondary shoe
and lining

Wheel cylinder
screws

Backing plate

Parking brake
strut

Shoe
guide

Strut spring

Adjuster lever

Actuating link

Hold-down pins

Hold-down
spring and cup

Parking brake lever

Brake shoe return spring

Lever return
springs

Hold-down
spring

Wheel cylinder

Primary shoe and lining

Adjusting
screw spring

Adjusting screw

(3)

Rear wheel cylinder

Master
cylinder

Tee fitting

Combination valve

Rear
brake hose

Front brake hose

Front brake caliper

except for some 1975-1976 Monza and 1976-1977 Starfire models, which use an expanding strut adjuster. Manual adjustment is required only after the brakes are serviced.

A dual hydraulic system (**Figure 3**) is used on all models, one for the front wheels and one for the rear wheels. Both are operated by a dual reservoir master cylinder. **Figure 4**

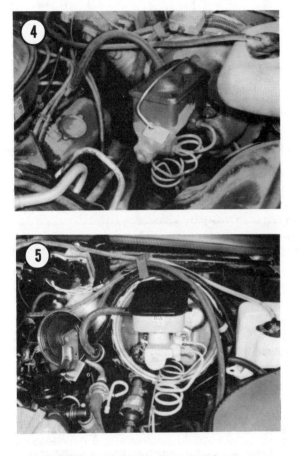

shows the master cylinder used on 1972-1980 gasoline and 1981-on diesel engine vehicles. **Figure 5** shows the master cylinder used on 1981-on gasoline vehicles. The reservoir nearest to the firewall provides brake fluid to the front brakes while the reservoir closest to the radiator supplies fluid to the rear brakes. Should one circuit fail, the other will bring the car safely to a stop.

A combination valve is connected to the master cylinder on all models. **Figure 6** shows a typical design and location. This valve contains a metering section, a proportioning section and a pressure differential section.

The metering section limits pressure to the front brakes until a predetermined pressure limit is obtained. The proportioning section balances braking pressure between the front and rear brakes to minimize rear wheel skidding during hard braking. The pressure differential section contains a brake warning light switch. When this section senses a pressure drop in either of the 2 independent brake systems, it turns the brake warning light on. The light shuts off when the system is serviced, bled and the brake pedal depressed to center the piston. If one of the 2 brake systems fails, a bypass feature sends full pressure to the other system.

An optional power brake booster utilizes engine intake manifold vacuum and atmospheric pressure for its power.

The parking brake is a mechanical type, operating the rear brakes through a cable linkage.

8

BRAKE INSPECTION

At the intervals recommended in Chapter Three, inspect the entire braking system. Check and adjust the parking brake when linings and pads are inspected. Replace linings and pads when worn to within 1/32 in. of the shoe or rivet head, whichever applies. Replace brake shoes and pads in axle sets (right and left sides). Disc brakes are checked by inspecting the outer shoe and lining at both ends of the caliper (**Figure 7**). If premature wear has occurred, check the inner shoes also.

FRONT DISC BRAKE PADS

Before removing the calipers for pad replacement, remove the master cylinder cover and use a large syringe to siphon about 50 percent of the fluid from the rear reservoir. Discard the fluid. This will prevent the master cylinder from overflowing when the caliper piston is compressed for reinstallation. *Do not* drain the entire reservoir or air will enter the system. Recheck the reservoir when the calipers are reinstalled and top up as required with fresh DOT 3 brake fluid. If no hydraulic line is opened, it should not be necessary to bleed the brake system after pad replacement.

NOTE
If pads are to be reused, mark them so they can be reinstalled in the same position. Reused pads must always be installed in the same position from which they were removed.

Removal

Refer to **Figure 1** for this procedure.
1. Set the parking brake. Block the rear wheels.
2. Loosen the wheel lug nuts.
3. Raise the front of the vehicle with a jack and place it on jackstands.
4. Remove the wheel/tire assemblies.
5. Install a 7-in. C-clamp on the caliper with the solid side of the clamp resting on the outer pad (**Figure 8**). Tighten the C-clamp and push the piston back into the caliper bore. Remove the C-clamp.
6. Remove the E-clips and washers from the mounting bolts holding the caliper to the support on Monza, Skyhawk, Starfire and Sunbird models. Remove the mounting bolts on all models. See **Figure 9**.
7. Remove the caliper from the rotor. Remove the inner pad from the caliper.

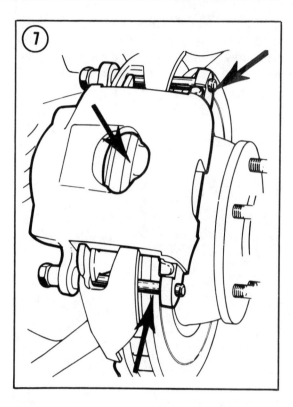

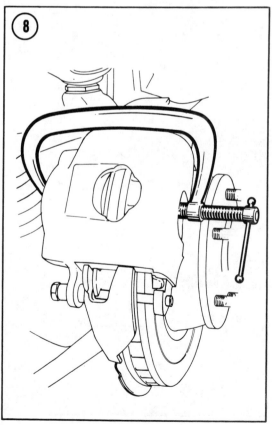

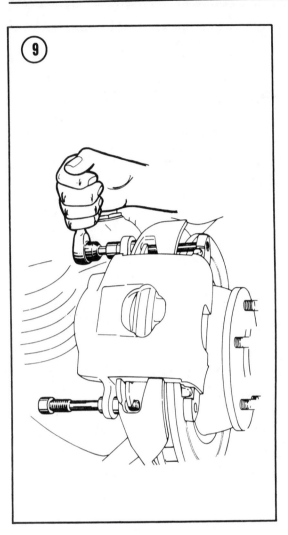

⑨

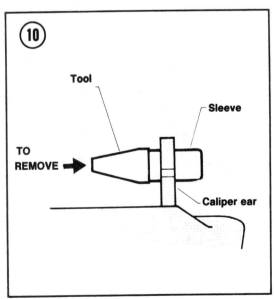

⑩

Tool

Sleeve

TO
REMOVE ➡

Caliper ear

8. Suspend the caliper from the front suspension arm with a length of wire to prevent stressing the brake hose. Remove the outer pad.

9. Use GM tool part No. J-22835 to remove the sleeves from the caliper inner ears (**Figure 10**). Remove the 4 rubber bushings from the caliper ear grooves.

Cleaning and Inspection

1. Inspect lining surfaces for wear. If the lining on either pad is worn to within 1/32 in. of the metal shoe, replace all pads.

2. Check pads for damage caused by overheating. If lining surfaces have been overheated (indicated by blue-tinted areas), replace the pads. Pads must also be replaced if the linings have been contaminated by grease, oil or brake fluid.

WARNING
If pads are replaced on one wheel, they must also be replaced on the other wheel to maintain equal brake action and avoid excessive brake pull.

3. Carefully clean the outside of the caliper. Clean the caliper ear holes and bushing grooves. Look for brake fluid leaks.

4. Check the condition of the dust boot. If the caliper is leaking or the dust boot is deteriorated or damaged, have the caliper overhauled by a dealer or brake shop.

5. Wipe the mounting bolts free of all dirt. Do not use abrasives to clean the bolts, as this will destroy the plating. If the bolts are damaged or corroded, replace with new bolts.

6. Inspect the flexible brake hose attached to the caliper. Replace the brake hose if it is swollen, cracked or leaking.

7. Check rotor condition. If excessively worn or scored, remove hub and have rotor refinished by a dealer or automotive machine shop.

Installation

Refer to **Figure 1** for this procedure.

1. Lubricate new sleeves, new rubber bushings, bushing grooves and mounting bolt

8

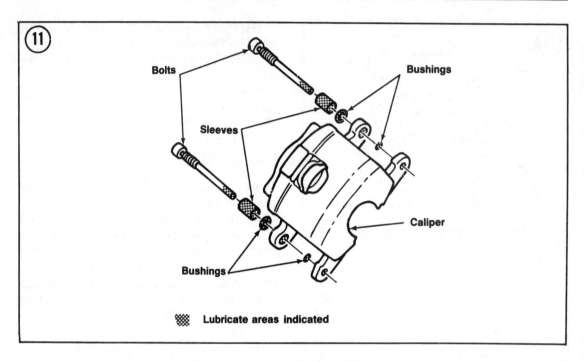

⑪ Bolts   Bushings   Sleeves   Caliper   Bushings

🞙 Lubricate areas indicated

ends with Delco Silicone Lube No. 5459912 or equivalent (**Figure 11**).

> *CAUTION*
> *New sleeves and rubber bushings must be used and lubrication instructions followed to ensure that the calipers function properly.*

2. Install new rubber bushings in all 4 caliper ears.

3. Use GM tool part No. J22835 to install new sleeves. Sleeve end facing pad should be flush with machined surface. See **Figure 12**.

> *NOTE*
> *Step 4 is not necessary on some Monza and Starfire models.*

4. Position single tang end of pad support spring over the notch in the center of the pad. Press 2 tangs at spring end of inner pad over bottom edge of pad. See **Figure 13**.

5. Install inner pad with spring attached in caliper with ear end of pad and lining facing down. See **Figure 14**.

> *CAUTION*
> *There is a specific left and right hand pad. The wear sensor should face the rear of the caliper when the pad is properly installed.*

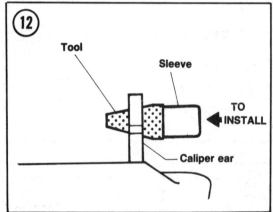

⑫ Tool   Sleeve   TO INSTALL   Caliper ear

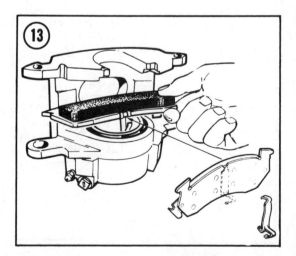

⑬

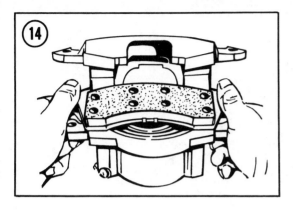

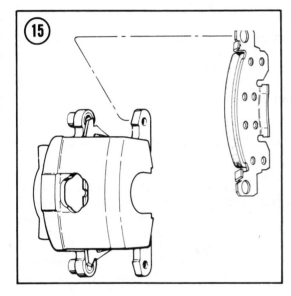

6. Install outer pad in caliper with the ears at the top of the pad over the caliper ears. The tab at the bottom of the pad should fit in the caliper cut-out. See **Figure 15**.

7. Install caliper on rotor with caliper ear holes and mounting bracket holes aligned. Check brake hose to make sure it is not kinked or twisted.

8. Insert mounting bolts through sleeves in inner caliper ears and mounting bracket. Bolt ends must pass under the retaining ear on the inner pad (**Figure 16**).

9. Engage holes in outer pad and caliper ears with mounting bolts. Thread bolts into mounting bracket.

10. On Monza, Skyhawk, Starfire and Sunbird models, install washers (if used) and E-clips. On all other models, torque mounting bolts to 35 ft.-lb. (47 N•m).

11. Add DOT 3 brake fluid to the master cylinder reservoir to bring the fluid level to within 1/8 in. of the top.

12. Pump the brake pedal several times to seat the linings against the rotor.

NOTE
Step 13 is not required on Monza, Skyhawk, Starfire and Sunbird models.

13. Bend upper ears of outer pad with channel lock (arc joint) pliers until no radial

8

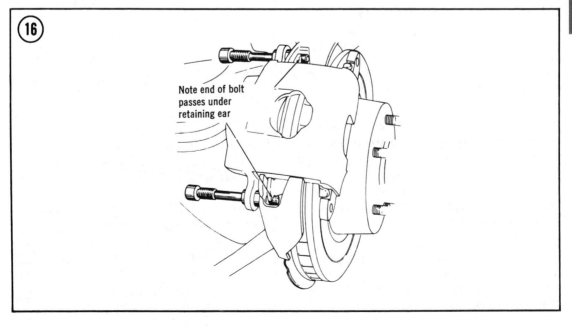

Note end of bolt passes under retaining ear

clearance exists between pad and caliper housing (**Figure 17**). Locate pliers on small notch of caliper housing during bending procedure.

> *NOTE*
> *Repeat Step 13 if radial clearance still*
> *exists after initial clinching.*

14. Install wheel/tire assemblies and lower vehicle to the ground.
15. Pump brake pedal several times to make sure it is firm. Recheck master cylinder fluid level after a firm pedal is achieved.
16. Road test vehicle to check for proper operation.

DISC BRAKE CALIPERS

Removal/Installation

1. Mark the left- and right-hand calipers with chalk or quick-drying paint for correct reinstallation.
2. Remove the caliper as described under *Front Disc Brake Pads* in this chapter.
3. Disconnect the flexible brake hose at the brake pipe fitting. Remove U-clip from bracket. Remove hose from bracket.

4. Remove bolt from caliper end of hose. Remove hose from caliper. Discard 2 copper gaskets on either side of fitting.
5. Installation is the reverse of removal. Install new copper gaskets. Wet bolt threads with brake fluid before installing in fitting. Check to make sure hose does not touch any part of the suspension, especially during extreme turn conditions. Bleed the brakes as described in this chapter.

BRAKE ROTORS

Inspection

1. Loosen the front wheel lug nuts.
2. Raise the front of the vehicle with a jack and place it on jackstands.
3. Remove the wheel/tire assemblies.
4. Check front wheel bearing adjustment as described in this chapter. Adjust if necessary.
5. Remove the caliper as described in this chapter, but do not disconnect the brake line. Suspend the caliper from the suspension with a length of wire to prevent stressing the line.
6. Inspect rotor for deep scratches. Small marks are not important, but deep radial scratches reduce brake effectiveness and increase lining wear. If deeply scratched, have

the rotor turned on a lathe to smooth the surface.

NOTE
Minimum rotor thickness after refinishing must not be less than the number cast on the inside of the rotor.

7. Install a dial indicator as shown in **Figure 18** and move the rotor one full turn to measure lateral runout. If runout exceeds 0.004 in. (0.10 mm), have the rotor turned or replace it.

Removal

1. Loosen the front wheel lug nuts.
2. Raise the front of the car and place it on jackstands.
3. Remove the wheel/tire assemblies.
4. Remove the caliper as described in this chapter, but do not disconnect the brake line. Suspend the caliper from the suspension with

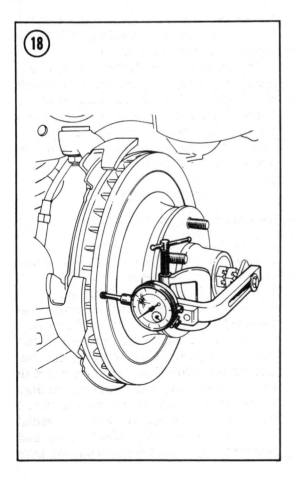

a length of wire to prevent stressing the brake hose.
5. Remove the grease cap, cotter pin and spindle nut.
6. Grasp the rotor in both hands and pull it off the spindle far enough to loosen the wheel bearing washer and outer wheel bearing.
7. Push the rotor back onto the spindle and take washer and outer wheel bearing off.
8. Pull the rotor/hub off the spindle, together with inner wheel bearing and grease seal.

Installation

1. If a new rotor is being installed, remove protective coating with carburetor degreaser. Install new wheel bearings as described under *Wheel Bearing Replacement* in this chapter.
2. If original rotor is being installed, pack wheel bearings with grease. The wheel bearing and grease seal must be in good condition. Keep braking surface of rotor clean.

CAUTION
Keep rotor centered on spindle to prevent damage to grease seal or spindle threads.

3. Install outer wheel bearing and washer. Install wheel bearing adjusting nut and tighten finger-tight. Make sure rotor rotates freely.
4. Install caliper as described in this chapter.
5. Adjust wheel bearings as described in this chapter.
6. Install wheel/tire assemblies. Lower vehicle to the ground and tighten lug nuts.

DRUM BRAKES

Drum Removal

1. Set the parking brake. Block the front or rear wheels as required.
2. Loosen the wheel lug nuts.
3. Raise the rear of the vehicle with a jack and place it on jackstands.
4. Remove the wheel/tire assemblies.
5. Remove the cover from the access slot in the rear of the backing plate.
6. Insert a brake adjustment tool through the hole and rotate adjusting screw upward.

8

NOTE
Some models may have an access slot in the drum instead of the backing plate. Rotate the adjusting screw downward on such models to permit drum removal.

7. Mark the drum so it can be reinstalled in the same position. Remove Tinnerman nuts, if used. Remove the drum.

Brake Shoe Removal

Brake linings worn to within 1/32 in. of a rivet on a riveted lining or the shoe on a bonded lining must be replaced. Brake linings contaminated by grease, oil or brake fluid must also be replaced. Replace linings on both wheels at the same time. Refer to **Figure 19** (front) or **Figure 20** (rear).

WARNING
Do not clean brake assembly with compressed air. Brake linings contain asbestos and the dust can be hazardous to your health. Clean assembly with a vacuum cleaner or use an old paint brush and wear a painter's mask over your nose and mouth.

1. Use a brake tool or large screwdriver to unhook the primary and secondary shoe return springs. See **Figure 21**.

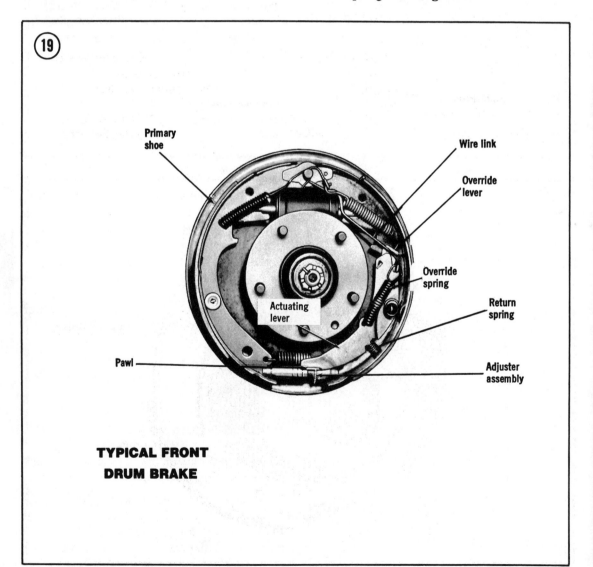

(19)

Primary shoe

Wire link

Override lever

Override spring

Actuating lever

Return spring

Pawl

Adjuster assembly

**TYPICAL FRONT
DRUM BRAKE**

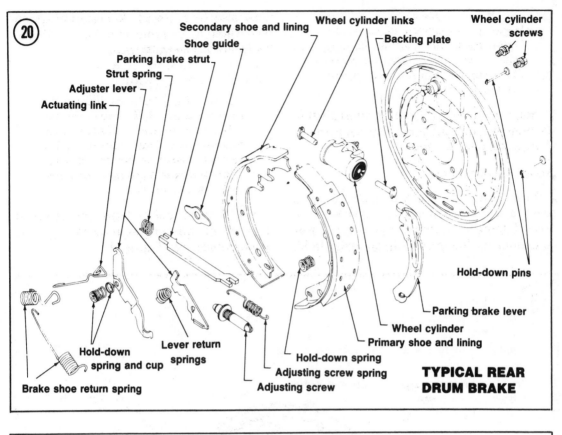

Secondary shoe and lining
Shoe guide
Parking brake strut
Strut spring
Adjuster lever
Actuating link
Wheel cylinder links
Backing plate
Wheel cylinder screws
Hold-down pins
Parking brake lever
Wheel cylinder
Primary shoe and lining
Hold-down spring and cup
Lever return springs
Brake shoe return spring
Hold-down spring
Adjusting screw spring
Adjusting screw

TYPICAL REAR DRUM BRAKE

8

2. Grasp the hold-down pin at the rear of the backing plate. Rotate the hold-down spring 90° with the brake tool or pliers. See **Figure 22**. Remove the hold-down spring and repeat procedure on other side.

3. Lift up on the actuator and unhook the actuator link from the anchor pin. Remove the actuator return spring, link and actuator assembly.

NOTE
Actuator, pivot and override spring are an assembly and should not be disassembled unless it is necessary to replace a broken part.

4. Expand shoes to remove from wheel cylinder connecting links.

5. On rear brakes, remove parking brake strut and spring, disconnect cable from parking brake lever and remove shoes from backing plate.

6. Remove adjusting screw and lock spring. Separate shoes.

7. On rear brakes, remove parking brake lever from secondary brake shoe.

Inspection

1. Clean all dirt from brake drum (avoid getting dirt into wheel bearings) and inspect for roughness, scoring or out-of-round condition.

2. If measuring equipment is not available, take all drums to a dealer, automotive machine shop or brake shop. Have them checked and turned on a lathe, if required. Brake drums that are more than 0.006 in. (0.152 mm) out-of-round must be reconditioned or replaced. If the drum is greater than the maximum wear diameter cast into it after refinishing, replace the drum.

3. Check the drum carefully for cracks and replace if any are found.

WARNING
Under no circumstances should a cracked brake drum be reused. Do not attempt to weld a cracked drum, as welding heat will cause deformation. Use of a cracked or deformed brake drum could result in brake failure, which could result in injury or loss of life.

4. Remove and inspect wheel bearings and grease seals. Replace parts as required. Repack and install bearings with new seals.

5. On wheel cylinders with external rubber boots, carefully pull lower edges of boot away from cylinders and check to see if interior is

wet with brake fluid. If excessive fluid is present, replace cylinder.

NOTE
Brake fluid on the piston inside the cylinder and on the end of the link pin removed from the boot is normal. The cylinder contains a porous piston impregnated with a corrosion inhibiting fluid.

6. On wheel cylinders with internal boots, carefully pull a small part of boot from the cylinder and inspect as in Step 5, observing the NOTE.
7. Check backing plate for oil leaking past the wheel bearing seals. If present, have a dealer install new oil seals.
8. Check backing plate attaching bolts for tightness.
9. Clean all rust and dirt from the backing plate shoe contact surfaces with fine emery or crocus cloth. Wipe all dust off with a solvent-moistened cloth.

Wheel Cylinder Removal/Installation

1. Remove brake drums and shoes as described in this chapter.
2. Clean all dirt and contamination from brake line fitting. Disconnect brake line and cover end of line with a clean, lint-free cloth to prevent contamination from entering hydraulic system.
3. Remove screws holding wheel cylinder to backing plate. Remove wheel cylinder.

CAUTION
Do not bend rear brake line away from wheel cylinder after unscrewing the nut. Bending the brake line will make it difficult to reconnect and may cause it to crack. The wheel cylinder will separate from brake line when it is lifted out.

4. Installation is the reverse of removal. Wipe ends of brake lines and hoses clean before reconnecting. Bleed brakes and center combination valve as described in this chapter.

Brake Shoe Installation

Refer to **Figure 19** (front) or **Figure 20** (rear) for this procedure.

1. On rear brakes, lubricate fulcrum end of parking brake lever with Delco brake lubricant or equivalent. Connect lever to secondary brake shoe. Make sure it moves freely.

NOTE
Install right-hand thread adjusting screw on left-hand side of vehicle and left-hand thread screw on right-hand side of vehicle.

2. Install adjusting screw spring to connect brake shoes and place adjusting screw in position. Spring should not touch starwheel. Make sure starwheel aligns with access slot in backing plate.
3. Lubricate all shoe contact points on backing plate with Delco brake lubricant or equivalent. See **Figure 23**.
4. Install brake shoes on backing plate and engage shoe ends with wheel cylinder links.
5. On rear brakes, connect parking brake cable to parking brake lever. Install strut and spring between primary shoe and lever.

NOTE
On full-size vehicles covered in this manual, the strut spring installs between the secondary shoe and lever on the right-hand side.

6. Install actuator assembly. Install guide pin over anchor pin and install wire link.

CAUTION
To avoid damage, fasten wire link to actuator assembly first and place other end over anchor pin stud by hand (do not use tool) while holding adjuster assembly in full down position.

7. Grasp guide pin at rear of backing plate and hold while installing hold-down spring. Rotate spring 90°. Install the other hold-down spring.
8. Install actuator return spring by easing it into place with a screwdriver or other suitable flat tool. Do not pry on actuator lever to install spring.
9. Install the primary and secondary shoe return springs with a brake tool or large pliers.

10. Make sure actuator lever works easily by hand-operating the self-adjusting feature (**Figure 24**).

11. Repeat Steps 1-10 on other side.

12. If wheel cylinders were removed, bleed hydraulic lines as described in this chapter.

13. Adjust service and parking brakes as described in this chapter.

14. Install drums and wheels. Lower vehicle to the ground. Pump the pedal several times and road test the car to make sure the brakes work properly.

Drum Installation

1. If a new drum is to be installed, remove protective coating with carburetor degreaser.

2. Place drum over brake assembly and into place. Adjust brakes as described in this chapter.

3. Install Tinnerman nuts (if used) and tighten securely.

4. Install wheel/tire assembly. Tighten lug nuts. Adjust brakes as described in this chapter.

BRAKE ADJUSTMENT

Disc Brakes

Disc brakes are automatically adjusted. No adjustment procedure is necessary or provided.

Drum Brakes

Drum brakes are self-adjusting during vehicle operation. Manual adjustment is necessary only after brakes have been serviced.

1. Disengage the actuator from the starwheel and rotate starwheel manually.

2. Rotate starwheel until brake drum will slide over the brake linings and rotate with only a slight drag.

3. Retract linings by rotating starwheel an additional 1 1/4 turns.

4. Install drum. Mark made in Step 7 of *Drum Removal* should be aligned to return drum to its original position.

5. Drive the car, making numerous forward and reverse stops to make the final

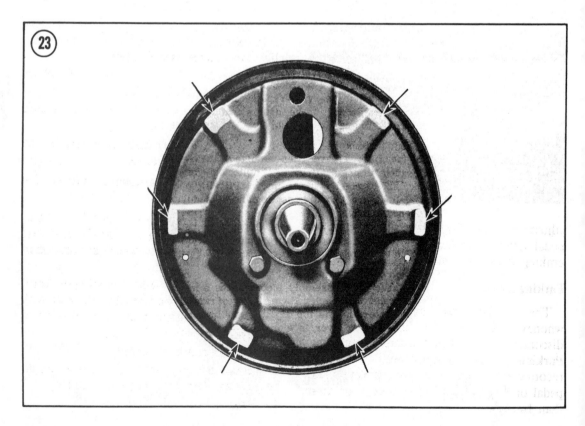

(23)

adjustment. Use firm pressure on the brake pedal until a satisfactory pedal height and braking action are obtained.

Parking Brake

The parking brake should be adjusted whenever the rear brake cables have been disconnected or when the cables are loose. Parking brake adjustment is also recommended whenever the parking brake pedal or lever travel is less than 9 or more than 16 clicks.

1. Fully release parking brake.

2. Pull parking brake handle or depress parking brake pedal exactly one notch/ratchet click from its released position.

3. Block the front wheels and place transmission in NEUTRAL.

4. Raise the rear of the vehicle with a jack and place it on jackstands.

5. Remove the driveshaft, if necessary, to gain access to the equalizer.

6. Loosen equalizer locknut (**Figure 25**, typical).

7A. Monza, Skyhawk, Starfire and Starbird–turn adjusting nut until a moderate drag is felt when the rear wheels are rotated in a forward direction.

7A. Full-size models–turn adjusting nut until left rear wheel can be turned to the rear with 2 hands, but is locked when forward rotation is attempted.

8. Tighten equalizer locknut.

9. Release parking brake fully. There should be no drag when the wheels are rotated.

10. Reinstall driveshaft, if removed.

8

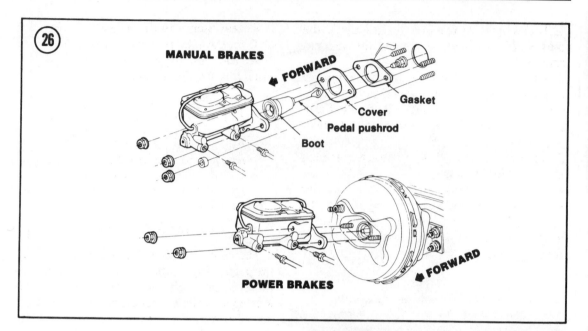

MANUAL BRAKES

FORWARD

Gasket

Cover

Pedal pushrod

Boot

POWER BRAKES

FORWARD

MASTER CYLINDER

Removal/Installation

Refer to **Figure 26** for this procedure.

1. Manual brakes–Disconnect brake pedal from master cylinder pushrod.

2. Disconnect primary and secondary brake lines from master cylinder (**Figure 27**).

> *CAUTION*
> *Brake fluid will damage paint. Place rags beneath master cylinder. If any brake fluid spills onto paint, wipe fluid off, then wash with soapy water.*

3. Remove master cylinder attaching nuts or bolts (**Figure 26**). Remove master cylinder.

4. Installation is the reverse of removal. Tighten master cylinder retaining bolts/nuts to 24 ft.-lb. (32 N•m) and brake line fittings to 150 in.-lb. (17 N•m). Fill master cylinder reservoirs to within 1/4 in. of reservoir tops with clean DOT 3 brake fluid. Bleed brakes and center pressure differential valve as described in this chapter. Depress brake pedal several times, then check master cylinder for brake fluid leaks.

BRAKE SYSTEM BLEEDING

The hydraulic system should be bled whenever air is suspected of entering it or

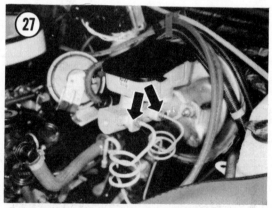

when braking effectiveness is reduced. If the pedal feels soft or if pedal travel increases considerably, bleeding is usually called for. Bleeding is also necessary whenever a hydraulic line is disconnected or the braking system serviced.

Because this procedure requires handling of brake fluid, be careful not to contaminate brake pads, shoes, rotors or drums with fluid. Clean all dirt from bleeder screws before beginning. Two people are required to bleed the system–one to operate the brake pedal and the other to open and close the bleed valves.

Bleeding should be conducted in the following order: right rear, left rear, right front, left front.

1. If equipped with power brakes, apply the brakes several times to exhaust the vacuum reserve.

2. Clean away all dirt around the master cylinder. Remove the cover and top up reservoirs with clean DOT 3 brake fluid. Leave the top off the reservoirs and cover with a clean shop cloth.

3. Fit an appropriate size box-end wrench over the bleeder screw.

4. Connect a rubber hose to the bleeder screw. Be sure the hose fits snugly on the screw. Submerge the other end of the hose in a container partially filled with clean brake fluid. See **Figure 28**.

NOTE
Do not allow the end of the hose to come out of the brake fluid during bleeding. This could allow air to enter the system and require that the bleeding procedure be done over.

5. Open the bleeder screw about 3/4 turn and have an assistant depress the brake pedal slowly to the floor. When the pedal reaches the floor, close the bleeder screw. After the screw is closed, have the assistant release the pedal slowly.

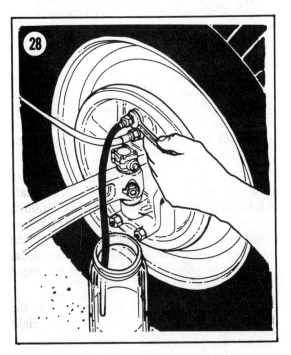

6. Repeat Step 5 until the fluid entering the jar from the tube is free of air bubbles.

7. Repeat this procedure at each of the remaining bleeder screws.

NOTE
Keep the master cylinder reservoir fluid level at least one-half full throughout the bleeding procedure. If either reservoir is allowed to empty, air will be sucked into the hydraulic system and the bleeding procedure must be repeated.

COMBINATION VALVE

The combination valve contains metering, proportioning and pressure differential/warning light sections. The valve is located near the master cylinder on the fender apron. If hydraulic pressure drops severely in either the front or rear brake system, the pressure differential section activates the brake warning switch. This switch then activates the warning light on the instrument panel.

The combination valve is serviced by replacement only. If any function of the valve fails, the entire valve must be replaced.

The pressure differential section valve must be centered whenever the brakes are bled. To do so, turn the ignition switch to the ACC or ON position, but do not start the engine. Press the brake pedal firmly until the warning light goes out (if it was illuminated). Turn the ignition switch OFF. Check brake operation to make sure a firm pedal is obtained.

POWER BRAKE UNIT

The power brake unit uses intake manifold vacuum and atmospheric pressure to reduce braking effort. The unit is repairable, but requires special tools and experience. If it does not operate properly, have the unit serviced by a dealer or brake shop.

Testing

1. Check the brake system for hydraulic leaks. Make sure the master cylinder reservoirs are filled to within 1/4 in. of the top.

2. Start the engine and let it idle for about 2 minutes, then shut it off. Place the transmission in NEUTRAL and set the parking brake.

3. Depress the brake pedal several times to exhaust any vacuum remaining in the system.

4. When the vacuum is exhausted, depress and hold the pedal. Start the engine. If the pedal does not start to fall away under foot pressure (requiring less pressure to hold it in place), the power brake unit is not working properly.

5. Disconnect the vacuum line at the unit (**Figure 29**). If vacuum can be felt at the line with the engine running, reconnect it and repeat Step 4. If the brake pedal does not move downward, have the power brake unit serviced by a dealer or brake shop.

6. Run the engine for at least 10 minutes at fast idle. Shut the engine off and let it stand for 10 minutes. Depress the brake pedal with about 20 lb. of force. If the pedal feel is not the same as it was with the engine running, have the power brake unit serviced by a dealer or brake shop.

Removal/Installation

1. Disconnect the negative battery cable.

2. Remove 2 nuts holding master cylinder to power brake unit and move it to one side without disconnecting any hydraulic lines.

3. Disconnect the manifold vacuum hose from the vacuum check valve located on the front of the power unit housing. See **Figure 29**. Cover hose with a clean cloth to prevent contaminants from entering.

4. Loosen the 4 nuts holding the power unit to the cowl.

5. Working inside the driver's compartment, disconnect the power brake pushrod from the brake pedal. Do not force pushrod to the side when disconnecting.

6. Remove the 4 nuts holding the power unit to the cowl.

7. Working inside the engine compartment, pull the booster forward until its studs clear the firewall. Rotate booster toward engine and remove from engine compartment. Remove gaskets, if used.

8. Installation is the reverse of removal. Install new gaskets, if they were used. Bleed brakes as described in this chapter, then road test the car.

WHEEL BEARINGS

Each front wheel and tire assembly is bolted to its respective rotor/hub or brake drum. A grease retainer is installed at the inner end of the hub to prevent lubricant from leaking into the drum or onto the rotor. The entire assembly is retained to its spindle by the adjusting nut, nut lock and cotter pin.

Wheel bearings should be repacked with grease each time the brakes are relined. New wheel bearings must be installed when drums are replaced.

The rear brake drum assembly is retained to studs on the rear axle shaft flange by 3 Tinnerman nuts. The wheel and tire assembly mounts on the same rear axle shaft flange studs and is held against the drum by the wheel lug nuts.

The rear wheel bearing is pressed onto the axle shaft just inside the shaft flange. The entire assembly is secured to the rear axle housing by the bearing retainer plate which is bolted to the housing flange. The inner end of each axle shaft is splined to the differential in the rear axle.

Replacement/Repacking (Drum Brake)

If bearing adjustment will not eliminate looseness or rough, noisy operation, the hub and bearings should be cleaned, inspected and

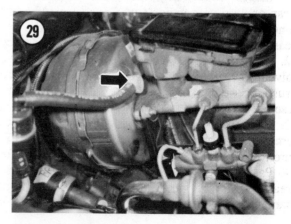

repacked. If bearing cups or cone and roller assemblies are worn or damaged, they should be replaced.

1. Raise the vehicle with a jack and place it on jackstands.

2. Insert a narrow screwdriver through the brake adjusting hole at the inner side of the brake backing plate. Disengage adjusting lever from adjusting screw. Back off adjusting screw with brake adjusting tool.

CAUTION
Be careful not to damage adjusting screw notches or the self-adjusting mechanism will not function properly.

3. Remove wheel cover or hub cap.

4. Remove dust cap from hub.

5. Remove cotter pin, spindle nut and flat washer from spindle.

6. Remove outer bearing cone and roller assembly.

7. Pull wheel/drum assembly off wheel spindle.

8. Remove grease retainer and inner bearing cone and roller assembly from hub with a drift.

9. Clean lubricant off inner and outer bearing cups with solvent and inspect cups for scratches, pits, excessive wear and other damage. If cups are worn or damaged, remove with a drift.

10. Soak new grease retainer in light engine oil at least 30 minutes before installation. Clean inner and outer bearing cones with solvent and dry thoroughly. Do not spin bearings with compressed air.

11. Inspect cone and roller assemblies for wear or damage and replace if necessary. If cone and roller assemblies are replaced, new bearing cups should be installed.

12. Clean spindle and inside of hub with solvent. Cover spindle with a clean cloth and brush loose dust and dirt from brake assembly.

13. If inner or outer bearing cups were removed, install replacement cups in hub. Be sure to seat cups properly in hub.

14. Pack inside of hub with wheel bearing grease until grease is flush with inside diameter of both bearing cups.

15. Clean all old grease from bearings. Repack bearing cone and roller assemblies with wheel bearing grease. If a bearing packer is not available, work as much lubricant as possible between rollers and cages. Lubricate cone surfaces with grease.

16. Place inner bearing cone and roller assembly in the inner cup and install new grease retainer. Be sure retainer is properly seated.

17. Install wheel/drum assembly on wheel spindle. Keep hub centered on spindle to prevent damage to the grease retainer or spindle threads.

18. Install outer bearing cone and roller assembly and flat washer on spindle, then install spindle nut.

19. Adjust wheel bearings as described in this chapter and install a new cotter pin. Bend ends of cotter pin around the spindle nut to prevent interference with the dust cap. Install dust cap.

20. If brake shoes were backed off to remove drum, adjust the brakes as described in this chapter.

Replacement/Repacking (Disc Brakes)

Refer to **Figure 30** for this procedure.

1. Raise the vehicle with a jack and place it on jackstands.

2. Remove wheel cover or hub cap.

3. Remove wheel/tire assembly.

4. Remove caliper as described in this chapter and suspend it from the suspension with a length of wire to prevent stressing the brake hose.

5. Remove dust cap from hub. Remove cotter pin, spindle nut and flat washer from spindle. Remove outer bearing cone and roller assembly.

6. Pull hub and rotor off wheel spindle.

7. Remove grease retainer and inner bearing cone and roller assembly from hub.

8. Clean lubricant from inner and outer bearing cups with solvent and inspect cups for scratches, pits, excessive wear and other damage. If cups are worn or damaged, remove with a drift.

8

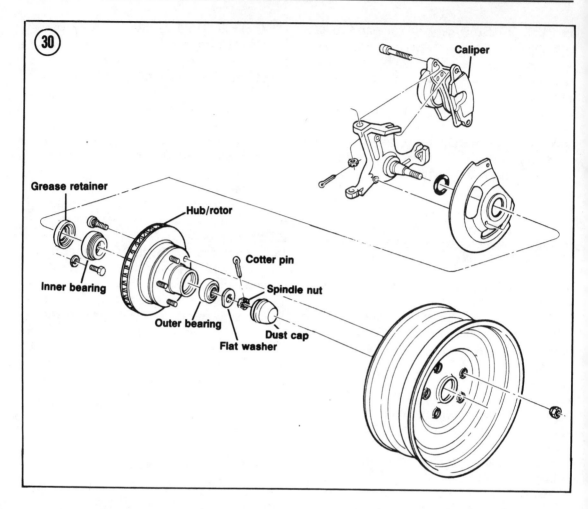

9. Soak new grease retainer in light engine oil at least 30 minutes before installation. Clean inner and outer bearing cones and rollers with solvent and dry thoroughly. Do not spin the bearings with compressed air.

10. Inspect cone and roller assemblies for wear or damage and replace if necessary. If cone and roller assemblies are replaced, new bearing cups should be installed.

11. Clean spindle and inside of rotor with solvent. Cover spindle with a clean cloth and brush loose dust and dirt from brake assembly.

12. If inner or outer bearing cups were removed, install replacement cups in the rotor. Be sure to seat cups properly in the rotor.

13. Pack inside of rotor with wheel bearing grease until grease is flush with inside diameter of both bearing cups.

14. Clean old grease from bearings. Pack bearing cone and roller assemblies with clean wheel bearing grease. If a bearing packer is unavailable, work as much lubricant as possible between rollers and cages. Lubricate cone surfaces with grease.

15. Place inner bearing cone and roller assembly in inner cup and install new grease retainer. Make sure retainer is properly seated.

16. Install hub and rotor on wheel spindle. Keep rotor centered on spindle to prevent damage to grease retainer or spindle threads.

17. Install outer bearing cone and roller assembly and flat washer on spindle, then install spindle nut.

18. Install caliper as described in this chapter.

19. Install wheel/tire assembly.

20. Adjust wheel bearings as described in this chapter and install a new cotter pin. Bend ends of cotter pin around spindle nut to prevent interference with dust cap. Install dust cap.

21. Install wheel cover or hub cap and lower vehicle to the ground. Pump the brake pedal several times to relocate the brake pads.

Adjustment (Front)

The front wheel bearing should be adjusted if the wheel is too loose on the spindle or if the wheel does not rotate freely.

1. Raise the vehicle with a jack and place it on jackstands.

2. Pry off wheel cover/hub cap and remove dust cap from hub.

3. Wipe excess grease from end of spindle. Remove and discard cotter pin.

4. Tighten spindle nut to 12 ft.-lb. (16 N•m) while rotating wheel assembly forward by hand to fully seat bearings. This removes any grease or burrs which could cause excessive wheel play.

5. Back off spindle nut to a "just loose" position.

6. Hand-tighten spindle nut, then back off until either hole in spindle aligns with any slot in nut (not more than 1/2 flat).

7. Install new cotter pin and bend ends of pin against spindle nut. Cut off extra length to avoid interference with dust cap.

8. Measure looseness in the hub assembly with a flat feeler gauge. End play should be 0.001-0.005 in. when properly adjusted. If it is not, repeat the procedure.

9. Check wheel rotation. If wheel rotates easily, install dust cap and hub cap/wheel cover. If wheel rotates roughly or noisily, clean or replace bearings and cups as necessary.

10. Pump the brake pedal several times to relocate the brake pads or linings.

8

CHAPTER NINE

CLUTCH

Proper clutch adjustment on models can add considerable length to the clutch's useful lifespan. All models except Monza, Skyhawk, Starfire and Sunbird use a linkage system. Monza, Skyhawk, Starfire and Sunbird use a cable system.

SLIPPAGE TEST (LINKAGE SYSTEM)

There is one linkage adjustment to compensate for all normal clutch wear. The clutch should have a specified amount of free travel before the throwout bearing engages the clutch diaphragm spring levers. Lash is required to prevent clutch slippage which would occur if the bearing was held against the fingers and to prevent the bearing from running continually until failure.

A clutch that was slipping before adjustment may still slip after adjustment because of prior heat damage. Allow the clutch to cool for at least 12 hours, then check for slippage as follows:

1. Drive in high gear at 20-25 miles per hour.
2. Depress clutch pedal to the floor and accelerate engine speed to about 3,000 rpm.
3. Snap foot off clutch pedal and at the same time, depress throttle pedal to floor. Engine speed should drop and then accelerate. If the clutch is bad, engine speed will increase before the vehicle accelerates.

NOTE
The clutch will overheat if this test is performed more than once in a 12-hour period.

LINKAGE INSPECTION

Several factors affect clutch performance. Check the clutch linkage to make sure that the clutch releases fully. This will help determine if the trouble is actually in the clutch.

1. With engine running, depress and hold clutch pedal about 1/2 in. from the floor mat. Move the shift lever between FIRST and REVERSE gears several times. If the clutch is releasing fully, this can be done smoothly.
2. Check pedal bushings for excessive wear or sticking.
3. Check for proper installation of clutch fork on ball stud. The fork can be pulled off the ball if lubrication is insufficient.
4. Check the cross shaft levers and support bracket for bending, cracking or damage.
5. Check clearance between cross shaft and engine mounts. If engine mounts are loose or damaged, the engine may shift its position

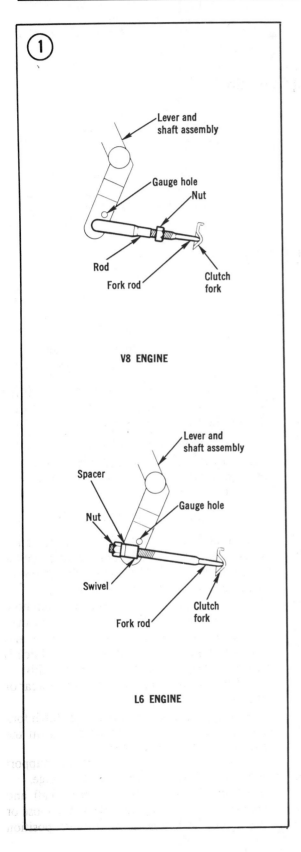

V8 ENGINE

L6 ENGINE

and cause the clutch linkage to bind at the cross shaft.

6. Check the throwout bearing clearance between the spring fingers and front bearing retainer on transmission. If there is no clearance, the fork may be improperly installed on the ball stud or the clutch disc may be worn.

LINKAGE ADJUSTMENT

Refer to **Figure 1** for this procedure.

1. Set the parking brake and block the rear wheels.
2. Raise the front of the car with a jack and place it on jackstands.
3. Disconnect the return spring at the clutch fork.
4. Raise the clutch lever and shaft assembly until the clutch pedal rests against the rubber bumper and dash brace.
5. Move outer end of clutch fork to the rear until the throwout bearing just contacts the pressure plate fingers.
6. Install the pushrod in the gauge hole and adjust length until all lash is removed from the linkage.
7. Remove the rod from the gauge hole and reinstall in the lower hole in the lever. Install retainer and tighten locknut. Be careful not to change the rod length.
8. Reinstall return spring and check pedal free travel. It should be 1 1/8-1 3/4 in. If not, repeat procedure.

SLIPPAGE TEST
(CABLE SYSTEM)

1. Check for loose or worn swivels or mounting bracket deflection.
2. With engine running, place transmission in NEUTRAL and engage clutch.
3. Disengage clutch, wait approximately 9 seconds and then shift the transmission to REVERSE. If the shift is smooth, the clutch is satisfactory. Any grinding noise indicates incorrect clutch adjustment, slippage, a misaligned clutch or internal problems.

CABLE ADJUSTMENT

Refer to **Figure 2** for this procedure.

1. Set the parking brake and block the rear wheels.
2. Raise the front of the car with a jack and place it on jackstands.
3. Disconnect the clutch return spring from the frame crossmember and remove the spring from the clutch fork.
4. Loosen the pin on the threaded end of the clutch cable (attached to the clutch fork) and pull on the cable until the clutch pedal is firmly snugged against the rubber bumper.
3. With the clutch pedal in this position, press the clutch fork forward until the throwout bearing is in contact with the clutch spring fingers.
4. Tighten the pin on the threaded end of the clutch cable until it comes in contact with the clutch fork surface. Tighten the pin 1/4 turn more and seat pin in clutch fork groove.
5. Install return spring and check clutch pedal free play. If not 0.65-1.15 in., repeat procedure.

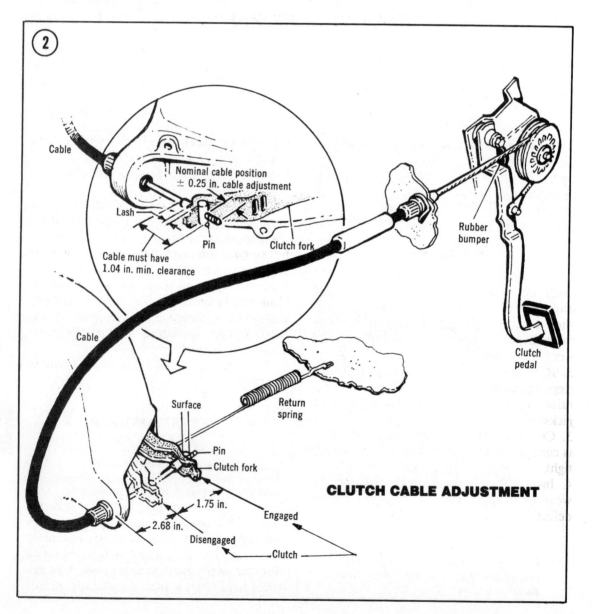

②

Cable

Nominal cable position ± 0.25 in. cable adjustment

Lash

Pin

Clutch fork

Cable must have 1.04 in. min. clearance

Rubber bumper

Cable

Clutch pedal

Surface

Return spring

Pin

Clutch fork

1.75 in.

2.68 in.

Engaged

Disengaged

Clutch

CLUTCH CABLE ADJUSTMENT

SHOCK ABSORBERS

Replacing shock absorbers is a relatively simple task. Although installation will vary slightly on different models, no special techniques or tools are required and the procedures in this chapter can be readily adapted to all models.

INSPECTION

1. To check the general condition of the shock absorbers, bounce the vehicle up and down several times and release. The car should not continue to bounce more than twice. Excessive bouncing is an indication of worn shock absorbers.
2. Raise the car on a hoist for the following steps if possible. If a hoist is not available, raise the car with a jack and place it on jackstands.
3. Check each shock absorber to make sure it is correctly installed and that all fasteners are tight.
4. Inspect the shock absorber insulators for wear or damage. Replace any that appear defective.

NOTE
If a defective insulator is an integral part of the shock absorber, replace the shock absorber.

5. Check the shock absorber for signs of fluid leakage. A light film of fluid is normal and does not mean the shock absorber should be replaced.
6. Disconnect the lower end of the shock absorber. Extend and compress the shock absorber as quickly as possible. Travel should be smooth on each stroke, with greater resistance on extension than on compression.
7. If the action of both front or rear shock absorbers is similar in Step 6, it is unlikely that either is defective. If one front or rear shock absorber is more erratic than the other, it is probably weak or defective.
8. Reconnect all shock absorbers and tighten fasteners.

FRONT SHOCK ABSORBERS

Removal/Installation

Refer to **Figure 1** for this procedure.
1. Loosen the front wheel lug nuts. Raise the front of the car with a jack and place it on jackstands. Remove the wheel/tire assembly.
2. Use an open-end wrench to hold the shock absorber upper stem from turning. Remove upper stem retaining nut, retainer and rubber

10

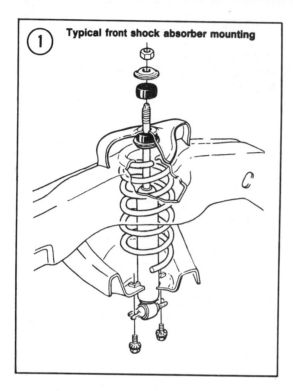

Typical front shock absorber mounting

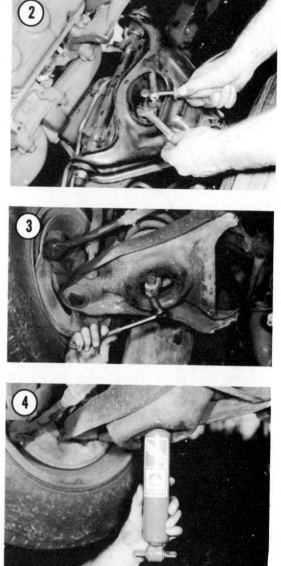

grommet. **Figure 2** shows removal with body removed for visibility.

3. Remove the 2 fasteners holding the lower shock absorber pivot to the lower control arm. See **Figure 3**.

4. Remove shock absorber from the bottom of the lower control arm (**Figure 4**).

5. If the shock absorber will be reinstalled, clean the shock studs with a wire brush to remove any rust or corrosion.

6. Place lower retainer and rubber grommet on upper stem (**Figure 5**).

7. Extend shock absorber fully. Install through lower control arm and spring so upper stem passes through mounting hole in upper control arm frame bracket.

8. Install upper rubber grommet, retainer and attaching nut on upper stem.

9. Hold upper stem from turning with open-end wrench and tighten nut to 7 ft.-lb. (10 N•m) for Monza, Skyhawk, Sunbird and 8 ft.-lb. (11 N•m) for all others.

10. Install lower fasteners. Tighten to 43 ft.-lb. for Monza, Skyhawk, Starfire, Sunbird and 20 ft.-lb. (27 N•m) for all others.

11. Install wheel/tire assembly. Remove jackstands and lower vehicle to ground.

6

REAR SHOCK ABSORBER MOUNTING

Wagons

Except wagons

REAR SHOCK ABSORBERS

Removal/Installation
(Except Monza, Skyhawk, Starfire and Sunbird)

Refer to **Figure 6** for this procedure.
1. Raise the rear of the vehicle with a jack and place it on jackstands with rear axle supported.
2. If equipped with superlift shock absorbers, disconnect the air line at the shock absorber.
3. Remove shock absorber upper bolts at mounting bracket. On some late model station wagons, disconnect the upper mounting bracket (**Figure 7**) by reaching between tire and frame and removing nuts with a wrench.
4. Disconnect shock absorber fastener at lower bracket (**Figure 8**).

CAUTION
If shock absorber has a hex surface on stud between the axle bracket and

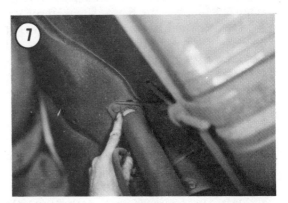

7

8

10

shock absorber, prevent stud from turning when removing lower attaching nut. Failure to do so can result in damage to mechanical bond between shock absorber bushing and mounting stud.

5. Remove shock absorber. If stud is rusted or corroded, it may be necessary to tap it free of axle bracket with a hammer as shown in **Figure 9**.

6. If old shock is to be reinstalled, clean stud threads with a wire brush to remove all rust and corrosion.

7. Loosely install shock absorber with upper attaching bolts.

8. Position lower attaching stud in axle bracket and loosely install lockwasher and nut.

9. Tighten upper attaching bolts to 20 ft.-lb. (27 N•m). If mounting bracket was removed, tighten nuts to 12 ft.-lb. (16 N•m).

10. Tighten lower attaching nuts to 62 ft.-lb. (87 N•m). See CAUTION after Step 4.

11. If equipped with superlift shock absorbers, connect air line at shock absorber. Add air to obtain 10 psi minimum to prevent damage to shock absorber.

12. Lower vehicle to the ground.

**Removal/Installation
(Monza, Skyhawk, Starfire and Sunbird)**

Refer to **Figure 10** for this procedure.

1. Raise the rear of the vehicle with a jack and place it on jackstands with rear axle supported.

2. Loosen and remove shock absorber lower mounting bolt.

3. Remove upper mounting bracket bolts. Remove shock absorber.

4. Loosely install shock absorber with 2 upper attaching bolts.

5. Insert shock absorber eye into lower bracket and secure with mounting bolt. Bolt head should face to front of vehicle. Tighten lower fastener to 42 ft.-lb. (57 N•m).

6. Tighten upper bolts to 18 ft.-lb. (25 N•m).

7. Lower vehicle to the ground.

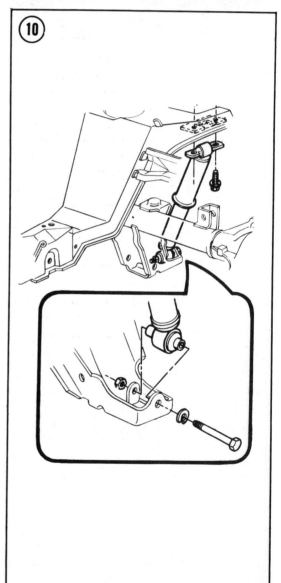

SUPPLEMENT

1985 SERVICE INFORMATION

This supplement contains service and maintenance information for the 1985 rear-wheel drive General Motors passenger cars covered in this manual. This information supplements the procedures in the main body (Chapters One through Ten) of the book, referred to in this supplement as the "basic book."

The chapter headings and titles in this supplement correspond to those in the basic book. If a chapter is not included in the supplement, there are no changes affecting 1985 rear-wheel drive models.

If your vehicle is covered by this supplement, carefully read the supplement and then read the appropriate chapters in the basic book before beginning any work.

CHAPTER THREE

LUBRICATION AND
PREVENTIVE MAINTENANCE

The following scheduled maintenance services reflect changes or additions to those specified in Chapter Three of the basic book.

Engine Oil and Filter

The 262 cid (4.3 liter) gasoline engine crankcase capacity is 4 qt. with or without a filter change.

Fuel Filter/Fuel Lines
(Fuel-injected Engines)

The fuel-injected 262 cid (4.3 liter) engine uses a disposable filter canister located in the fuel line underneath the vehicle and bracket-mounted to the right frame rail. See **Figure 1**.

Use the following procedure to change the filter.

1. Relieve the system pressure as described in the Chapter Five section of this supplement.
2. Raise the car with a jack and place it on jackstands.
3. Place one wrench on the rear filter (inlet) nut. Place a second wrench on the fuel line connector nut. Hold the filter inlet nut from moving and loosen the connector nut.
4. Disconnect the fuel line from the inlet nut fitting. Plug the line to prevent leakage.
5. Repeat Step 3 and Step 4 to remove the fuel outlet line at the front of the filter.
6. Remove the attaching bracket bolt. Remove the filter and bracket from the frame rail.
7. Installation is the reverse of removal. Check the condition of each fuel line connector O-ring and replace as required.

Unplug the lines before connecting them to the new filter. Start the connector nuts carefully by hand to prevent cross-threading and tighten to 22 ft.-lb. (30 N•m) while holding the inlet or outlet nut with a wrench.
8. Remove the jackstands and lower the vehicle to the ground.
9. Start the engine and check for leaks.

Fuel Filter/Fuel Lines
(Diesel Engines)

A new diesel engine fuel system was introduced as a running change during the latter part of the 1984 model year. See **Figure 2**. The system is designed to improve cold weather operation and provide increased

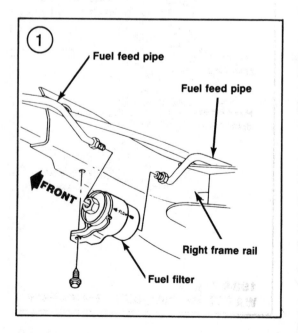

① Fuel feed pipe

Fuel feed pipe

FRONT

Right frame rail

Fuel filter

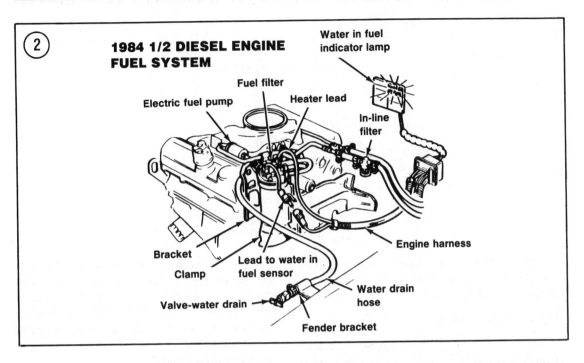

② **1984 1/2 DIESEL ENGINE FUEL SYSTEM**

Water in fuel indicator lamp

Electric fuel pump

Fuel filter

Heater lead

In-line filter

Bracket

Clamp

Lead to water in fuel sensor

Valve-water drain

Water drain hose

Fender bracket

Engine harness

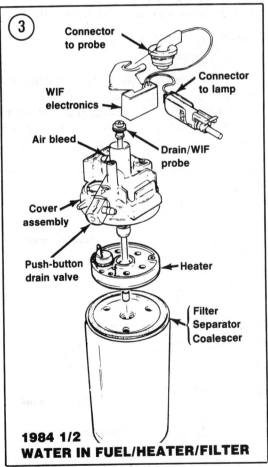

③

Connector to probe

Connector to lamp

WIF electronics

Air bleed

Drain/WIF probe

Cover assembly

Push-button drain valve

Heater

Filter Separator Coalescer

1984 1/2 WATER IN FUEL/HEATER/FILTER

protection from water contamination. The water-in-fuel detector, fuel filter and optional fuel heater are combined in a single engine-mounted filter assembly. See **Figure 3**. A second inline sight glass filter is used to allow spot fuel checks for signs of fuel contamination.

The filter assembly should be drained at each oil change. Both fuel filters should be replaced at the intervals stated in **Table 5**, Chapter Three of the basic book, or whenever the inline sight glass filter shows signs of contamination. The engine-mounted assembly uses an AC TP-1000 spin-on filter. The inline sight glass filter is a GM 22524298 (V8) or GM 22522452 (V6).

Draining filter assembly

1. Set the parking brake. Place the transmission selector in PARK.
2. Turn the ignition key to the RUN position (do not start engine) to energize the electric fuel pump. The "Water-in-Fuel" light on the instrument panel should come on.
3. Open the hood and locate the bracket-mounted drain valve on the left wheel house. A drain container furnished with the car is bracket-mounted either on the radiator support or the wheel house.

11

4. Place the drain container (or a suitable substitute that will hold at least 16 ounces) under the drain valve.

WARNING
The water and fuel mixture is flammable and may be hot if the car has been driven recently. Do not touch the fuel coming out of the drain valve in Step 5 and do not drain the system in an area where sparks or flames can ignite the mixture.

5. Open the drain valve 2 full turns. Depress the red drain valve button on the engine-mounted filter assembly (**Figure 3**).
6. Let the system drain until the fuel flowing from the valve is clear. This should require 15-20 seconds. Do not drain more than 12 ounces of the mixture.
7. Close the drain valve. Dispose of the drained water and fuel safely. Clean the container and reinstall in its bracket.

Engine-mounted filter replacement

1. Disconnect the negative battery cable.
2. Disconnect the inlet/outlet fuel lines at the filter assembly. Remove and discard the fuel line O-rings.
3. Disconnect the drain hose. If equipped with a fuel heater, disconnect the electrical harness.
4. Remove the 2 clamp-to-bracket screws holding the filter assembly. Swing the clamp open and remove it from the bracket. See **Figure 4**.
5. Disengage the filter from the bracket with a rotating motion and remove from the engine compartment.
6. Wrap the filter assembly in a shop cloth and carefully clamp it in a vise with protective jaws. Clamp at the line openings and the flat on the opposite side of the cover.
7. Unscrew, remove and discard the spin-on filter.
8. Wipe the filter cover gasket sealing surface.
9. Coat the gasket on the new filter with clean engine oil or diesel fuel.
10. Thread the filter onto the cover until the sealing surfaces just touch, then tighten another 2/3 turn by hand.

11. Reverse Steps 1-5 to complete filter installation. Use new O-rings when installing the fuel lines to the filter assembly. Tighten the clamp screws to 71 in.-lb. (8 N•m). Tighten the fuel inlet fitting to 17 ft.-lb. (23 N•m) and the outlet line to 20 ft.-lb. (27 N•m).
12. Replace the inline filter as described in this supplement.
13. Loosen the air bleed screw on the filter assembly (**Figure 3**) and turn the ignition switch to the RUN position (do not start the engine) to energize the fuel pump.
14. When fuel starts to flow from the bleed screw ports, close the bleed screw and wipe up any discharged fuel.
15. Start the engine and check for leaks.

Inline filter replacement

1. Disconnect the negative battery cable.
2. Expand each clamp holding the fuel hoses to the inline filter and slide the clamp back on the hose about one inch.
3. Disconnect the hoses from the filter and remove the filter from the engine compartment.
4. Installation is the reverse of removal. Be sure the embossed arrow on the filter points toward the engine.

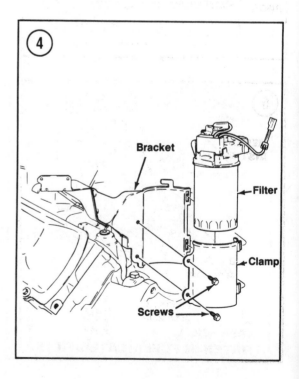

CHAPTER FOUR

ENGINE TUNE-UP

CYLINDER HEAD BOLTS

The head bolts on the 262 cid (4.3 liter) V6 engine should be tightened to 65 ft.-lb. (88 N•m) following the sequence shown in **Figure 5**.

HIGH ENERGY IGNITION SYSTEM

A smaller HEI/EST distributor and high efficiency remote coil with plug-in connectors are used on the 262 cid (4.3 liter) V6 engine.

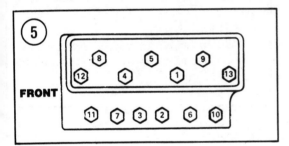

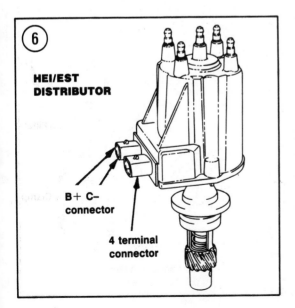

See **Figure 6**. The electronic module design differs from the larger HEI distributors and is not interchangeable.

DIESEL ENGINE TUNE-UP

Idle Speed Adjustment

NOTE
A special tachometer with a magnet probe (part No. J-26925 or equivalent) must be used on diesel engines. Most tachometers for gasoline engines operate from the electrical ignition pulses and will not work on diesel engines.

1. Set the parking brake and block the drive wheels.
2. Place the transmission selector in PARK.
3. Start the engine and let it reach normal operating temperature (upper radiator hose hot).
4. Shut the engine off and remove the air cleaner cover.
5. Remove the retainer clip holding the MAP sensor to the air cleaner housing. See **Figure 7**. Place the MAP sensor to one side.
6. Remove the air cleaner housing. Install air crossover cover (part No. J-26996-1) in its place.
7. Insert the tachometer probe in the timing indicator hole. Connect the red and black tachometer leads to the positive and negative battery terminals respectively.
8. If equipped with air conditioning, disconnect the AC compressor clutch lead at the compressor.
9. If equipped with cruise control, disconnect the servo throttle rod retainer.
10. Make sure all electrical accessories are OFF. Start the engine and place the transmission selector in DRIVE.

11

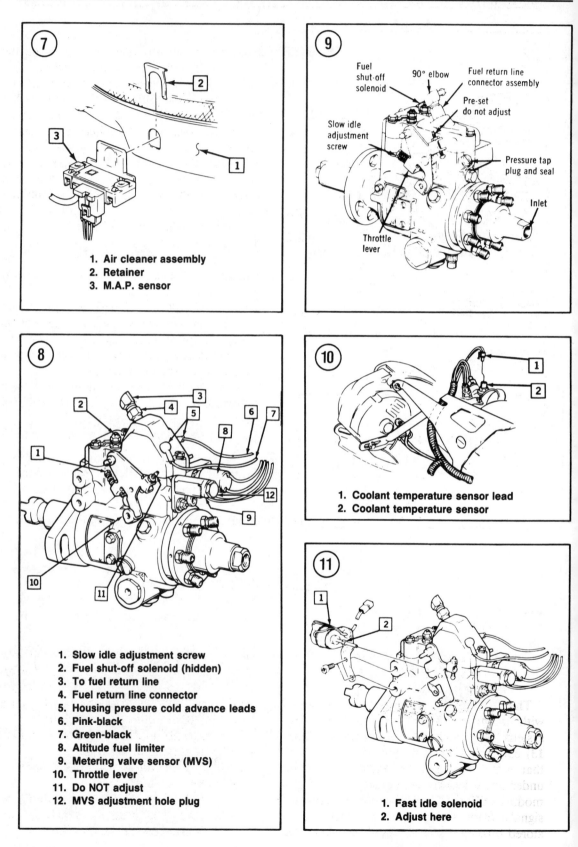

7

1. Air cleaner assembly
2. Retainer
3. M.A.P. sensor

9

Fuel shut-off solenoid
90° elbow
Fuel return line connector assembly
Pre-set do not adjust
Slow idle adjustment screw
Pressure tap plug and seal
Inlet
Throttle lever

8

1. Slow idle adjustment screw
2. Fuel shut-off solenoid (hidden)
3. To fuel return line
4. Fuel return line connector
5. Housing pressure cold advance leads
6. Pink-black
7. Green-black
8. Altitude fuel limiter
9. Metering valve sensor (MVS)
10. Throttle lever
11. Do NOT adjust
12. MVS adjustment hole plug

10

1. Coolant temperature sensor lead
2. Coolant temperature sensor

11

1. Fast idle solenoid
2. Adjust here

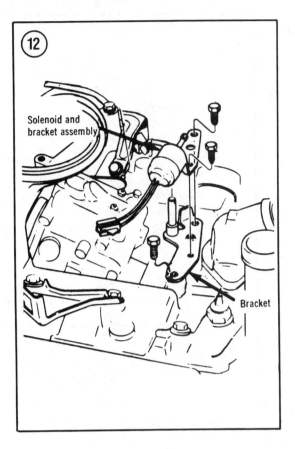

11. Note the tachometer reading and compare to the slow idle speed given on the Vehicle Emission Control Information (VECI) decal in the engine compartment.

12. If the slow idle speed is not within specifications, adjust the slow idle speed screw. See **Figure 8** or **Figure 9** for screw location according to type of pump used.

13. Shut the engine off. Disconnect the engine coolant temperature sensor. **Figure 10** shows the V8 sensor; the V6 is similarly located.

14. Restart the engine and place the transmission in DRIVE.

15. Note the tachometer reading and compare to the fast idle speed given on the VECI decal.

16. If the fast idle speed is not within specifications, adjust the solenoid plunger to obtain the specified fast idle speed. See **Figure 11** or **Figure 12** for solenoid location according to type of pump used.

17. Reconnect the engine coolant temperature sensor lead, then recheck the slow idle speed. Reset, if required.

18. Shut the engine off and reverse Steps 1-9.

CHAPTER FIVE

FUEL SYSTEM

THROTTLE BODY FUEL INJECTION

The 262 cid (4.3 liter) engine is equipped with a throttle body fuel injection (TBI) system. The throttle body assembly (**Figure 13**) contains 2 electrically operated injectors that meter fuel into the intake air stream under the direction of the electronic control module (ECM). The ECM receives electrical signals from various sensors, refers to its stored program memory and calculates the precise amount and timing of fuel required by the engine. Fuel delivery time of the injectors is modified to accomodate special engine conditions such as cranking, cold starts, elevation, acceleration or deceleration.

The basic throttle body assembly consists of 2 major aluminum castings:

a. A throttle body containing a valve to control air flow.

b. A fuel body assembly containing an integral fuel pressure regulator and solenoid-operated fuel injector.

11

System Operation

Filtered fuel is supplied to the TBI assembly by an electric fuel pump mounted in the fuel tank. When the ignition switch is turned ON, a fuel pump relay bracket-mounted on the fender near the coolant recovery tank (**Figure 14**) activates the in-tank pump for 1.5-2 seconds to prime the injectors. If the ECM does not receive a reference signal from the distributor, it then shuts down the fuel pump.

Fuel flow is controlled by varying the duration of injection according to signals from the ECM. Excess fuel passes through a pressure regulator in the fuel meter assembly and is returned to the fuel tank. A throttle position sensor (TPS) informs the ECM of throttle valve position. An idle air control (IAC) assembly maintains a pre-programmed idle speed according to directions from the ECM.

Since the system is electronically controlled, no attempt should be made to adjust the idle speed or fuel mixture. Owner service should be limited to replacement only. If the TBI system is not working properly, take the car to a GM dealer for diagnosis and adjustment.

System Pressure Relief

A bleed in the pressure regulator relieves system pressure whenever the ignition is turned OFF. However, residual fuel pressure should be relieved before opening any fuel connection on a TBI-equipped engine to reduce the risk of fire and personal injury.

1. Place the transmission in PARK.
2. Set the parking brake and block the drive wheels.
3. Remove the fuel pump fuse from the fuse block.
4. Crank the engine. The engine will start and run until the fuel remaining in the lines is used up. When the engine stops, crank the engine again for 3 seconds. This will dissipate any remaining fuel pressure and permit safe disconnection of the fuel lines.

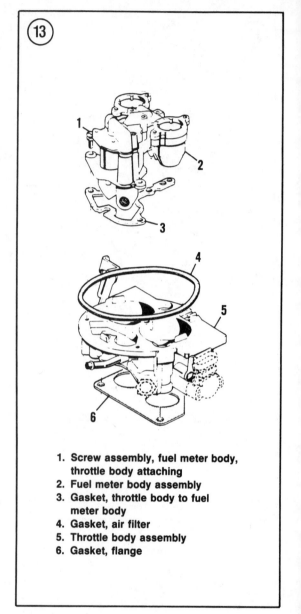

1. Screw assembly, fuel meter body, throttle body attaching
2. Fuel meter body assembly
3. Gasket, throttle body to fuel meter body
4. Gasket, air filter
5. Throttle body assembly
6. Gasket, flange

5. When fuel system service has been completed and all lines reconnected, install the fuel pump fuse in the fuse block.
6. Turn the ignition switch ON, but do not start the engine. Inspect the system connections for leaks and repair if necessary before starting the engine.

Throttle Body Removal/Installation

1. Relieve system pressure as described in this supplement.
2. Remove the air cleaner.

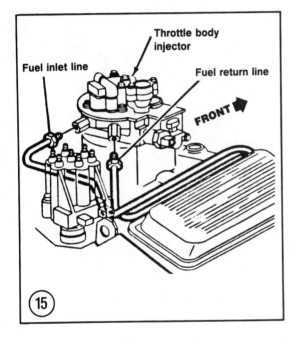

3. Disconnect the electrical connectors at the idle air control assembly and throttle position sensor.

4. Carefully disconnect the wiring harness from each injector to prevent damage to the electrical connector pins.

5. Disconnect the throttle linkage and return spring. Disconnect the downshift and TV cables. If equipped with cruise control, disconnect the cable.

6. Label and disconnect all vacuum lines at the throttle body.

7. Disconnect the fuel supply and return lines at the throttle body (**Figure 15**). Plug the lines to prevent leakage.

8. Remove the bolts holding the throttle body to the engine. Remove the TBI assembly and gasket from the manifold.

9. Installation is the reverse of removal. Use a new gasket and tighten the throttle body attaching bolts to 120-168 in.-lb. (14-19 N•m). Tighten fuel and return line fittings to 19 ft.-lb. (26 N•m).

FUEL FILTER

The TBI-equipped 262 cid (4.3 liter) V6 engine fuel filter is bracket-mounted to the right frame rail just ahead of the fuel tank. Refer to the Chapter Three section of this supplement for filter replacement.

CHAPTER SIX

ELECTRICAL SYSTEMS

CHARGING SYSTEM

Regulator Test

To test the voltage regulator on the car, connect a fast charger and a voltmeter to the battery terminals, observing correct polarity.

Turn the ignition ON and slowly increase the charge rate. When the indicator lamp on the instrument panel starts to dim, read the voltmeter scale. The lamp should dim at a reading between 13.5-16 volts. If it dims at a voltage setting outside this range, the regulator is defective and must be replaced.

11

INDEX

12

12

T

V

W